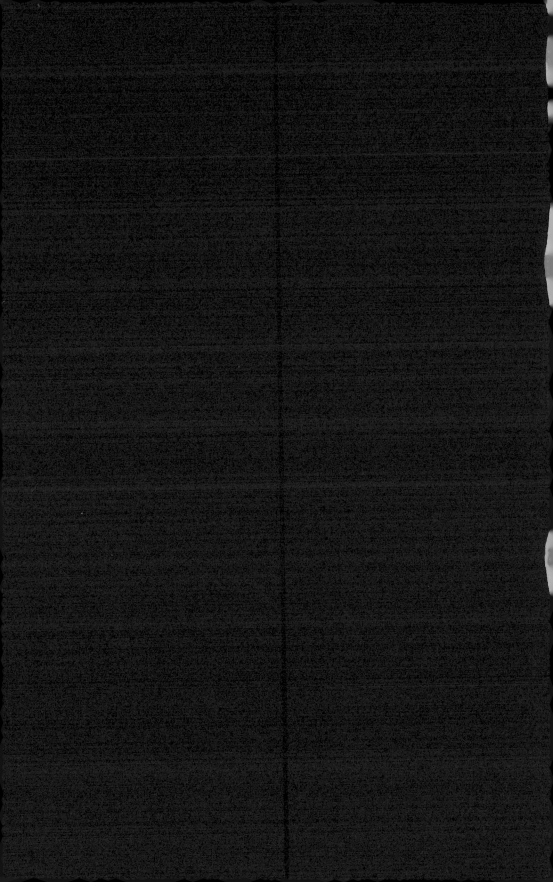

ODE TO THE GRAND SPIRIT

ECHOES AND REFLECTIONS
THE SELECTED WORKS OF DAISAKU IKEDA

Showcasing some of the most potent and far-reaching spiritual works of our times, this major new series brings together – for the first time under the banner of a single imprint – twelve classic dialogues between modern spiritual master Daisaku Ikeda and a distinguished roll-call of discussants, who are uniformly thinkers of global stature and reputation. *Echoes and Reflections* ranges widely across the fields of religion, politics, economics, science and the arts, and in each instance puts a profound and searching new perspective on some of the most pressing issues of our age. Topics covered include: the search for worldwide social justice; the challenges posed by climate change and diminishing natural resources; the perils of religious misdirection; the urgent need for inner growth and harmony; the importance of learning and education; and, above all, the significance of the human quest for meaning and value in life.

Titles in the series:

Choose Life, Arnold Toynbee & Daisaku Ikeda

Dawn After Dark, René Huyghe & Daisaku Ikeda

Human Values in A Changing World, Bryan Wilson & Daisaku Ikeda

Search for A New Humanity, Josef Derbolav & Daisaku Ikeda

Before it is Too Late, Aurelio Peccei & Daisaku Ikeda

A Lifelong Quest for Peace, Linus Pauling & Daisaku Ikeda

Ode to the Grand Spirit, Chingiz Aitmatov & Daisaku Ikeda

Human Rights in the Twenty-first Century, Austregésilo de Athayde & Daisaku Ikeda

Dialogue on José Martí, Cintio Vitier & Daisaku Ikeda

Compassionate Light in Asia, Jin Yong & Daisaku Ikeda

Global Civilization, Majid Tehranian & Daisaku Ikeda

Moral Lessons of the Twentieth Century, Mikhail Gorbachev & Daisaku Ikeda

ODE TO THE GRAND SPIRIT

A Dialogue

CHINGIZ AITMATOV
and
DAISAKU IKEDA

Translated by Richard L. Gage

ECHOES AND REFLECTIONS
THE SELECTED WORKS OF DAISAKU IKEDA

I.B. TAURIS
LONDON · NEW YORK

Echoes and Reflections is a new series that repackages twelve classic dialogues held between Daisaku Ikeda and a variety of interlocutors, which took place from 1972 to 1996. The texts of these dialogues are presented in this series substantively in the form in which they were originally published. For the sake of verisimilitude, and to preserve the integrity of the series, the events, persons and dates referred to in the texts reflect the original periods and contexts in which the conversations were first held, and so have not been altered or edited to mirror subsequent developments in international affairs or the changed worldwide circumstances of later years.

Published in 2009 by I.B.Tauris & Co Ltd
6 Salem Road, London W2 4BU
www.ibtauris.com

Distributed in the United States and Canada Exclusively by Palgrave Macmillan
175 Fifth Avenue, New York NY 10010

ISBN: 978 1 84511 987 4

A full CIP record for this book is available from the British Library
A full CIP record is available from the Library of Congress

Library of Congress Catalog Card Number: available

Typeset by Ellipsis Books Limited, Glasgow
Printed and bound in Great Britain by CPI Antony Rowe, Chippenham

FSC
Mixed Sources
Product group from well-managed
forests and other controlled sources
Cert no. SGS-COC-2953
www.fsc.org
© 1996 Forest Stewardship Council

Contents

Preface

by Chingiz Aitmatov

Fireside Dialogue with Daisaku Ikeda

No word is homeless. Each individual is the home and the lord of the word. Even when turning to God in the secret hope of hearing His voice, we actually hear our own words. The word lives in us. Parting from us and returning to us, it serves us from birth to death. It bears on itself the creation of the spirit and the grandeur of the universe, which at present we can imagine only in the magic of the word. At the same time, the word carries almost photographic images of our personalities.

The Japanese thinker and writer Daisaku Ikeda and I are separated by immense geographical distance – he is in Japan, and I in Turkestan. But we share a common property: the word. The word dies unless shared with others. But how can we make our words attractive to interested conversation partners? I ask this to clarify the issue. Not everything in life makes interesting subject matter. Not all texts are read with absorbed interest. In this sense, dialogue is a difficult genre demanding great patience and thoughtfulness on the part of the reader. That is why, from the very outset, I want to make clear to myself and to the reader how this dialogue came about and what it means to me.

I long dreamed about such a dialogue and waited for the right occasion. I knew that, at sometime or another, a conversation embracing all my life experiences was bound to take place. It would include recollections, analyses and confessions in one channel. Now I can say that fate predetermined and preordained it. I believe that Daisaku Ikeda and I have been walking towards each other for a long time. His personality played the major role. For me, he is a powerful magnet.

As a child, I was often surprised to hear old men in our Kirghiz village complain about having no one to talk to, no one to open their hearts to. But there were people everywhere. How could they lack somebody to talk to? Now I understand what they meant. They had in mind the thirst for that one irreplaceable companion. Sooner or later, I was certain to find the person my soul had yearned for all those years, the person in whom I could see and understand myself clearer and more accurately because, as Schopenhauer put it, I am all people and all people are I.

I hope that Daisaku Ikeda yearned for the same thing. To what can I compare my meeting with him? I am seeking an image. I only know that he can reveal and explain to me the consistency of predestination from an everyday and, at the same time, from a philosophical viewpoint. Perhaps this picture, emerging suddenly in my imagination, will concisely transmit my inner striving for something that human beings long for, if only instinctively. Suddenly a human face comes into view; I experience the extraordinary happiness of epiphany. Conversation starts on its own – from heart to heart, from intellect to intellect.

This is how it was. Imagine two travellers, each of whom has been on the road for years. Both are exhausted because the way has been a long and hard path of life. Many thorns have pierced mind and body. Thirst and an intolerable hunger torment them. I am talking, not about physical hunger, which is easily appeased, but spiritual hunger – the trials of attempting to comprehend existence. I am reminded of the words of Antoine de Saint-Exupéry who expressed his own physical experience in words to the effect that, in a desert, a person is worth what he really is worth. When the silence becomes intolerable, when the desert of the quotidian is ready to swallow one up, life, which is wiser and more compassionate than we are, brings salvation from despair.

As I imagine it, we came across each other on some occasion. I was walking for whatever reason, as the day was drawing to an end. Then I encountered Daisaku Ikeda, who was calmly sitting down by the fire on the roadside. I do not recall how our conversation started. Perhaps it did not start at all but only continued because we had already been talking to each other even before we met. Each of us had been talking to himself. Then our thoughts united and melded, sending off inadvertent sparks. And for this reason the soul felt lighter. The world around unfolded and unfurled as our revelations expanded.

Our talk lasted until morning. I call this a fireside meeting with Daisaku Ikeda. We met by his camp fire in extremely complicated historical times, when the space of the twentieth century was undergoing unheard of changes not only in forms of existence, but also in the evolution of the very type and structure of contemporary thought. Similes decline, absurdity is on the rise. And no one can say whether for better or worse.

I also want to comment on the nature of dialogue. Some people assume that dialogue is always an argument between people of diametrically opposed views of life. I, on the other hand, consider conversation – even when restricted to half a word or half a glance between people who think the same and understand each other – much more fruitful.

Dialogue is a wise way of coming close to shared truths of great importance for everybody. It absolutely is not a way of satisfying personal ambitions or the achievement of selfish aims as often occurs in reality. In the past in Russia, during our period of stagnation, we either kept our mouths shut or reacted in a servile fashion to such things. Later, given the liberty afforded by *perestroika*, we have, unfortunately, been forced unwillingly to witness, even in parliaments, mirror-shattering displays of public loutishness and personal insult. To make the matter worse, there are not a few participants who welcomed those displays with cheers and applause, stimulating their low-minded instincts. We know what this leads to. It begins with elementary contempt and unwillingness to listen to other opinions. It ends in terror, which is one theme of the dialogue in this book.

I should like to conclude this brief preface with a comment on the nature of one aspect of dialogue: tension, which is the result of cooperative striving for truth, before which all are equal and in which all unite.

I hope our dialogue will be as bright and useful as the flames from Daisaku Ikeda's bonfire. Seen from afar, such a fire is good news and hope for the traveller who, perhaps exhausted in the dark, is dying of thirst for the human word.

CHAPTER ONE

Three Days that Shook the World

Victory Over the Self: The Supreme Victory

My Dear Friend Daisaku Ikeda,

Recently it occurred to me that, as work on the dialogue contained in these pages has evolved, the world around us has been virtually recreated. As it was being written, translated, and in general prepared for the press, geopolitical changes took place that no book of its time can ignore. This is all the more true of a book like ours, which ought to comment in a timely and lasting way on recent global changes.

At one time, I thought of putting such comments in a postscript. But, after mature consideration, I decided that there is no need for a special postscript. The telegrams you sent me during the August putsch in Moscow in 1991, provide us with a personal occurrence, simultaneous with the coup d'état, with which to update the foreword of our book, thus eliminating the need to add anything at the end.

I was taken completely unawares by those unforgettable days in August 1991. Perhaps I believed too deeply in *perestroika* as divinely predetermined and irreversible. I could not imagine that anyone would raise a hand in violence against our long history of suffering. I was shocked. I did not know what to do with myself. Disturbed by the situation in the Soviet Union, friends telephoned me from Turkey, Germany and America. Your aides in Soka Gakkai telephoned from Japan. All this concern cheered me somewhat. Then, on the evening of 19 August, near the end of the first day of the coup, I received from you, my friend, a facsimile-telegram expressing your, as you phrased it, 'limitless grief' at what was happening.

By nature, I am not a sentimental person. But I could not help being moved by your sincere message, a reply to an SOS sent out into global space to save my soul. I immediately understood that, contemporaries and co-authors, we two are bound by the spiritual confession we make before our era. We are not merely commentators on, but also living participants in history.

Then suddenly, on 23 August, when unarmed democracy had triumphed decisively over the tanks of the putsch instigators, I received a second telegram from you, joining your voice with the worldwide celebration of justice and historical progress represented by events in Moscow.

Behind the bare facts as set forth here, this episode embodies much more and many phenomena of both a personal and a general nature.

As I write this, summer is dying. The leaves are dropping from the trees. I recall that, earlier this same summer, we met and talked together in Europe. Your visit to Luxembourg, where I was ambassador at the time, was a significant event for our family and for the Soviet embassy.

Discussions started in Luxembourg then continued later when you opened the Victor Hugo House of Literature near Paris. The honour of participating in that unique undertaking enabled my wife and me to witness first hand the cultural cooperation taking place between the contemporary East and West on a new, integrated level. After opening ceremonies in that historic mansion, we went on talking and interpreting everyday events in the light of our experience. I mention this here to point out how far our thoughts and outlooks were removed from events that were to take place in the Soviet Union, the land of *perestroika*, not long afterward.

After the failure of the Moscow junta brought, at least provisional, relief from the danger of a recurrence, we found ourselves forced to ask why neo-Stalinists had openly succeeded as far as they had. The superficial pursuit of this incident is easy. Newspapers everywhere noised them abroad. Television broadcasts were devoted to them. Actually, however, the putsch entailed a whole syndrome of causes and consequences extending back a century to the birth of Marx-Leninism as a class ideology. But that problem belongs in the sphere of historians and political scientists. Here I shall limit myself to setting forth my own living reactions to the August coup d'état mainly on the personal plane.

In the middle of the summer of 1991, not long before the putsch, Soviet newspapers and radio newscasts announced the discovery of yet another secret burial place of victims of the Stalinist executions of 1937. On this occasion, the communal grave was discovered at Chon-Tash, in my homeland Kirghiz. As you and I mention in the main text of this book, my father, Torekul Aitmatov, was repressed and then destroyed during the Stalinist terror. In 1991, just as the August putsch was gaining head, fate once again took up the threads of an old story: my father's remains were discovered in the Chon-Tash communal grave. Relatives, close friends and the Kirghiz government made contact with me in Luxembourg to arrange for me to conduct a public re-burial. Shortly thereafter, I was to participate in a fateful, extraordinary emergency assembly of peoples' deputies that was to decide the continuance or eradication of the government of the USSR, a millstone around the neck of twentieth-century history.

As you will readily imagine, this whole series of events and their consequences weighed heavily on all of us, and especially so on me: the putsch, the downfall of the junta, the re-burial of clandestinely buried Stalinist victims, and, to top it all off, the extraordinary peoples' deputies assembly and the pending fate of a government that, for us, symbolised Soviet totalitarianism. I expressed my reactions and reflections on these events in an article in the 2 September 1991 issue of the *Literaturnaya Gazeta* (Literary Newspaper).

My father was killed during the horrifying years when independently thinking people in our country were liquidated. The staggering history of the discovery of the remains of some of them convinces me of the existence of a higher justice, which may be limitless, strict and beyond our own daily existence. Just think. After half a century, fifty-four years to be precise, in what could be called another Katyn, a sheet of paper bearing my father's indictment turns up together with his remains. A bullet hole in the paper suggested it had been in his pocket. Everything else, the bodies of all the victims, their footwear, clothing, had rotted away. But this document bearing the name *Torekul Aitmatov* survived. The type-written text was still legible. With my own eyes, I read this paper left behind by fate to help establish the truth.

To us today, the absurdity and peremptoriness of the document's style are shocking. Barbarous! But, for all that, it was a death sentence, one of many similar sentences handed out in those days. To give an idea of how many, I might comment that, not too long ago, Soviet newspapers published an incredible, top-secret telegram seized from KGB archives. Sent from Moscow in 1937, it ordered the destruction of ten thousand 'enemies' in each republic of the Union. It was signed by N. I. Yezhov, Stalin's bloody purge director. In the light of things like this, it is surprising that our people survived without losing their humanity.

At her death, twenty years ago, we raised a gravestone to my mother, bearing her name and my father's. In our despair, for our own sakes, we tried to convince ourselves the two of them lay there together. Then, beyond all expectation, Father's remains were discovered. Of course, I was stunned. That terrifying piece of paper, which had lain in the earth half a century to re-appear, from beyond the grave, brought countless memories in its train. *Abysmal inhumanity* are the only words I can find to describe what was done to my father and the others who died with him.

I recall the day when a man in KGB uniform galloped up to our house. I was nine, going on ten. The whole incident engraved itself deep in my memory. The visor of his service cap glittered. His boots had been cleaned. Hearing a loud clatter of hooves, Mother and we four children, of which I was oldest, ran to the front door. The messenger reined his snorting horse in short, pulled an envelope from his bag, handed it to Mother and galloped away.

Mother began to read. I could see something was wrong. She was confused. The envelope contained an answer to her request for information about my father and his whereabouts. It said he had been sentenced to ten years and was forbidden to write or receive letters. Actually, he had already been shot.

They hid everything; they betrayed us. Everything was done in secret. The victims were led to a deserted place in the foothills in secret. And there, on the eve of 7 November, the day on which the Soviet Union commemorated the October Revolution of 1917, they were shot. The following day was given over completely to celebration. Brass bands and victory parades through street and plaza extolled the devil in the shape of Stalin. Having murdered 138 people in a single night and tossed their corpses into a pit, the perpetrators felt free to feast at banquet tables. They were guilty of intellectual genocide that destroyed the best young minds – all the victims were between thirty and thirty-five, my father being just thirty-five – in the Kirghiz of the time.

Of course, all witnesses held their tongues. They had to. Not long ago, a certain old woman related what she, as a young girl, had witnessed on that frightful night. Her father had been a guard at a nearby Pioneer camp. Everything took place before her young eyes. Her father strictly forbade her to talk about it to anyone. 'Otherwise,' he told her, 'we're dead!' Nonetheless, years later, just before her own death, she resolved to tell what she knew. By then, the KGB could do her no harm.

The re-burial inspired a great popular mourning. Thousands took part in a memorial meeting held in the mountains. I tried to explain what had happened. But the social attitudes prevailing at the time of the killings had been so distorted that no one, let alone young people, could grasp the significance of what I said. Power in the Soviet Union in the era of the purges was totalitarian in the truest sense. Stalin wielded a power so total that, at will, he could destroy millions.

When time for the emergency congress, as it was called, came round, my thoughts were bitter. [Incidentally, in Russian, an emergency congress is called an *avariiny s'ezd*. But the word *s'ezd* can mean either a coming together (congress) or a descent. Steep slopes on roads are sometimes indicated by signboards bearing the words *Avariiny S'ezd*.] In the Soviet Union, we had been indoctrinated to assume unconditionally that any *s'ezd* (in this case, congress) by nature was triumphant. There could be no doubt of this at all. The emergency congress of peoples' deputies I am describing, however, was anything but triumphant: it was truly an emergency in the full sense of the word. We had reached a critical point, from which we had to advance with the greatest circumspection.

In the twentieth century, no other people have undergone as many trials as ours. Everything has rolled over us: revolution, war, famine, dictatorship, inquisition, ecological poverty. Now a new age of fresh trials has fallen to our lot. We find ourselves at the junction of two historic epochs. Adherents of the old ways want revenge; they cling to a system that dominated us for nearly a century. To the reform-minded, the nascent epoch promises a new way of life. While many people interpret the incident in a negative way and regard it as a collapse or destruction, some other people are immersed in the feeling of happiness brought about by the general reform. Perhaps both represent reality. However, since we are carrying out the reform in the middle of battles and conflicts, it is impossible for us to give an objective answer to the series of the events. Future historians alone will be able to tell what we are experiencing now and what we are revealing toward the end of the twentieth-century. What comes to my mind is that a calendar completion, the end of the century, and a new epoch-making incident are happening simultaneously.

The problem is that the promise makes nothing easier. Of course, we can explain it and philosophise and theorise about it, but the painful, glaring reality persists. We are living human beings, and the events of today reflect on our living fates, both large and small. Who could have thought a short while ago that we would find ourselves in the situation we are in today? Few could have foreseen it, least of all President Gorbachev. The putsch was as big a shock for him as it was for the rest of us.

Our experiences during those three days in August disturbed both the surface and the depths of the waters. We all ended up in the same mael-strom. Although these events may constitute a subject of gripping interest for future historians, philosophers and writers, as I said, they make nothing easier for us.

The idea that our general governmental structure could disappear affected me powerfully. While realising the possibility, I hoped things would not go that far. In the newspaper article I contributed to my paper, the *Literaturnaya Gazeta*, I tried to express my innermost thoughts about the preservation, or to speak more accurately, the transformation, of the Union. (I think of the *Literaturnaya Gazeta* as *my* newspaper because I always read it and have been on the editorial staff for decades.) Such statements were unpopular, but I made them all the same.

I support national self-determination, independence and sovereignty. Everyone wishes his own people, great or small, to be a worthy partner sharing equal rights with other nations. I have the moral right to speak out on this topic since I was the first in our republic to point out the extreme danger posed by a process of assimilation that had reached an incredible scale. At the time, bringing up such issues was by no means simple. Many people held their tongues and hid in corners, leaving me alone to face both the republican and the national party bureaucracy and the press, including *Pravda, Komsomol'skaya* and *Sots-industriya*. I was reviled then as a nationalist by the very same people who now use nationalism as a vehicle for their own populist excursions. These neo-nationalists are interested, not in nations, but in their own national reputations. The two things are not the same. Such self-seekers transform nationalism from an ethno-patriotic incentive into an anti-force, a self-inflicted blindness. In such circumstances, the intelligentsia pays less attention to scientific and cultural creativity than to the creation of its own image against a back-ground of limitless nationalism. Conflicts arise not only among, but also within nations, which collapse into tribal and even geographic fragments. This all leads to a distorted view of the relationships between the indi-vidual and the nation. The individual's possibilities, one's intellectual, professional and moral qualities and services to general national interests become less important than a person's position in a tribal and topo-graphical hierarchy.

Such an attitude toward the individual cannot fail to influence politi-cal policies in sovereign republics, especially in the Turkistan region. In so far as I have been able to observe, on all levels of democratic govern-ment, priority in power apportionment can be determined, not according to the qualities of individuals, but on the basis of local-geographical bias. This practice is an area in which we are backward and may remain so for a long time yet. Instead of devoting too much energy to localised agitation, as many people, especially the young now do, nations must concentrate on improving themselves and cooperating in the global process of human development as fully worthy, historical, civilised, ethnic members of the world community. A nation bogged down in exclusively down-home concerns isolates itself from this world movement.

But to return to an issue common to everyone in the former Soviet Union, what do we do now? The Union may have been wicked, but it was a whole, united, governmental structure. We were born there. Suffering with the Soviet Union and in a sense struggling with ourselves, we developed into what we are today. Inevitably and necessarily we must now say goodbye to that political structure. Still, before crossing the threshold of our own home for the last time, we ought to pause and reflect a moment.

My own, admittedly not uncontroversial, idea is this. As paradoxical as it may sound, the more independent the republics of the former Soviet Union grow, the more they are going to require a new form of coexistence, a new all-union integration, based on fundamentally different principles. The old central government outlived itself. Good riddance! The newly emerging collective categorically rejects centralisation, which is regarded as a vicious phenomenon. In these circumstances, how are we supposed to create a new form of coexistence? It seems to me that our dilemma is unique in the history of humanity and that it was predestined by fate, which, as everybody knows, is inescapable.

The Communist Party of the Soviet Union applied the brakes to democratic development. Its collapse, degradation and self-dissolution were the historical prerequisite for seeing things in a new light. An act of great self-liberation of social forces, the dissolution of the party promoted the good, not only of the people as a whole, but also of the party itself and of the millions of people connected with it. The party's passing removed the pivot of totalitarian integration, thus opening up new conditions and possibilities for integration of the component governments of the former union into a voluntary Euro-Asian association of independent republics based on completely new, contemporary principles.

Naturally, participation must be entirely voluntary. Perhaps achieving this will take a long time, but we already have a possible model in the European Union, which is taking form before our eyes and represents the most outstanding achievement of world democracy and civilisation in the second half of the twentieth century.

In the big view, the collapse of such a great empire as the Soviet Union was, and is, relatively painless. In this, I see the goodwill of a higher fate. After all, things might have followed a totally different historical scenario. No past imperial structure has left the arena without a bloodbath and the sacrifice of millions of human lives in what might be called the nuclear fission of cataclysm. To illustrate my meaning, I need only compare what happened in the Soviet Union with events in India, Pakistan, Bangladesh and then Sri Lanka when the British Empire fell. Even now, half a century later, this region continues to be a hotbed of globally important problems.

Developments in the former Soviet Union, on the other hand, indicate that *perestroika*; no matter how much it is reviled by right and left, by dispossessed parasites and honest workers – prepared us, adapted us and saved us from ourselves. Without it, the totalitarian, communist way of thinking, to which we were all hostages, would certainly have unleashed a civil war of such destructive, world-scale force that current occurrences in the former Yugoslavia would seem like child's play in comparison. (Of course, in bloody warfare, scale is not the only important thing: the perishing of a single soul is an immeasurable loss.)

In spite of all the stones hurled at it now, *perestroika* saved us. Like Christ, abused and trampled on by the very people to whom it brought light and freedom, *perestroika* fulfilled its mission to the very end. For this reason, bowing my head in respect to our saviour from civil grief, I have this to say.

In the calamities that an ominously tolling bell now proclaims on Earth and beyond its confines, we, mad humanity, alone are guilty. Whether of friend or foe, the life-giving blood shed in battle once flowed in the veins of a creature born in God's world with the universal mission and supreme right to happiness. Human life loses none of its value and significance even if, in the grips of passion, we underestimate or even disdain it. Its meaning does end, however, when life ends. At the instant when a person, victim of chance or martyr to faith, falls to the ground dead, all motivations leading to this outcome, everything that incited him to the violence that killed him, falls to dust. The reason is simple: there can be no meaning in life without life itself. When this has been said, we find ourselves left with bitter questions. Could the conflict have been resolved through conciliation and strategy without loss of life? Was there

no civilised alternative to war? Was a fiercely one-sided, therefore generally barbarous, terrorist, radical and bloody means the only way to reach
the desired goal?

Perestroika may represent a leap forward for worldwide development.
After our experience with it, surely we should stop evaluating the significance of a battle in terms of numbers of heads lost and degree of human
torment and suffering. Is the bloodletting between classes and nations
that we poetically describe as 'the struggle' inescapable? Is there no blood-
less way to justice? Surely the Everest of murdered corpses marking
humankind's way is enough. Surely we do not need to scale the crags of
suffering over and over again. Where do we go from here? Outer space?
In the light of these considerations, I find revolutions and civil wars
unjustifiable. Pathetic exclamations about the millions of lives sacrificed
on the altar of victory awaken in me no flood of inspiration or pride.
Instead, I pray God to give us no more such costly victories. Unfortunately,
even for the formulators of ideas that spawn war, pre-death insights, those
apocalyptic flashes of penetration into the inaccessible depths of things,
occur only at the final threshold, from which there is no return. Once
they have been experienced, it is too late to convey information about
them to others.

No one has spoken from beyond the grave to express satisfaction with
this life or with the fate of even the most cherished causes. Survivors explain
things according to their own lights. Filled with righteous fury, they swear
vengeance, and take it. Revenge evokes retaliation, and so on. Satan exults.
Calling the tunes, he inspires us with evil and substitutes intolerance and
xenophobia for good sense. Evil spreading in our souls like mould destroys
virtue, while a banner floating on high proclaims violence to be justifiable. Saddest of all, the ordeals incumbent on this topsy-turvy philosophy
produce nothing. The way of bloodshed leads, not to an enrichment of the
historical experience of one generation over its predecessors, but to regres-
sion, cruelty and the destruction of past achievements.

Matured now in the course of historical evolution, we in my country
thirst for democracy, respect for the individual and national and governmental sovereignty. Such things are achievable only through *perestroika*,
which, bestowed on us by fate, is the image of humanism at the end of
the second millennium. It is our contribution to the noble cause of
humanity.

Appearances to the contrary notwithstanding, my past few years have
not been devoted entirely to *perestroika*. During them, I have been compelled

to examine everything called the 'literary process', including my own work, in a new light. The people, the milieu I was accustomed to, have changed. Criteria are different. It is as if all my former readers had moved to other worlds, to other spheres. Once, even a short article, not to mention a short story or novel, stimulated instantaneous response. My words fell on listening ears. It is no longer that way. And I know why: people are too much in the grips of political madness to have time for literature.

What about the years to come? Will literature dominate our minds, souls and feelings? Or has its era ended? To my grief, I no longer see in the literary life the significance and energy that was once characteristic of it and that once gave my work meaning. How are we to augment and elevate the word afresh? I have not laid my pen down; I continue to work. But I have been forced to make a fundamental re-examination of everything I had stored up, foreseen and written down. For me it required tremendous effort and fearsome torments to orient myself again in my own field.

To conclude, in giving this letter the title 'Victory Over the Self: The Supreme Victory,' I had in mind confrontation between the self and its responsibility before history. In the final analysis, this confrontation is of fundamental importance because society is the sum of its individual members. The individual is a repository of social consciousness. The original dispositions of its individual members determine the total aspect of the collective. Totalitarianism prevailed in the Soviet Union as long as it did because it denied human freedoms and rights and completely repressed and dominated the individual to party, state and utopian ideological interests. Thanks to the August 1991 victory of democratic forces over the neo-Stalinists, we have broken through into a new epoch, a qualitatively different set of circumstances for society, government and, most important of all, each individual and the people as a whole.

The hour has struck. History has delivered its verdict: with increasing prevalence, democracy is becoming the guiding principle of contemporary life. Nothing prevents a person from realising his own abilities and strivings in private life and on the level of social activity. All the prerequisites for free development are on hand. Now it is up to each human being and to society.

Democracy has become a reality. But socialism converted a centuries-old heritage of Russian egoism into universal hypocrisy and lies accepted as norms, all-pervading and hopeless dependence, and massive disinclination to work. Can we overcome this heritage? Will we be able to beat down within ourselves all the viciousness that brought us to cultural and social degeneration?

We must put the fruits of labour and science to use for our own good. At last, scorning the absurd idea of global domination, we must cease being hostages to ourselves. We must liberate ourselves from the military–industrial oligarchy. But can we accomplish all these things? My bitter words are inspired by apprehensions about our ability to rise from the ashes by triumphing over ourselves.

Hope and Friendship: The Wise Man's Orders of Merit

To my respected and dear friend Chingiz Aitmatov,

Permit me to begin my remarks on a personal note. I sympathise with the shock and pain you felt when, after having lain in obscurity for years, your father's remains, together with his death sentence, were discovered immediately before the August putsch. Hearing of this, I recalled with special poignancy a dedication to him in one of your books: 'To my father, Torekul Aitmatov, whose burial place is unknown to me.' I remembered, too, being deeply moved by your description of your parting with him at Kazan Station in Moscow, how you raced along the station platform in pursuit of the train carrying away the father you might never see again. The savage slaughter of those innocent people, most of them in the prime of youth, enrages me. Still I am consoled to an extent to know that, at long last, your father has returned to his family. This must be a source of consolation to his spirit, too. I offer a sincere prayer for his repose.

Now to pick up the general thread of our discussion. In spite of the victory of democracy in Moscow, in August 1991, the confiding letter I received from you not long afterward was far from exuberant in tone. In fact, it struck me as sad and pained. This was only natural in the light of the many difficulties that confronted your homeland, including the collapse of the Soviet Union itself.

Your oblique reference in the title 'Three Days That Shook the World' to the famous book *Ten Days That Shook the World*, by the American journalist and revolutionary John Reed (1887–1920), suggested the anxiety with which you observed events during and after the attempted coup. Certainly, the situation was very distressing; nonetheless, we must be true optimists because, given identical circumstances, optimism is more productive than pessimism. It is always darkest before the dawn. The chaos and pain experienced by the Soviet Union and Russia are harbingers of the birth of a great new *cosmos*, in the Greek sense of order.

On the personal and national level, the experience was a wrenching one. President Gorbachev himself, as many commentators noted, was shaken by the attempted putsch and his own virtual imprisonment. I already knew Mr. Gorbachev from two previous meetings. But seeing him on television, unable to conceal his exhaustion from the cameras, distressed me deeply. True, glimpses of the appealing Gorbachev smile now and again shone through, but it was hard for him to hide his gloom.

Then, as now, many people took both Gorbachev and *perestroika* too lightly. Some claim it is already finished. Others have branded Gorbachev's attempts to balance right and left as self-serving. Some even stooped low enough to accuse Gorbachev of being behind the attempted coup d'état. Only people with small minds could publicise such absurd opinions. As the old Japanese saying has it, 'The crab digs a hole that fits its own shell.' Like the crab, such petty people conform all situations to themselves.

If his own interests had been paramount in his mind, President Gorbachev could easily have retained his position of absolute authority as first secretary of the Communist Party of the Soviet Union. No one forced him to pull what Fedor Burlatsky, a member of the supreme Soviet, called the 'hot chestnut' of *perestroika* from the fire. Gorbachev deserves too much respect to be called an apparatchik and a self-server. People who criticise him as such are incapable of sensing his suffering and loneliness at being betrayed.

He himself is fully aware of their incapability. When I met him in July 1990 – you were present at the time – he said that the people of the Soviet Union did not know how to use the freedom *perestroika* gave them. They are like prisoners long incarcerated in the dark: the glare of the sun of liberty hurts their eyes. Gorbachev was morally compelled to sow the seeds of *perestroika*, although he and his contemporaries may never live to enjoy its fruits.

As the lowdown on the failed putsch was gradually revealed, it became clear that Gorbachev stuck by his convictions throughout the whole affair. His close advisor Anatoly S. Chernyaev reported that, during house arrest, far from giving in to intimidation, he shouted orders to the coup leaders to 'cut out the kidding'. Still, as deluded as the crab suiting the hole to his own shell, the plotters firmly believed that, as long as they had the government, the military and the KGB on their side, they could force Gorbachev to meet their demands. They failed to understand that the old power structure was irreparably damaged. The philosophy of *perestroika* denied the very existence of any former power bases that lacked popular support. Blinkered as they were, the plotters continued serving vested interests, never dreaming of the changes *perestroika* had worked in the very nature of the Soviet people.

I agree fully with you that, no matter how many stones are cast at it, *perestroika* was the salvation of your people. Its course of development was inevitably tortuous. It is too new and unfamiliar for a straight path. Further trial-and-error implementations of its principles lie ahead. But, as an irreversible part of the tide of world history, it continues to exert a decisive influence on human fate.

Perhaps, as you say, a higher destiny ordained the relatively peaceful breakdown of the Soviet empire. It is certainly true that, had the Soviet Union been plunged into civil war, events in the former Yugoslavia would pale in comparison. And, had Soviet civil strife turned nuclear, the survival of humanity would have hung in the balance.

In this connection too, President Gorbachev laudably stuck to his principles. Of course, Boris Yeltsin showed his mettle by courageously withstanding the forces of the coup. But he alone could not have prevented civil war had not Gorbachev, virtually imprisoned, betrayed by close associates and isolated from outside news, remained true to his convictions and refused to resign the presidency. His firmness appears all the more praiseworthy when we remember that the coup leaders were people he had once trusted enough to put in positions of high authority.

The collapse of the Soviet Union rang down the curtain on the Cold War. When this happened, the United States found itself groping for a new world order in which military power could be de-emphasised. My own agreement with this general policy inspired me to develop the doctrine of soft power. This idea attracted enough attention for me to concentrate on it in a speech entitled 'The Age of Soft Power', which I delivered at the John Fitzgerald Kennedy School of Government, at Harvard University on September 26, 1991.

On that occasion, I explained my belief that we are now witnessing a shift from such hard-power factors as military might, violence and money in the direction of the soft power manifested in knowledge, information, systems and public opinion. Consequently, we require a philosophy that truly applies soft power and that, like the philosophy of Socrates, evokes inner-generated human energy for the sake of consensus and general agreement.

Interestingly, immediately after I finished my speech at the Kennedy School, President George H. Bush, in Washington, proposed sweeping, unilateral nuclear-arms reductions. Professor A. B. Carter, director of the Science and International Affairs Centre at the Kennedy School and consultant to then President Bush and Secretary of Defense Richard B. Cheney, had hurried to Boston to hear my speech and to comment on it before returning to Washington. Perhaps he and others reacted favourably to my ideas particularly because they were in keeping with the then-prevailing American enthusiasm for disarmament.

In the former Soviet Union, *perestroika* drastically shifted emphasis from hard to soft power. Bureaucratic control under the one-party Communist dictatorship, barracks socialism as it was called, was built on profound distrust of the people. Perhaps inspired by a belief in inherent human depravity and propensity to evil, its rigid system incorporated such repugnant practices as informing, which engendered and encouraged widespread mutual suspicion. Certain notorious cases of informing on close relatives were held aloft as laudable models. For example, the little boy Pavlik Morozov, whose tale-carrying resulted in his parents' execution, was regarded as a hero. As you say, such things cannot be justified; they are categorically evil. Turning a father in to the authorities for being a well-to-do farmer, as little Morozov did, destroys morality in the parent-child relationship. The icy ideology that made such things possible relied on widespread dread of hard political and military power.

Perestroika, on the other hand, abandoned arid, stereotyped, Soviet-style officialese and employed the policy of openness – *glasnost* – to restore popular faith in words and in interpersonal relations. Gorbachev's achievement in championing *glasnost* is satirically illustrated by a list of successive secretary generals of the Soviet Communist Party drawn up by a certain Japanese intellectual: Stalin, lord of fear; Khrushchev, lord of recklessness; Brezhnev, lord of stagnation; and Gorbachev, lord of honesty. This designation of President Gorbachev is especially apt since he made trust in the honest words of honest people a driving power for social reforms. I sense similar honesty in your intense faith in *perestroika* as a divinely determined, irreversible deterrent to violence.

Surprisingly, belief in honesty's ability to evoke honesty from others reformed the Soviet Communist Party from within. Earlier experiences in other East European nations had suggested that external force was the only way to effect internal reformation of communist parties at the head of highly centralised, one-party-dominated systems. In the summer of 1991, party reform in the Soviet Union was out of the question. With the exception of Gorbachev himself and a few supporters like Deputy Secretary General Vladimir Ivashko, the party either actively or passively sided with the coup leaders. While rejecting the plotters' demand for his resignation, President Gorbachev sincerely believed in the Communists' capability of self-purification. It remained for others to dissolve the party, temporarily.

I understand how bitterly the disgusting betrayal of faith and friendship behind the coup must have shocked you and Mr. Gorbachev. Still, there is a bright side to the affair. Only a few years ago, the mere use of words like *friendship* and *trust* in connection with occurrences in the Kremlin would have been grotesquely inappropriate. Thanks to *perestroika*, the Kremlin seems much less monstrous and more human than before.

The distrustful person is unable to profit from defeat. Setbacks and frustrations born of trust, however, teach valuable lessons. Long experience with life and faith has proved to me that a person who fails through trusting is not defeated: he has triumphed over himself, the most difficult of all victories, as you justly say. Such a victor can find his way out of any difficulty. In the limitless expanse of his spirit there is no frustration, only hope. With this in mind, I have named my part of our preface 'Hope and Friendship: The Wise Man's Orders of Merit'.

Nationalism embodies certain natural demands and rights; but its egoistic aspects spark localised conflicts that, if unchecked, can expand to the global scale. The roots of nationalist sentiment go deep. You, for example, while realising from experience what nationalist conflicts are like, nonetheless feel enough nostalgia for the former Soviet Union to express the poignant desire to pause and reflect before parting with it forever.

Parting with home affects different people in different ways. The Austrian author Stefan Zweig (1881–1942) was driven from his home by the Nazis and compelled to spend the remainder of his life in exile in Brazil. He wrote:

> Inevitably, all forms of exile destroy balance. When a person does not have his own earth under his feet, he loses, and this must be experienced to be understood, his upright posture. He becomes less sure and more self-suspicious.[1]

Like Zweig, a Jew, Albert Einstein (1879–1955) also suffered persecution at the hands of the Nazis and was driven from his homeland. But this experience exerted slight influence and left no scars on his spiritual world. Indeed, the more he wandered and travelled, the more his cosmopolitanism flourished. Perhaps this in part explains the vigour with which he championed the idea of world government in his late years. The roots of individual identity are important, but cosmopolitanism transcending national identity is more important still.

The Soviet Union swept nationalistic problems under the carpet, pretending Communism had solved them all. When the Union collapsed, separatist and independence movements broke out in counteraction to this inherently oppressive approach. You insist that a new union of a different kind, perhaps similar to the European Union, is now needed. No matter what form it takes, however, to be truly harmonious, the new union must embody the open spirit of cosmopolitanism so thoroughly manifested in Albert Einstein and the soft-power factors of spirituality and humanism that I have long advocated.

Because contemporary humanity is too quick to undervalue the intangible world, our spiritual life has been impoverished, trivialised and glaciated. Human beings can no more tolerate such barren circumstances than nature can tolerate a vacuum. The vacuum in people's hearts was taken advantage of by devils, leaving their spiritual life devastated by pseudo-religious ideology.

You ask whether your people can overcome the unsavoury aspects of their heritage. Some knowledgeable people in Russia and other parts of the former Soviet Union think they cannot. Still, as *perestroika* taught us, history often turns the tables on the commentators. Ten years ago, no one would have dreamed that the Berlin Wall would come down during this century. Obviously, avoiding both empty platitudes and narrow biases, we must observe the changing times with calm and humility. The British historian Arnold J. Toynbee (1889–1975) advised me to concentrate on the quiet depths of history without being distracted by busy surface currents. We must learn to hear the beating of the heart of the people in the depths of the flow of time.

That profound heartbeat is now telling us of the imminence of the age of soft power, of intangible factors like the religious spirit, spirituality and humanism. Russia, with its great nineteenth-century tradition of humanist literature, cannot help playing an important role in guiding the current of the age.

Because you are a brilliant writer and my close friend, I must sympathise with you for being unable to find the old vitality in contemporary writing. Undeniably, the flood of information unleashed by *glasnost* has cheapened words themselves. The greater the verbosity, the less the content. In Japan today, too, verbiage often swamps a modicum of meaning. In the Soviet Union, with its curbs on freedom of expression, people thirsted for verbal truth even in dribs and drabs. Today, Russia is flooded with words that few people heed. But this situation will probably pass quickly.

Not as a bystander, but as a participant in the events of our times, I believe in historical selection. In 1991, in Luxembourg, that green heart of Europe, you said to me, 'I do not agree with people who called Victor Hugo's school of romanticism old-fashioned. As a matter of fact, it ought to be revived today.' With this dialogue as part of the undertaking, let us begin patiently reviving it right now. Like Hugo, let us speak freely of goodness, justice, friendship and love.

CHAPTER TWO

War, Literature, Youth

First Books

IKEDA: Familiarity with superior literature during the sensitive years of youth can strongly influence character formation throughout life. Reading is a joy at any age. But I think the sensitivity cultivated by concentrated reading early in life is unique. I know this is true in my own instance. Reading does more than inform, it inspires self-discovery.

You turned your attention to literature while a young student of stockbreeding at an agricultural university. What aroused your interest? What books and authors, then or later, made especially strong impressions on you?

AITMATOV: I am sincerely happy you have asked this question at the very start of our conversation. There can hardly be anyone among our contemporaries who, during the young years of life, failed to come into contact with a book that left an indelible trace. After all, youth is an epoch in itself. Children everywhere, including, I am sure, Japanese children, find books like Daniel Defoe's *Robinson Crusoe* or Rudyard Kipling's *The Jungle Book* exciting discoveries. The attraction suggests to me a natural predilection for the good that has evolved in human beings everywhere. Precisely for this reason, romances, adventure stories and didactic writing exert enormous influence on pure, naïve souls. Recollections of the thoughts and dreams inspired by such remarkable books and of the connections they inspired in later life could constitute a whole human history.

But our bookish worlds are turned topsy-turvy when aspirations for the nobility and courage literature inculcates run afoul of the bitterness, fears, deceptions and enmities of real life. In spite of the disappointments of maturity, however, a child's first book radiates light that lasts, as an ideal, throughout life. I hope something like this is to be found in my own stories *Early Cranes (Rannie zhuravli)* and *Piebald Dog Running along the Seashore (Pegy pes, begushchii kraem morya*). As adults, even in today's mass-culture jungle, we can still reap the benefits of the aesthetic and social experiences embodied in world literature. For this to happen, we must, as children, be gradually introduced to serious reading, artistic analysis and philosophy.

For each of us, truly, 'in the beginning was the Word', both in the beginning of all beginnings and in the beginning for each individual born into God's world. In happiness or sorrow and in cool investigations of the essences of matters, the polysemantic, all-defining Word is God. Therefore, God must be sought in the all-encompassing Word. Our whole lives, all our examinations of good and evil, concentrate on God. Without the Word, we would be incapable of taking a single step. This is why we must exert all our efforts, of book and Word, in cultivating young people to appreciate the light of their youthful experience and to preserve it as long as possible. As God, and therefore the most important goal in life, the Word must serve the Good exclusively. It takes strength to affirm the Good. Power that affirms Good must grow ceaselessly if it is to overcome Evil, which has primordial world superiority.

Unlike Good, Evil is tenacious and always commands enormous potential for self-production and reproduction. In all things, large and small, Evil is at work treading the Good down and trying to destroy it. Only the God-Word can withstand Evil, day in day out, from age to age.

When the Tower of Babel was thrown down, no doubt by Satanic curse, the Word-God was ripped asunder with the result that peoples lost the ability to understand each other. The burden of this sundering has oppressed us for too long. But the situation cannot last forever. In their torment, the fragments of the Word-God struggle to re-unite. Perhaps, this insuperable, ineluctable striving constitutes the genetic basis, the fundamental nature, of the inexpressible torments and mystical fears experienced keenly and painfully by a humanity threatened with catastrophe and possible annihilation.

Though geographically far from each and other, you and I are united by the Word; which for us is literature. Can it save the world? What constitutes salvation? Can literature somehow avert ruin? Can it go beyond merely postponing 'the end of history' and eliminate the very idea of such a tragic, alas, all too conceivable, outcome? Of course, it would be naïve to put our trust in literature as the sole, universal means of resolving the problems confronting us. It would *not* be naïve, however to put faith in a *new* Word in which all human beings are one, as we are in God, and equal, as we are before God.

Whence will such a Word appear? Is there any hope that it will appear at all? I make bold to suggest that what is called the *new thinking*, the *perestroika* philosophy of seeking solutions to problems from the standpoint of all humanity and not merely in connection with social class, plus new attitudes and understandings, no matter how stubbornly resisted by some people, will beget the new Word. In spite of the contemporary tendency to regard it as an innovation, the new Word is not actually new at all. In its literary applications it has existed from the very first as the embodiment of values common to all humankind. These values are the source of the accessibility of great art to all peoples. They characterise what Goethe proclaimed to be world literature.

I have departed from your question. But, for me, reflection on the topic you propose is far more valuable than a mere pre-planned reply to your words. It is one thing to examine the problem of introducing young people to literature from the everyday view. It is quite another to interpret it from the philosophical standpoint. In the latter case, the issue assumes the enormous scale of general human aims. To what kind of literature should we introduce young people? How should we go about it? This is a matter of the greatest moment because, to a decisive degree, the fate of the whole world depends on the nature of the humanity of tomorrow.

In seeking an answer, suppose I permit myself to indulge in free fantasy? Perhaps we might profitably consider founding an international research institute of books. It could assume responsibility for working such projects as publication of a Library of World Literature for Young People to which citizens of all nations could subscribe. The Prussian statesman, educational reformer and philologist Wilhelm von Humboldt (1767–1835) provides a suitable motto for such an undertaking: 'To think means to join one's thought to the thought of all humankind.'

IKEDA: The idea of a research institute making great literature available to everyone everywhere is fascinating. I should like the Victor Hugo House of Literature, the *Maison Littéraire de Victor Hugo*, in France to serve such a function. I agree with you wholeheartedly that literature, especially literature for young people, must serve the interests of the good exclusively. Indeed, helping literature serve those aims was one of our goals in setting up the Hugo House.

No writer demarcates good and evil as clearly as Victor Hugo. His novels are no mere shallow didactics. As he proceeds through their broad expanses, following the complications of their plot lines, the reader experiences an increasingly clear awareness of the ultimate, and convincing, victory of good.

Of the many scenes from Hugo's novels that I recall from childhood, the suicide of Inspector Javert in *Les Misérables* remains undyingly fresh in my memory. Confronted with the immense compassion of the hero, the ex-convict Jean Valjean, Javert loses the code-bound certainty that had guided his every act.

> An entire world appeared to his soul; favour accepted and returned, devotion, compassion, indulgence, acts of violence committed by pity upon austerity, respect of persons, no more final condemnation, no more damnation, the possibility of a tear in the eye of the law, a mysterious justice according to God going counter to justice according to man. He perceived in the darkness the fearful rising of an unknown moral sun; he was horrified and blinded by it. An owl compelled to an eagle's gaze.[1]

For all of us, this 'moral sun' is the only thing combating the threatening power of Evil of which you speak. Now, at the end of the twentieth century, signs of the impending victory of Evil are apparent on all sides. Victor Hugo should be more widely read by people of all ages because he turns our attention to the sun that can drive the threatening clouds away. Our jaded contemporaries who dismiss him as out-of-date are like people who condemn the sun for shining too brightly.

As the poetic soul of the Romantic movement, Victor Hugo belongs to all times and all places. My familiarity with his all-embracing themes inspired in me a desire to build a Hugo memorial on French soil. The result is the *Maison Littéraire de Victor Hugo*, which we hope will stimulate the budding imagination and develop the immense potential of today's young people, who are too often exposed to the desiccating influence of the adult world. I feel certain that, in addition, it can be a milestone on the way toward the restoration of the global spiritual culture your international library and research centre would serve. Do you have any specific plans in connection with your idea? Where will you start work?

AITMATOV: At a ripe age, Leo Tolstoy (1828–1910) drew up a list of books that, read in childhood, adolescence and youth (he divided his own life into these phases, each of which lasted a decade), had strongly impressed him and decisively influenced his life. Surprisingly, in early youth, he was fascinated by Rousseau and Schopenhauer, whose works, conceivably, would be neither accessible nor, to our way of thinking, interesting to a teenager. In similar, much later lists, we find fairy tales. Force of habit almost led me to call this, too, surprising. But surely it is time for us to stop being surprised by things that, sensibly viewed, are simply normal. The really important thing is that the Bible, the book of books, appears as essential reading in all Tolstoy's lists.

IKEDA: Tolstoy no doubt compiled his lists from among those 'eternal' books that have always been indispensable to spiritual development. I should very much like to hear your opinions on those books and on the kind of reading you consider important to the psycho-biological formation of young people, who demonstrate more concern with the meaning of life and death than adults do.

In spite of the dissatisfaction they may find in contemporary society, young people demand sincere answers to sometimes very difficult questions. I remember your telling me how, when you once found your son Eldar looking perplexed and asked him what the matter was, he replied that the book he was reading said our sun will go out and life on Earth will become extinct in one-and-a-half-billion years. With the innocence of youth, he asked you how to prevent the catastrophe and, I am certain, expected you to have an answer.

AITMATOV: I am touched by your remembering something so trivial. It was the knowledge embodied in the Word that stimulated Eldar to ask such a question.

But to return to reading at an early age. The desire was awakened in Tolstoy by the spiritual atmosphere he breathed, the atmosphere of Russia and Europe, the Enlightenment, a sense of nationality and so on. My own generation did not experience such a milieu; dominating theories of social class robbed us of it. We were permitted to read only what corresponded to revolutionary awareness, in other words, to narrowly political aims. This restriction seriously hampered our reading and our creative activity; in both areas we came up very short. We had no idea what kinds of books existed outside our realm. Still, theories of class proved incapable of isolating us completely from the world. Reading attracted us enormously. It is only natural to be attracted to humanistic literature. Parents must protect their children from ideological incursions and totalitarian pressures that would stifle the response to this attraction.

What was the source of the attraction for me? For their time, my father and mother were educated people. Apart from the examples set by my parents, I enjoyed another source of introduction to finer things: the tales my grandmother Aimkan told me. To my good fortune, she loved telling stories and cultivated a taste for them in me. The Russian writer Yuriy Olesha (1899–1960) said that the person protected in youth by a wise mentor is fortunate. My grandmother was my wise mentor.

Finally, I must address the issue of books and the theme of war in relation to children. In societies dominated by rigid ideologies, more than anything else, books prepare younger generations to condone wars conducted by the state. I know this from experience, since my own childhood and adolescence coincided with the years of the Second World War. Only many years later did I come to see the extent and scale to which propaganda preaching the need, the inevitability, of subjugating normal life to military needs took root in our half-childish minds. Propagandist literature raised self-sacrifice on the altar of war to the status of supreme patriotic valor.

You and I are of the same age. I imagine that you remember how the Japanese ultra-militarists put juvenile literature to the same use. As far as I can gather, the policy of dealing with war in heroic and poetic terms reached great heights in Japan in the 1930s.

I sometimes try to imagine a situation in which, with shouts of hurrah, soldiers killed in war rise from the dead. I suspect that neither the most enthusiastic recruiting nor the most speciously convincing reasons could make them willing to fall in battle a second time. Only people just emerging into conscious life evince rash readiness to die. And this is precisely why ideologues hurry to get a grip on the soul as early as possible. Certainly that is what happened to us during the totalitarian era.

As a rule, Soviet books took only a near-sighted view of war as heroism, victory and sacrifice. The soldier heroes of such literature neither had nor strove to have their own personal views of the nature of war. The individual as such totally lacked historical significance. This ideological interpretation remained unshakable in all evaluations of the war theme until recent years.

In the course of my own literary development, I, too, encountered the power of this mindset. Thirty years after its initial publication, I added a chapter to my very first book, *The Deserter's Wife* [original Russian title *Litsom k litsu*, or Face to Face]. The additional material deals with the fate of the deserter and his family and a psychological analysis of his desertion. For ideological reasons, I had been unable to write about this earlier.

IKEDA: I was once called on to explain your *The Deserter's Wife* to an audience of tens of thousands. The response was tremendous. The single-mindedness, suffering and strength of its heroine moved many women in the audience to tears. I was surprised and glad to learn that emotional reactions to such traits have not been dulled in my compatriots by the unprecedented peace and material prosperity we have enjoyed during the past few decades.

The conflict between a mother's strength and political authority constitutes the core of *The Deserter's Wife* and of such others of your works as *Mother Earth and Other Stories* (*Materinskoe pole*) and, in a sense, *The White Cloud of Genghis-Khan* (*Beloe oblako Gengis-Khana*). Your heroines' firm pacifism arises from their own experiences of the evil of conflict and not in response to the high-sounding propaganda that, as you point out, has all too often been employed by political regimes to condition the general populace to obedience and self-sacrifice. Totalitarian regimes try to compel the people to fit one pattern: the one that suits state political ends. As the mythical Greek Procrustes did by lopping parts off victims too large to fit his bed, such regimes try to amputate all popular rights that contradict their rigid political agendas. Tremendous loss of life under the Stalinist regime, and at the hands of the Nazis, has taught the peoples of the former Soviet Union what sacrifices are entailed in too readily swallowing glib governmental propaganda. The people of Japan, too, were deceived by militarists who led them into a war that caused horrifying losses at home and in other countries as well.

Throughout history, governments have put the cart before the horse by affording precedence to the interests of the state system over those of the people. We must now get our priorities right and put an end to this evil once and for all. Your task and mine are to contribute to the restoration of a true humanism that will achieve this goal.

Spiritual Support in Troubled Times

IKEDA: You and I were both born in 1928. Although our environments were different, we both belong to a generation whose value criteria were violently upset by the Second World War. As Socrates said, human beings must strive not merely to live, but also to live right; that is, constantly to seek meaning in life. When our value criteria are confused, our need to search for meaning intensifies. As we both know from experience, in youth, the need amounts to a compelling thirst. This is why I always advise young people to question the purposes of all their actions. I realise that they require spiritual support in this process. Certainly, I did when I was young. And I suppose you did too. What was your source of spiritual support in those troubled years when you began trying to make a difference to society? I found it in Buddhism and in the guidance given me by Josei Toda, the second president of Soka Gakkai and my personal mentor.

AITMATOV: I am sure I gave no thought to my own subjective relations to society in my early days. Our society was too cruel and merciless for that. The totalitarian regime in which we grew up, and to which we unquestioningly submitted, did not permit consideration, at least, not open consideration, of social problems from the individual's standpoint. The people accepted complete subjection of the individual to the dictates of state power not only as axiomatic and natural, but also as a positive achievement of the revolution. According to this postulate, no one was indispensable. And this, our fatal tragedy, was open to neither interpretation nor appeal.

The individual could only serve meticulously, could only be a means toward the attainment of ideological and political aims. Everything that failed to conform to the principles of class interests, everything, including spiritual and moral traditions, ethics, and even family relations, was repudiated as a leftover from the past and the lawless whims of bourgeois individualism. For example, conducting burials according to ancient customs and ceremonies was considered a symptom of political immaturity incurring persecution. The ruling party, which held a limitless monopoly on power, claimed to be the mind, conscience and honour of the epoch. It was the epoch's punitive force as well. In such conditions, the kind of mentor you mention cannot exist.

We lived in accordance with the principles of an artificial, coercive power, unique in the history of the new world. I bring all of this up in order to explain why I am unable to name a teacher who was for me the kind of spiritual mainstay that Josei Toda was for you. I can, however, name a few people who, in my young years, played a decisive part in the renewal of our society and its spiritual aspirations. First, Nikita Krushchev (1894–1971). Then, Alexander Tvardovsky (1910–71), editor-in-chief of the journal *Novy Mir* (New World). Though difficult at the time, his work as a publisher opened the road to great literature to me. Among Central Asian cultural figures, I recall with gratitude the classical Kazakh author Mukhtar Auezov (1897–1961), who participated directly in my literary formation.

Yes, of course, there were real people in those days, people whose whole way of life embodied a lofty understanding of honour, nobility and courage. I can only wonder how they managed to survive and preserve those traits under the inhuman conditions of totalitarian narrow-mindedness and patriotic cant. According to the fanatical logic of a time when informing, even among family members, was encouraged, such people should have been pulled up by the roots, like weeds, and destroyed. We have already mentioned the case of Pavlik Morozov, a little boy who was held up as a hero and model for emulation because he turned his father in to the officials for being politically suspect. Streets, children's organisations and schools were named for Pavlik. His father was shot.

The circumstances we lived in may explain why my generation of Soviet writers finds dealing with our tragedy painful. In this connection, the superb short story called *The Roundup* (*Oblava*) by the Belorussian writer Vasily Bykov (1924–2003), recommends itself to the international reader. More than thirty years ago, in *The Deserter's Wife*, I too tried to talk about it. We learned from our tragedy. Now we want to tell others how much the lesson cost us, what a terrifying price humanity has had to pay for it.

IKEDA: The liberal policies associated with *perestroika* opened the way for the publication of fiction of kinds strictly forbidden by the Communists. Of the numerous new Russian novels already available to us in Japanese translations, I found Anatoly Naumovich Rybakov's (1911–98) *The Children of the Arbat* (*Deti arbata*) especially impressive. In soul-searching fashion, the author tells the story of Sasha, a young man with a strong sense of justice, who is exiled because someone informed on him. At one juncture, Sasha says,

> What is morality? Lenin said morality is what is in the interests of the proletariat. But the proletariat is people and proletarian morals are human morals. To leave children in the snow is inhuman and, consequently, immoral. And it's also immoral to save your own life at the cost of somebody else's.[2]

Although Sasha's sentiments indicate no more than the way ordinary human beings ought to feel, his need to soliloquize on what would seem to be only normal attitudes suggests the ferocity of the totalitarian system he lived under. Honest self-awareness and common sense morality are the most important things. The French philosopher Henri Bergson (1859–1941) said that philosophy is only profound common sense. No ideology should be allowed to derange or obscure good common sense, a value shared by the individual and society as a whole. The philosophers' duty is to refine and enhance it.

Though to a lesser extent than in the Soviet Union, fanatic ideology once crippled Japanese society, too, especially in connection with education and freedom of expression. Even in those trying times, however, right-thinking people went on inconspicuously cultivating common sense. As long as some human beings remain true to their humanity, fanatic ideologies must sooner or later be exposed for what they truly are.

AITMATOV: To my great good fortune, in my early youth, I came into contact with people who, inwardly, rejected totalitarian ideas. They gave me courage and taught me to be, and always to remain, a human being in spite of everything; to place a higher value on my own noble human worth than on anything else.

I will always remember a country-school teacher who told me sternly: 'Never hang your head when you mention your father's name!' As I have said, my father, Torekul Aitmatov, was repressed and executed in 1937, and our family was forced to live deep in what could be called the sticks. It was perilous even to entertain certain thoughts, even silently, in those days. And here was this school teacher, not only thinking them, but actually saying them out loud.

Although at the time I only sensed it, I now fully understand his meaning. He was telling me to take pride in my father. The lesson was unforgettable. Of course, there were many others who instructed me, though without words. But, after all, the simple working man's wisdom is the man himself. Often you never even recognise his word's as instructions.

In short, I too had teachers of life. I bow my head in profound respect for the pure people of my homeland. They remain a spiritual mainstay for me to this day. Nor do I have to go back home to be reminded, in moments of happiness, rapture and, forgive me, glory, of my sources and of my immense debt to people who, for some unknown reason, love me.

In the Soviet Union, a fearsome poison found its way into our blood. Many people of my own generation know from experience how unbelievably, agonisingly hard it is for us to find the way to true culture and to the spiritual sources of the good. But without teachers of life on our path, we would find no salvation. In the past, I devoted my life to the search for the spiritual good. I shall go on doing so for as much time as remains to me. Fortunately, I still meet people who help me learn how to live. I find it bitter, however, to be compelled to say that many of my contemporaries, unable to break from the ideological shadows of Stalinism, still cling stubbornly to obsolete dogmas.

In our complicated, contradictory world, I too want to do as much as I can to help young people, even through my own mistakes, find the true road. I think it was Bismarck who said that fools learn from their own mistakes and wise people from the mistakes of others.

IKEDA: With your humanity and perceptiveness, you have a great deal to offer the young. I was only nineteen when I first met Josei Toda. At our first encounter, I let fly with three tremendously weighty questions about the nature of a just person and of true patriotism and his opinions of the Japanese emperor system. My inquiries were the natural outcome of the perplexities of youth and experience with the crushing weight of militaristic fascism. As the subtitle of Plato's *The Republic*, 'An Inquiry into the Nature of Justice', would have told me, humanity had been tussling with my first question for a very long time. I arrived at it intuitively. I vividly remember how Mr. Toda said, 'Now those are tough questions!' and then, without the slightest hesitation, proceeded to answer them fluently and wittily, avoiding abstruse philosophical terminology and speaking in accessible language ringing with unshakable faith. Won over by his convincing powers, I realised that he was the man I wanted to be my mentor. Subsequent experiences with Mr. Toda proved my intuition correct. Through him, I learned about society and humanity. He showed me the truth about life. I can say joyfully, proudly and boldly that my mentor was everything to me.

Expectations of Youth

IKEDA: In a less than affluent environment, young people in my day were greedy for reading and education in general. Times were hard and printing materials scarce. When word of a new edition of something got out, long lines formed in front of bookstores. I often joined them. As a way of sharing our limited supply of books, my friends and I organised reading groups. Now when I think back on it, I realise that shortages of books actually made us all the more determined to read voraciously. Perhaps this helps account for the clarity with which I remember things learned then. Indeed, it is not rare for restrictions to intensify effort. The French philosopher and author Jean Paul Sartre (1905–80) once said paradoxically about life in Nazi-occupied Paris: 'We have never been as free as under the German occupation.'[3]

Young people in the materialistic society of today are surrounded by a plethora of information generated by unprecedented economic prosperity. Instead of learning all they can, however, they ignore universal values and give themselves over to spiritually empty, loose living. On the basis of your own experience, how do you evaluate contemporary young people? Where can they find sound reasons for living?

AITMATOV: The very simplicity of the pressing question you pose conceals eternal factors that are very ancient and that are related to the interpretation of the meaning of life itself. We are compelled to ask ourselves whether living for the sake of children like the ones we see today is really worth it. History is supposed to manifest a tendency to progress. If this is indeed true, what progressive, new and better things do today's young people display?

Parents pass away. Their children are at once their greatest and their most contradictory legacy. Successors always arouse a complex of feelings including alarm and even despair in their predecessors. I am afraid even to take the matter up. Because I share the general alarms and doubts, I fear I will seem only another run-of-the-mill moralist. But I cannot help it. After all, you cannot run away from yourself.

Although I once barely ever noticed them, now, with each passing day, I sense the gaps between age groups more strongly. Maybe these very distances increasingly exacerbate generational disagreements about the struggle between the rational and the bad, between the permissible and the forbidden, and among socially elected modes of development. In such circumstances, deciding who is right and wrong becomes extremely complicated. For example, the older generations in Russia today innocently strayed and in doing so led the young people of the eighties and nineties into a dead-end street. How should we interpret the guilt the older people feel? We fathers rushed headlong into *perestroika* with the hope that posterity would carry the work on. But will young people justify our expectations? What do they think about our expectations of them? Will the youth of today appreciate our motives and actions for the sake of the democratic reconstruction of society? Or will the sufferings of the fathers be subjected to mockery and even vengeance by young people who have despised them from their earliest years? I have no simple answers to these questions.

Contemporary life has become so complicated that ordinary domestic moral teachings can hardly be effective. Of course, I might make some bitter, perplexed comments on, for example, the current pervasive fascination with all kinds of sexual play and its connection with a misunderstood notion of freedom. Such actions are actually dissipation, pornography – wretched, starved interference with a nature-given, extremely intimate possession. Everyone everywhere blames visual media like films, the stage, painting and so forth. But there would be no supply without a demand. Enough about that . . .

IKEDA: No, the point you bring up is too important to drop just yet. Besides, I have some thoughts on the generation gap that I want to mention. During the quarter of a century that has passed since the Austrian-born American economist Peter F. Drucker (1909–2005) coined the phrase, the generation gap has grown conspicuous enough to pose a grave social problem. The phenomenon itself, of course, is not new. Since the days of the ancient Greeks, older people have been complaining, 'I don't know what's wrong with these kids today . . .' In the past, instruction in the home helped bridge the gap. But recent dramatic alterations in society have greatly lowered its ability to fulfill that function with the result that the generation gap now seems too wide to bridge. Before long, today's kids will be the older generations. The rapid pace of change diminishes the general social sense of history. And, as this happens, words like *ideals, goals* and *aspirations*, symbolising traits that once seemed beautiful, natural accompaniments to youth, fade away.

Many people in the industrialised nations share your admitted reluctance even to discuss the matter. Middle and high-school teachers in Japan complain that moral instruction is their hardest task. They claim the greater their efforts, the greater student apathy.

How are we to deal with this situation without becoming, as you say, run-of-the-mill moralisers? I feel we must adopt two fundamental attitudes. First, we must avoid unilaterally criticising young people. Second, we must trust them. For better or worse, adults are the creators of society, which children reflect like mirrors. All the failings and faults we see in young people correspond to anomalies in society itself. How many adults can self-confidently assert trust in the younger generations? The ability to trust is unconditional; it does not depend on the other party. The trustworthiness of the young is beside the point. All human beings are worth trusting.

Instead of being guided by pre-judgements or outside opinions, we must live according to our own lights. Older people who condemn the young outright are often too much influenced by the lights of third parties.

My trust in young people arises from intimate conversations and direct cooperation with millions of them. They repay trust with trust. Older people who lament the diminished capacities of the young may only be revealing the meanness of their own abilities.

AITMATOV: I have quite simple things to say to young people. First, always remember that youth, like everything splendid, passes quickly. Today you are young; tomorrow you are middle-aged. Consequently, it is wrong to regard the world from the position of infantile privileges and peculiarities particular to given age groups. Good and evil are the same for people of all ages. Young people must not demonstrate the egoism of youth for too long. At a very early stage, they must begin to realise that they bear adult responsibilities. For a person with common sense, this in no way prevents young people from being young.

Second, a piece of fatherly advice: revolution is riot. Young people, put no trust in social revolutions! For nations, people and society, it is mass sickness, mass violence and general catastrophe. We Russians have learned this fully. Seek instead democratic reformation as the way to bloodless evolution and the gradual rebuilding of society. Evolution demands more time and patience, more compromises than revolution. It requires the building and cultivation of happiness, not its forceful establishment. I pray to God that younger generations will learn from our mistakes!

Finally, what is the meaning of life? This will remain an eternal question as long as humankind survives on Earth. Far from eliminating it, war, revolutions, all kinds of theories and teachings, profound internal shocks and insights, like those manifested by the critically thoughtful people in the Soviet Union or, in reverse, like the tragedy of democratic thought unfolding in China, intensify and complicate the inquiry, making it all the more keen and pressing. In short, in all situations, the flame of eternal inquiry never dies. We will go on thinking about the meaning of life and about reasons why human beings live. The duty of each generation is to try to answer this inexhaustible question as well as permit its insights.

Young people must think about the goals of life for themselves. Still, I should like to express my thoughts on the matter. Always immediately apparent, the needs of the moment generally take first precedent. In life's immutable struggle, in labour and vigil, in chaos and order, spiritual culture is one of the main achievements, if not the main achievement, justifying human life and fate.

Fyodor Dostoyevsky (1821–81) agonised over what would follow if everything in the world were so well arranged that everyone had enough to eat, clothes and shoes to wear, a fire on the hearth and a roof overhead. Assume that, with the aid of technological civilisation and post-industrial discoveries putting humankind on a par with the universal creator, all the sufferings of economic backwardness, poverty and abjection now gripping enormous regions of the Earth were to be overcome. Suppose that human material well-being were as certain as the rising and setting of the sun. Would not we, or our distant descendants, discover that material stimulus is far from an end in itself? Willy-nilly we consider it one now; indeed, in comparison with it, everything else is mere rhetoric. In a future, materially secure world, however, would we not see that material motives themselves are not the goal? Would we not understand that, like the things experienced in the torments of insight and self-expression, the higher goal is endless advance? By this, I mean moral, ethical and spiritual improvement from generation to generation. Perhaps eternal improvement of this kind is an approach toward a distant providence, in other words, toward the awakening of the divine-human in all members of humankind.

Justice

IKEDA: In describing your youth, you have written, 'In every house, hunger, want of the basic necessities, sickness and mourning for the dead . . . All this cruelty caused me incalculable suffering. But it also enabled me, relying on my own experience, to think deeply about the meaning of human life . . . My heart burst with pain when I saw how they took away the last lamb from a widow and orphans who had nothing else to eat. Yes, it was a cruel time . . .' Witnessing social injustice inspires a burning longing for justice in young minds. It must also have done so in you.

In my own late teens, when I eagerly absorbed everything around, I was profoundly moved by Victor Hugo's description of the awakening of conscience and philanthropy in the heart of Jean Valjean, hero of *Les Misérables*. Valjean's love for the poor and oppressed and his devotion to social reform, taught me the meaning of justice, strictness and kind-heartedness and suggested ways to seek justice under the layered anomalies of society.

AITMATOV: Socialist ideas can be said to have arisen from a dream of justice; that is, the dream that, no matter what his birth or social class, each human being should have the right to self-realisation, to a way of life worthy of his humanity. Championing justice is a relatively modern development, but the dream itself dates from time immemorial and may even be built into the human genetic code. The ancients, at least those about whom historical evidence has survived, dreamed of a 'Golden Age'. Later, Christianity, the religion of the poor, took up the idea. What stimulated early Christians to suffer horribly for their faith? The dream of justice! They were certain that, after earthly pain and suffering, they would go to heaven, which is as difficult for a rich man to enter as it is for a camel to go through the eye of a needle. Christian ideals have inspired magnificent art and literature. Dostoyevsky, one of your favourite writers, began his literary career with a novel called *Poor Folk (Bednye lyudi)*. Tolstoy divided all literature into Christian and non-Christian; that is to say, humane and anti-humane.

This is all splendid, but what does the Soviet socialist experiment have to show for itself? After destroying the rich, we failed to enrich the poor. Poverty remains just as it was. What am I trying to say? Just this: perhaps attainment of justice does not depend on a rigid separation of the 'rich' from the 'poor'. Do we struggle with frenzied rage, giving ourselves over to blind instincts, solely so that everyone can be equal and affluent? I think the proposition should be restated in this way: it is just as shameful to be rich as it is to be poor. We are not talking about a crust of bread. Any society, no matter what name it goes under, is shameful if it manifests poverty. Such a society cannot claim to be just. Perhaps I can explain my meaning better by referring to the Roman Stoic philosopher Seneca (4?BC–AD65), who said that the man who wants more, not the man who has little, is truly poor. Indisputably, having more is achieved at the cost of those who have less.

What do we mean by 'more' and 'less'? Unfortunately, in our incomplete, divided, and cruel world, we are limited to talking about our 'daily bread'. This is inescapable. The millions of hungry and hapless on this Earth are a living denunciation and curse to any social system permitting humans to live in such circumstances. They are the clearest and bitterest possible examples of an injustice that cries to the heavens: an injustice that stifles discussion. Nonetheless, we must speak out. The evil of social injustice predates Biblical times and extends back to the creation of humanity. What is its source?

IKEDA: Great thinkers and writers have seen that evil is often perpetrated in the name of superficial considerations that are by no means its true causes. Seneca gets to the heart of the matter by saying that poverty is not the lack of property but the, ostensibly grasping, desire for more possessions. In Shakespeare's *Othello*, the evidence of Desdemona's faithlessness slyly planted in Othello's mind by Iago is entirely too flimsy to be the true cause of Othello's raging jealousy. The real cause lies much deeper in Othello's profoundly passionate soul. In passing, Iago's wife Emilia remarks that some spirits are jealous innately:

Emilia: Pray heaven it be state matters, as you think,
   And no conception nor no jealous toy
   Concerning you.
Desdemona: Alas the day, I never gave him cause!
Emilia: But jealous souls will not be answer'd so;
   They are not ever jealous for the cause,
   But jealous for they are jealous. 'tis a monster
   Begot on itself, born on itself. (Act III, Scene 4)[4]

Nazism and Stalinism, two looming evils of the twentieth century, habitually advanced superficial reasons for perpetrating the most horrendous crimes against humanity. In the case of the Nazis, it generally had something to do with Aryan purity and the eradication of so-called inferior races. This patently insignificant consideration spawned the Holocaust. Stalin and his henchmen spilled the blood of vast numbers of people in the name of such shallow ideas as party loyalty. In the furore created by Nazis and Stalinists alike, thoughtful people must have found it hard to penetrate to and confront the real causes of the horror. Japanese militarists also led the people into war in the name of fanatic, state Shinto chauvinism superficial enough to brand all Americans and Englishmen as 'fiends'.

As Western artists, including the Greek tragic dramatists and Saint Augustine, have clearly shown, the first step in delving to the true cause of evils is to cast off superficialities and to concentrate on what is deep inside us.

AITMATOV: Sometimes, however, deep inside there is only contemptuous intolerance that breeds injustice and leads people unable to recognise higher values to consider whole other races as no more than slaves. Self-proclaimed prophets claim the right to make others happy but, if the favours they proffer are rejected, grow so disgruntled that, in the grips of ineffable fervour, they become, not gracious benefactors, but merciless hangmen. Many examples of such a thing might be cited.

I recall how my heart bled at the sight of humiliated and insulted human beings. It still bleeds for them today. My pain is all the stronger because, and this is worst of all, the insulted person may not understand what humiliates him, mocks his human worth, and insolently tramples underfoot his sacred rights as a free-born human being; at least in so far as is set forth in the Universal Declaration of Human Rights.

When I wrote about the starving widow and orphans, I was moved by compassion and pain. Later, I learned that the people who took away their last sheep did not even understand the so-called Great Idea in the name of which they were supposed to be acting. Far from justifying their acts, the perpetrators' ignorance makes what they did a grave, an unforgivable, crime. In fact, their 'Great Idea' was misanthropy as state policy.

It is my duty as a writer to understand all psychology, even criminal psychology. But, as a human being, although perhaps incapable of actually punishing them, I cannot condone the crimes of the guilty. As a writer, I must understand even the philosophy of leaders who either found suitable accomplices ready to hand or converted ordinary human beings (granted they once were ordinary humans) into blind tools of their own satanic will. How are such people to be judged? As human beings? As non-humans? Does a way to describe such people even exist? Confronted with this dilemma, whether we want to or not, we must turn to God: 'Yes, there is divine judgement!' But this knowledge brings no peace to a mind awaiting, not vengeance, but *justice*.

You ask about the sources of justice and standards for discriminating between the just and the unjust. I wish I knew how to locate them. I should like to think they are to be found in love for the human being innately entitled to happiness. In the face of this consideration, all ideologies and governmental systems are beside the point. Or, if they count at all, it is only when they value and affirm justice above all else.

IKEDA: Humanity has cried out for justice throughout history. With mental and physical misery heaped on him, Job, the 'perfect and upright' man was seeking justice from God when he demanded, 'Make me to know my transgression and my sin.' (Job 13:23). In China, Sima Qian (*c*.145–90BC), the author of the *Records of the Grand Historian*, was castrated for alleged disloyalty to the throne. In his pain and shame, he, too, demanded to know whether his fate was just; that is, whether it accorded with the Way of Heaven. Your own sincerely expressed reactions to the injustices you have witnessed belong in this same tradition. I agree wholeheartedly that the source of justice is love for the human being innately entitled to be free and happy. You express the essence of the matter with the appropriately weighty, penetrating simplicity born of experience. Your words shed light on both the sources of justice and the spiritual essence of humanism.

As you say, it was the tragedy of the peoples of the Soviet Union to be dominated for seventy years by the so-called 'Great Idea'. And, now that the idea has been discredited, everyone who experienced it is at a loss to find a replacement. To an extent, it is understandable that, as some of my

Russian acquaintances claim, hatred now rules the public mind. The gap that seventy years of materialistic education created may be too wide and too deep for the leap to divine salvation and the establishment of justice. The problem is rendered more difficult by the irreversible secularisation that modernisation is causing, not only in Russia, but also throughout the world.

The topic naturally invites discussion of religious faith, but we must postpone that for a while. I suggest concentrating now on the idea of humanity. The noted French writer André Gide (1869–1951) visited the Soviet Union in the 1930s. He went with high expectations but returned shocked by the threat of totalitarianism he sensed there. Back in France, he expressed his fears in the book *Retour d l'U.R.S.S.* (*Return from the USSR*). The political and philosophical Left ganged up to criticise the book severely. Still, refusing to give in to them, Gide continued celebrating the importance of *humanité*. Let us follow his example.

The Cultural Agora

IKEDA: Public poetry readings are a venerable, still thriving, Russian tradition. In the past, people read their own poems publicly in cafés. Nowadays, trained actors give poetry readings on the stage and on television. I envy you this. Once upon a time, poetry meetings and gatherings to compose and recite haiku were common in Japan. But in recent years they have grown rare.

Perhaps it is necessary to have a specific place where literature can be read aloud and shared by a participating audience in a way that enlivens the word's soul-liberating effect. In the ancient Greek theatre and in Shakespeare's theatre, where the stage projected deep into the groundlings' unroofed pit, actors and audience were close enough together to share the same emotional experiences. The absence of barriers between them facilitated stirring communications striking mutually sympathetic chords. The rarity of similar places for communications in modern society hampers the essential operations of literary art. This is why poetry readings of the kind the Russian people love deserve great respect.

AITMATOV: Democratic culture is characterised by direct communications with art and in places like the market place or agora and by joint participation in drama (or play).

All this together [tales, epics, touring theatrical troupes, *mushair* (poetic competitions of improvising bands)] constitutes a hypostasis of folk art.

Profoundly ethnic in content, it embodies common human spiritual values that, alas not too long ago, our official Soviet class ideology called feudal and patriarchal and strove to uproot and discard as antagonistic to the new socialist culture.

They would have succeeded in this task, had the roots of folk culture been shallow. Because they are deep, however, oral epic poetry, as one example, survived in the innermost folk spirit. A striking artistic phenomenon, the oceanlike epos flows on from generation to generation, from age to age. Although it seems unlikely, single human beings can memorise this whole sea of verses. For many years I was on friendly terms with Sayabkai Karalaev, an outstanding and, alas, unique narrator of folk poetry, who knew a million lines of the Kirghiz epic *Manas*. The last great bards of this epic, whom I knew, were truly great personalities uniting in themselves poetry and folk wisdom.

Allow me to relate an incident I was fortunate enough to witness. By chance, I travelled with Karalaev to a collective farm, or *kolkhoz*, in the Chuiskaya valley. An outstanding *Manas* minstrel was scheduled to perform there. Word spread at once throughout the village and surrounding settlements. Because the *kolkhoz* club was too small to hold everyone who wanted to attend, Karalaev performed outdoors. A chair was set for him on a platform, and audience members sat wherever they could. Suddenly storm clouds gathered. A horrendous downpour! Still Karalaev went on performing; not a single person left. They all sat there listening to the *Manas* in the pouring rain, completely engrossed in what they were hearing. I shall never forget it.

How can I explain this unlikely occurrence? Listening to ancient tales embodying a whole people's history, world knowledge and poetic gifts, the audience members not only remembered what they used to be like, but also came to know their present selves better.

IKEDA: Your interesting comments on bards in your country call to mind the blind minstrels who once travelled all over Japan, reciting epic tales while accompanying themselves on the four-string lute (the *biwa*, introduced into Japan from China). Though known as early as the tenth century, these minstrels were most active during the thirteenth and fourteenth centuries, when they specialised in reciting the *Heike Monogatari* (The Tale of the Heike), a long, romantic telling of the rise and fall of the Taira clan, who for a while dominated the ruling military class. As time passed, emendations and additions swelled the original six volumes of the tale to twelve.

The blind minstrels who compiled, memorised and popularised the *Heike Monogatari* played an important part in taking good literature out of the aristocratic circles to which it had formerly been restricted and introducing it to warriors and ordinary people, who constituted the major part of their audiences. A familiar seven-and-five syllable meter in combination with distinctly rhythmical recitation and the reverberating lute accompaniment intensified the impression of their performances, which involved cooperative audience-artist interchanges like those you characterise as belonging in the agora.

Another Japanese example of cooperative literary creation and enjoyment is the literary genre known as *renga* (linked verse), which was popular from about the twelfth into the sixteenth century. At *renga* gatherings, one poet would compose and recite the first half of a poem, usually of either three lines of five, seven and five syllables or in two lines of seven and seven syllables each, and another would compose and recite the second half. *Renga* parties, often held out of doors under the trees, especially at cherry-blossom time, are said sometimes to have produced thousands or tens of thousands of verses at a sitting. Unfortunately, however, this tradition has largely died out. Ironically, the age of convenient transport that brings us all closer together physically has isolated us from each other spiritually.

AITMATOV: In the agora art of medieval Europe, proximity facilitated specific dialogue between performers and spectators. In such circumstances, the observer is included in the action of the performance. Instead of merely watching what others perform, he creates. With or without his purposeful intention, his reactions saturate the performer's words, thus impassioning the performer himself. The fascinating and ever-new question of interactions between performers and spectators demands different answers in different epochs. It would be interesting to hear the opinions of actors and directors in connection with it, and of audiences as well. Celebrated Russian stage directors like Vsevolod Meyerhold (1874–1940) and Nikolay Okhlopkov (1900–67) dreamed of theatre in the ancient Greek spirit. And, if I am not mistaken, Yuri Lyubimov (1917–) has tried, and continues to try, to do something similar at the Taganka Theatre in Moscow.

Oriental theatrical traditions, in particular those of Japan – the kabuki theatre, for instance – strike me as truly democratic. Wherever it has been fortunate to survive, so-called folk culture provides the grounds for the creation of such theatre. In this connection, I might mention the singing holidays of the Baltic countries. During these inspiring festivals, citizens unite spiritually. Similar festivals are held in Georgia, Moldova and elsewhere.

IKEDA: A thorough understanding of a contemporary culture requires consideration of relations between the intelligentsia and the ordinary people. In Russia after the time of Peter I (1672–1725), a great gap opened between the upper-class intelligentsia and the people. Although sometimes regarded as the first page in the process leading to the Revolution of 1917, the Decembrist uprising of 1825 was actually carried out, not by ordinary citizens, but by politically disaffected upper-class officers. At a later time, other upper-class intellectuals reacted to the failure of the Decembrists by fomenting a 'back-to-the-people' movement. When he set out on the path of democratisation, President Gorbachev found that, in spite of Soviet egalitarianism, the old gap persisted, compelling him to take great authority into his own hands. Like Peter I, he faced the dilemma of having to become an enlightened despot.

AITMATOV: In Western European culture, on the other hand, no such gap seems to have existed. If it had, why would muleteers in Florence sing Dante's canzoni? Why did merchants shut up shop and dash to hear the poet Bernardo Oscoldi when he passed through Rome? Behaviour of this kind occurs when the upper crust and the lower echelons of society reverberate together.

IKEDA: Yes, as the Swiss art and culture historian Jakob Burckhardt (1818– 97) insisted, it is wrong to assume that the masses of the ordinary people played no part in the Renaissance. After all, as he pointed out, the very poorest Italians read the poetry of Torquato Tasso (1544–95). This only indicates that richly valuable culture can grow only in the fertile soul of the people.

AITMATOV: Of course, a discussion of this kind requires a definition of the word *culture*, even if only as a working term. Perhaps culture can be called the unity of style in all artistic manifestations of a given people.

IKEDA: I can agree with that but should like to add the element of religious zeal. The American-born British poet, critic and Nobel laureate T. S. Eliot (1888–1965) said, 'We may ask whether any culture could come into being, or maintain itself, without a religious basis.' and 'the culture being, essentially, the incarnation (so to speak) of the religion of a people.'[5]

Culture expresses an inner human voice. It aspires toward lofty spiritual values. But it must include a religious element if it is to reach great heights. The poetry of Matsuo Bashō (1644–94) usually embodies a religious approach, which, as in the following haiku, may not be in any sense self-assertive. 'Viewed in calm, all things are self-enlightenment.'

AITMATOV: Art was an inalienable part of the lives of illiterate Tadzhik farmers, who knew by heart great quantities of poetry including the quatrains (*ruba'i*) of the Persian poet Omar Khayyam (*c*.1050–1122) and works by the Iranian poets Firdausi (*c*.940–1020) and Nezami (twelfth century), the Turkish poet Mehmed bin Süleyman Fuzuli (*c*.1495–1556) and the Turkmen Mahtum Quli (eighteenth century).

Culture is related to the problem of ethnic memory. In our day, when connections with the past have been severed, this problem has assumed a tragic nuance. The fearsome illness of our age, ethnic amnesia, is the root of all the evils that have crashed down on the head of humanity in the form of totalitarian regimes and dictatorships. The cruel experiments of revolutionising oracles require a state of 'cultural revolution'. But the revolutions they laud as noble human activities only lead the masses into spiritual and cultural nihilism, impoverishment and, consequently, barbarism.

The attempt, or more accurately, the ideological state policy, of creating a *new* culture – as in the Soviet Union – not only arrogantly rejects so-called 'bourgeois' culture, but also, confined within the rigid frame of some political system with peremptory doctrines, ultimately destroys *all* culture. Their essence and their aims doom such new cultures to failure. Why? First and foremost, because culture is not created overnight in the service of an ideology. It is neither instituted by decree nor created on order. True culture is always in a process of development continuing from time immemorial. This is the only reason why a history of culture exists. A sense of the unbroken continuity of history is embodied in the culture of a people. Cherished in the popular spirit, culture finds expression in songs, poetry and dances, which, in their turn, depend on a people's traditions.

IKEDA: Yes, traditions are essential. During a period of intense borrowings and learning from the West, the Japanese laboured long and hard over the problem of balancing modernisation and tradition. Leading thinkers and writers said illuminating things on the subject. Profoundly versed in the cultural traditions of his own country, the scholar, author and translator

Ōgai Mori (1862–1922) said, 'If I examined it honestly, there was no reason to assume that the Japanese, who had progressed satisfactorily through some thousands of years, had followed an unreasonable way of life. It had been obvious from the very beginning.'[6] The poet and novelist Tōson Shimazaki (1872–1943) wrote, 'Something survives within us (Japanese) that is not to be found in Europe, a certain stylishness or dashing manner. An innate love of beauty and cleanliness. I think these things have harmonised relations between our poor and our rich.'[7]

People like Sōseki Natsume (1867–1916) and Ōgai Mori were able to understand Western culture well because they had a firm understanding of their own tradition. By like token, their understanding of the West intensified the traditional flavour of their works.

Japanese thinkers and writers like these attained an admirable level of cultural inter-relation. Our task today is to expand international cultural cooperation with the aim of attaining the global. Creative culture was envisioned by Goethe. In speaking to his friend and editor Johann Peter Eckermann (1792–1854), after commenting on the vicious nature and pertinacity of inter-nation hatred, Goethe explained where such feelings are most likely to be found and how he himself relates to them:

'Actually,' Goethe went on, 'national hatred is something particular. You will find it at its most intense and violent on the lowest cultural levels. There is a level, however, where it disappears and where people, so to speak, stand above nations and feel the joys and sorrows of neighbouring peoples as if they were their own. This cultural level accorded with my own nature, and I fortified myself in it for a long time, until I attained my sixtieth year.'[8]

We today must strive to live on this level and to create a global culture oriented toward universal understanding and spiritual solidarity.

Incidentally, as the first introduction to the West of the work of the fourteenth-century Persian poet Hafez (1315–90), Goethe's own *West-Eastern Divan* contributed to the development of such a culture.

AITMATOV: The culture issue, particularly the culture dialogue, of which the Russian thinker Mikhail M. Bakhtin (1895–1975) dreamed, is pre-eminently important. And, in connection with it, I entertain the hope of establishing a new, international, cultural program designed to influence world society.

Culture in the Country

IKEDA: You are often compared with the younger Siberian writer Valentin G. Rasputin (1937–). Perhaps this is because, like yours, his stories deal with simple human love and emphasise the importance of inherited traditions. He also draws freely on folklore and proverbs. To an extent, the vitality of your writing, and of his, arises from your sources, Kirghiz in your case and Siberian in his, both of them far from what is generally considered Russia's cultural centres.

As is illustrated by current vigorous literary production in Latin America and the Third World nations, deep-rooted traditions bear rich artistic fruit, even in the face of standardisation brought on by the spread of sophisticated means of travel and communication. Modernisation and population concentration inevitably put urban culture in a position of dominance. Now, however, as that culture reaches an impasse, more and more people are turning their attention toward what is happening far from the great conurbations. Literature in the big cities has fallen on bad times. Whereas this alone does not necessarily indicate degradation of the entire urban civilisation, it is nonetheless a significant phenomenon.

AITMATOV: The French say genius is born in the country and dies in Paris. If the heart of your question is the inevitability of renewing so-called traditional culture 'produced' in the city and then disseminated to the 'provinces', what does the concept of 'Paris' stand for? The vile process of urban cultural concentration did not start yesterday. Once again, we must take the historical view. Why has cultural activity gradually and, equally as important, un-deviatingly become 'urban' merchandise and a means of, as you accurately point out, standardisation? Today people are so afraid of being called countrified that they are willing to renounce their own roots for the sake of seeming up-to-date and cultivated.

The whole matter is a complicated, intractable knot. Why does so-called new culture exercise such a monopoly? I think the reason is directly connected with the techno-scientific revolution and, first of all, with population urbanisation, which, while creating vast megalopolises with lifestyles completely at variance with older peasant traditions, has restructured morality to suit the new ways. In fundamentally changing circumstances, laws for community life are born and the laws define and regulate social behaviour and ideals of the human being.

The American novelist John Steinbeck (1902–68) perspicaciously remarked, 'The present universal fear has been the result of a forward surge in our knowledge and manipulation of certain dangerous factors in the physical world.'⁹ The sense of danger becomes all the more powerful because we do not understand what is happening.

It is often said, and not without some grounds, that you Japanese already live in the twenty-first century. That is one reason why I should be happy to learn your thoughts on this subject. How do the effects of the techno-scientific revolution influence Japanese culture?

IKEDA: To speak frankly, the influence is destructive. Traditional Japanese culture evolved in harmonious symbiotic relations with the world of nature. In addition to finding expression in aesthetic treatments of the beauty of the changing seasons, this harmony has permeated daily life in various manifestations of both love and fear of natural forces and in accommodating practical activities to natural rhythms.

In the latter part of the nineteenth century, Western influences began flooding Japan. The national government adopted a policy of industrialisation for the sake of what was called a 'Wealthy Nation and a Mighty Military'. For a while, without eradicating traditional relationships with nature, Westernisation merely appended the blessings of the new to the old.

After the Second World War, ruthless pursuit of economic growth and wealth upset the old balance. Galloping environmental destruction was the result. Familiar, beloved scenes of hillside and stream were spoiled beyond recognition. Pollution of air and water took high tolls in human sacrifices. The apparent prosperity enjoyed by the Japanese archipelago concealed environmental pollution exceeding natural capabilities of self-purification and recovery. Modern rationalism is founded on the concept of subjugating nature. The relative mildness of the Japanese environment, plus a plexus of other contributory factors, enabled this concept to manifest its powers in extreme forms in our country.

We are now compelled to revise our whole view of nature. Instead of opposing and attempting to subjugate it, we must strive to harmonise and unite ourselves with the natural world. The threats ecological problems pose for the future of the whole human race make this change of attitude all the more pressing. While we cannot return to primitive ways of life, we must strive to harmonise the enjoyment of the fruits of civilisation with moderation and respect for the needs of the non-human world of nature.

AITMATOV: That is unquestionably true. A people's culture is founded on irreplaceable spiritual and moral values evolved in the course of thousands of years. Today those values are being horribly corroded and are being declared, or at least were declared in the former Soviet Union, to be outdated feudal or bourgeois prejudices. They were called 'provincial.'

Mythology was treated the same way. But fairy tales, legends and myths are folk art in which the people express and preserve truths that, while eternal, are always new in that each emerging generation has great need of them. They constitute a spiritual immortality that has always helped us survive and preserve our humanity in the face of the most improbable cataclysms. As no doubt everyone agrees, culture continually evolves; old cultures are not replaced *in toto* by new ones.

IKEDA: Because of the great importance of history and tradition to it, culture by its nature embodies continuance and continuity. It is the height of modern presumption and arrogance to imagine that the past can be severed from the present and that one culture can be exchanged for another as easily as we change one garment for another. Culture must not be so grossly underrated.

Culture embodies the accumulated wisdom of our forefathers. The proverbial three score years and ten are too short a span to amass enough wisdom to deal with all the contingencies of existence. This is why culture, or knowledge, selected and refined over many generations, is indispensable.

As part of the inevitable process of cultural evolution, new accretions may sometimes seem to obliterate the old. Actually, however, the old is always present at deeper levels, where it exerts a powerful influence on thought and behaviour. With the passing of time, the new grows old, undergoing selection and refinement ultimately to take its place in the cultural continuum. Coercive attempts to perform the impossible by brutally annihilating one culture and replacing it with another always leave only chaos and anarchy behind.

AITMATOV: Still, some people think total replacement is the only way to deal with the civilisational changes taking place in the Soviet Union now. Such attempts disturb me. To my way of thinking, though we travel in ultramodern vehicles, we must remain provincial in the sense of professing faith in the rules of behavioural and moral laws bequeathed to us by our ancestors. First among those laws is this: some things are forbidden.

But how is the contemporary human being to fix the bounds between the permitted and the forbidden? What role does culture play in this process?

IKEDA: Culture applies the brakes to ensure that we answer the voice of conscience when it tells us 'some things are forbidden'. In the following passage from *Doktor Zhivago*, the Nobel laureate Boris Pasternak (1890–1960) speaks with the voice of conscience. Addressing some hot-headed young Bolsheviks, Zhivago says,

> Re-do life? Maybe that's the way people who have seen a few sights but have never known life or felt its smell and soul can talk. For people like that, existence is a lump of coarse material not yet ennobled by their touch and needing to be worked over by them. But life is never matter or a substance. Life is, if you like, a beginning that is constantly renewing and re-shaping itself. Life is always re-doing and transub-stantiating itself. It is far above our obtuse theories.[10]

Like you, when you say that some things are forbidden, Pasternak warns arrogant contemporary humanity against mistaking license for liberty.

Culture preserves moral standards evolved by our forefathers. Serving as the axis around which we may all unite spiritually, it provides common criteria of good and evil, behavioural patterns and grounds for identity. It gives individuals a daily-life guide and sets priorities. If they want to be progressively effective, reformers must keep cultural patterns in mind. Merely tossing out the old and replacing it with something new illustrates the kind of arrogance Pasternak characterises as regarding human life and culture as no more than raw material.

AITMATOV: I agree. In the years to come, non-urban regions; that is, 'the country', will vitalise culture founded in common human values. A tendency to return to nature, the mother of all things and the source of our spirituality, is now just emerging. We must also take this into consideration. Who knows, perhaps humanity will one day want to flee from the monstrous megalopolis. If so, what will happen then?

IKEDA: What will happen? I wonder. The ultimate outcome of urbanisation and modernisation is a very big topic. Nonetheless, I suggest dialectics, not nostalgia, must characterise our approach to it. Modern cities may be heinous, but we cannot go back to the past, as the American philosopher Henry David Thoreau (1817–68) and the French philosopher Jean Jacques Rousseau (1712–78) seem to have wanted to do. For one thing, it would demand reducing global population to half or two-thirds its present size.

Modern civilisation has its good points. Some progress has been made, at least in parts of the world, in dealing with poverty, hunger and illness. Undeniably serious problems remain. Instead of throwing the baby out with the bathwater, we must apply the best of our achievements to their solutions in a dialectic fashion. Navigating the ship of humanity through the troubled waters of the future is a difficult, but inescapable, task.

Learning is Light; Ignorance, Darkness

IKEDA: At one time, when word got out of the imminent publication of something of great popular interest, say a full edition of Dostoyevsky, Soviet citizens lined up in front of bookstores as much as ten days in advance. During the hard times of the immediate postwar period, we Japanese, too, stood in long lines to buy the latest good books, like *Zen no Kenkyu* (An Inquiry into the Good), by the celebrated philosopher Kitarō Nishida (1870–1945).

But in today's more affluent society, young people demonstrate less interest in time-tested literature than in frivolous, trendy, purely commercial writing. Such shallow writings may titillate but cannot thrill deeply because they never deal with fundamental questions about the nature of life and the way we ought to live it. Reading for pure entertainment has its place; but young people need and, I think, demand chances to pit their minds and hearts against great books that broach profound issues.

AITMATOV: Reading matter for young people is a major concern to the family and to society as a whole. From day to day, letter to letter, reading forms the juvenile mind. As the pertinent popular aphorism has it, show me what your young people read and I'll tell you what awaits you in the future. Cooperation between family upbringing and books is important. Often, however, the relation between the two is disharmonious. At the risk of championing extremely primitive views, I insist on my own, very likely conservative, convictions.

First of all, reading must prepare the young to avoid inevitable encounters with evil. This is important: we must not allow ourselves to forget it for a single moment. Rearing young people has been, is, and always will be preparation for encounters with evil, which waits around every corner for everyone, young and old alike. Evil is ubiquitous, but good must be created through the constant labour of the soul.

The best-intentioned book may be undistinguished, unattractive and simply uninteresting. As simple as it might seem, it takes time and effort to be able to predict from the first paragraph, from word arrangement and phrase construction and content, whether what lies ahead justifies reading a book to the finish. How often we find ourselves struggling through grey jungles of banal, run-of-the-mill writing! I want to save young people from straying in this thicket and keep them from sinking in swamps of dialectic, rhetoric and bare pretentiousness. But how? I am fully aware that my starry-eyed idyllists about teaching youth how to be good readers are not always realistic. Nonetheless, I am convinced that there is only one way to achieve this end: deliberate hard work. Goethe, when an old man, said he had been studying how to read all his life. This from a man like Goethe!

And what is meant by 'studying to read'? It means cultivating an ability to experience things vicariously. I consider reading a special kind of emotion-moral life, which is all the more vivid the greater and deeper the reader's gift for vicarious experience.

IKEDA: Goethe's life-long studying to read was a process of cultivating the imagination, or to use your words, the ability for vicarious experience. Always difficult, this undertaking grows even harder after the passing years have abraded and diminished vigorous, youthful imaginative powers. The French poet and philosopher Paul Valéry (1871–1945) once said, 'The thing that strikes me more than anything else about Goethe is his very long life.'[11] Perhaps Valéry was referring to the full maturation of imaginative powers that Goethe's longevity permitted.

Like the writer, the reader, too, if he wants to be good at his task, must preserve a vigorous, youthful imagination throughout life. Neither powers of imagination nor the gift for vicarious experience is innate. Occurring to greater or lesser extents in different people, they must be discovered and cultivated. At all stages of the cultivation, the reader must remain on his guard, as my mentor Josei Toda repeatedly cautioned me, to remain in control of reading matter without ever allowing it to get the upper hand. Too many young people today allow junk-writing, trafficking in explicit sex and violence and holding up as role models ruthless self-servers who stop at nothing to achieve their selfish aims, to gain too strong a hold on their minds.

AITMATOV: That is indeed a disturbing phenomenon. Among young Russians, as is only to be expected, impoverished, ideological Soviet literature is no longer in demand. Its day has passed. Fortunately, the young no longer accept empty admonitions, pretentious declarations or false optimism. It is nonetheless distressing to observe the massive attraction, and I am not exaggerating, of low-level writing of the kind you describe: pornography, justifications of violence, mysticism and so on. Fruits that were once forbidden seem sweet. But unscrupulous people are taking advantage of the young. Flooding the market with trash, they inundate immature, susceptible, young minds with obscene writing inciting wild, primitive instincts. This is a manifestation of eternal, multifaceted Evil. Of course, it is all done under 'revolutionary' slogans like 'Freedom of Speech', '*Glasnost*' and so on. What can we do? Prohibitions will not help. Quite the contrary. Still, we must do something.

IKEDA: Cheap publications have plagued many others in the past, too. In his *Gespräche mit Goethe* (Conversations with Goethe), Johann Peter Eckermann reports the poet's comments on the topic:

> Through the bad, chiefly negative, aesthetical and critical tone of the journals, a sort of half culture finds its way into the masses; but to productive talent it is a noxious mist, a dropping poison, which destroys the tree of creative power from the ornamental green leaves, to the deepest pith and most hidden fibres.[12]

What would Goethe have to say about the publishing and media situation prevailing in much of the world today? At his most pessimistic, he could not have imagined the extents to which the meretricious media of our times pander to carnal passions by concentrating on sex, scandal and violence. The situation is probably similar in both Japan and Russia.

You are correct in advising against prohibitions. The press ought to regulate itself. But their prevailing greed leaves little hope that the mass-media will change their ways. Young people are impatient. Cruel as it may appear, as long as the media fail to act responsibly, perhaps we have no recourse but to expose youth to coverage of contemporary abuses in the hope that it will generate antibodies against actual evil.

AITMATOV: At the opening of his poetic novel *Evgeniy Onegin*, Aleksandr S. Pushkin (1799–1837) sets a line by his contemporary Prince Pyotr Vyazemsky (1792–1878) that describes the impatience of youth as rushing to live and hurrying to feel.

IKEDA: Yes, young people are like that. They fear time will run out before they have absorbed everything life has to offer. But the headlong, hedonistic, carpe-diem attitude can lead to nihilism, a kind of inversion of traditional Russian Messianism.

AITMATOV: In spite of the destructive force of contemporary mass culture, many young people refuse to submit, can tell good from evil and prize chastity in love above everything. Unafraid to appear passé to their peers, they value old-fashioned ideas like honour, nobility and self-sacrifice.

Many people find recreational reading attractive because it makes no demand on the heart or the mind. I am worried, however, that such people might someday come to consider that living without thinking is normal. That would be socially dangerous. Scope and choice of reading matter depend largely on prevailing evaluations of the human being. What is the good of learning if the ignorant and uncultivated live in clover while the scholar is looked upon as an oddball? Why learn to read at all, then?

IKEDA: Because learning is light and ignorance darkness. Today, young people are beginning to understand the value of the well-rounded, harmonious personality, something beautifully expressed by the Russian word *vse-chelovechestvo*. They must be prepared to live in the complex and fascinating world of the future in a way that does honour to the best of their humanity. Reading is indispensable to acquiring the ability to live in such a way. Good books do more than expand knowledge: they facilitate the creation of a new self.

The Highest Responsibility

IKEDA: Out of a sense of social responsibility, you expand your field of activity beyond literature by participating in projects of wide significance. For example, in 1987, you invited writers like the American futurologist Alvin Toffler (1928–) and the playwright Arthur Miller (1915–2005) to take part in the Issyk-Kul International Forum held on the shores of Lake Issyk-Kul in your homeland, Kyrgyzstan, to discuss human survival in a world free of nuclear weapons.

Writers and all other intellectuals must be acutely aware of their social responsibilities and, without favouring factions, must set their goals on universal values like philanthropy, justice and peace. According to the celebrated Russian writer Maksim Gorky (1868–1936), intellectuals must ask themselves daily what they are doing, and what they will do, to keep civilisation from relapsing into barbarity.

AITMATOV: Essentially, the development and sustenance of society as a whole is their responsibility. For intellectuals, their duty to culture is the paramount issue. The mass culture of the era of the scientific-technological revolution is both our destiny and our sorrow. How are we to survive and preserve genuine values in the conditions of mass culture?

In my opinion, barbarity, bitterness and cynicism constitute the greatest threat to contemporary humanity. Ignorance, pornography and the cult of violence dominate the arts. Young people have nothing with which to fill their spiritual emptiness, nothing on which to spend their genetic energy. Many of the great ideas for which humanity has struggled and died and which represent the heroic acts of whole generations are either forgotten or betrayed.

In Russia today, with the rejection of God and the transgression of the law, we are reaping the harvest of seeds sown with the destruction of our hereditary intelligentsia, peasantry and cultural monuments. Publicly recognised political, economic and cultural ignorance is the wages of these acts and the source of our current crisis. The major responsibility of the intelligentsia, if we, writers in particular, decide to describe ourselves in this way, is to determine clearly for ourselves the causes of what has happened and continues to happen to us, report to the people, and find a way out of our impasse. We must penetrate to the heart of the matter. The writer's responsibility is to utter sorrow-engendered words embodying the torment, pain, faith and hope in whose name he is charged to speak.

Everything that happens in the world happens to the writer and willy-nilly reflects in his art, which, no mere occupation, like, for example, music or painting, is his fate, his means of understanding and expressing a truth higher than he is and necessary to all. In the face of such a responsibility, 'narrow party interests' pale into insignificance.

IKEDA: As I suspect you recall, the *Maison Littéraire de Victor Hugo*, in France, displays a collection of letters from home and abroad congratulating Hugo on his eightieth birthday. One of them is from the French novelist Émile Zola (1840–1902). Although little is known for certain about relations between them, the two novelists, one a great romanticist, the other a fervent naturalist, exchanged communications from time to time, on important occasions.

In the broad sense, Hugo and Zola were both moralists incapable of remaining unaffected by suffering and consistently opposed evil and corruption in high places. Hugo stubbornly opposed the autocratic measures of Napoleon III and relentlessly fought for freedom of expression. Zola's heroic stance, exemplified in his famous article '*J'accuse*', against the government's false accusations and sentencing for treason of the innocent Captain Alfred Dreyfus (1859–1935), is well known. In your country, Tolstoy opposed the autocracy and the Russian Orthodox Church for most of his life.

With some exceptions, writers today rarely speak out boldly enough to awaken great international response. Especially in the industrialised nations, although it is perhaps unfair to lump them all together, writers and intellectuals, embarrassed or too hesitant to join the common cry against injustice, tend either to retire into an autistic world or to become cynical. Recent conversations with Nelson Mandela (1918–) and the South African poet Oswald M. Mtshali (1940–) suggest that the voice of anger against evil and injustice is being raised louder in the Third World.

AITMATOV: Ten years ago, I was asked to define the problems facing the Association of Asian and African Writers. At the time, I spoke of the 'mission' of psychologically and morally emancipating humanity from the results of colonialism. If asked the same question today, I would answer in a broader vein. The pertinent issue concerns not just specific regions, but all of us, all people who in one way or another were hostages to a system of slavery, no matter what name it went under.

If we are to liberate humanity from what might be called an under-evaluation complex, awaken a sense of human worth and make the spirit of brotherhood real, we must consider the consequences of colonialism, and of totalitarianism, feudalism, socialism and so on, which seriously impeded the development of the human spirit. We can only guess what immense stretches of time will be needed to cleanse the human mind and soul of all this.

Colonialism was humankind's gravest experience in self-enslavement. The artist today must reflect on it socially and philosophically. Only after thinking deeply about these things can we write with conviction about the absurdity of all conceptions of superiority – national, state, or racial. The kind of unification of peoples that Tolstoy regarded as his mission is possible only on the basis of values shared by all humanity. The artist can have no higher responsibility before history than this.

Reviving Words

IKEDA: At certain stages in their developments, all peoples have evolved traditions of oral literature in the forms of legends and myths constituting compendia of experience and wisdom. For centuries before they acquired a writing system after the Russian Revolution, your own Kirghiz people had an exclusively oral literary tradition. With the aid of specialist story-tellers, African peoples have preserved thousands of years of tribal memory in purely oral form. Today, similar story-tellers explain the cultural achievements of their peoples to outsiders. Incidentally, in 1986, in recognition of my poetry collections and dialogues, I was awarded the Kenya Oral-literature Prize by the Kenya Oral Literature Association (KOLA).

Of course, traditions kept alive through orally-transmitted literature are not limited to Africa. I have already mentioned ancient Japanese minstrels who travelled all over the country reciting the *Heike Monogatari*, accompanying themselves on the lute. At a somewhat later period, reciters of what was called *sekkyō-bushi*, originally Buddhist sermons, carried literature to the largely illiterate masses. The traditions and mythological images interwoven in your own writing suggest the influence of the oral-literature tradition.

AITMATOV: All expatriates share the need to talk, to unburden the heart with someone who speaks the same language. What has this need to do with literary art?

First, and to me decisive, is this: the modern writer who sets out to create an image of real life in a bygone time has an unquenchable longing for the taste and smell of things that, though now forgotten, live on in the genes of memory and language bequeathed to us by our forebears. In inspired songs, in the past, the poetic word and music were inseparable. Bards, including the *manaschi* of Kyrgyzstan, the rhapsodes of ancient Greece, the Russian reciters of *byliny*, the *ashugi* minstrels of the Caucasus and the *kobziri* of the Ukraine, portrayed their peoples' spirit, world view and sense of oneness and harmony with nature in an astonishing fashion. They described the inner cosmos, without which humanity would be incapable of spiritually and, consequently, physically surviving in the vastness of the universe unbowed by the elements that created him: Heaven, Earth, Fire and the Unknown concealed beyond the horizon.

In our souls, all of us at one time or another become pilgrims and wander in a secret place where it is impossible to avoid the dead noise and clamour of the surroundings. When this happens, we cannot survive without reviving words, on the lips of old or young, that cause the weary soul to blossom afresh.

IKEDA: You imply using history as a ground on which to generate the strength needed for a leap into the future.

AITMATOV: Maybe. I sometimes entertain a, perhaps strange, desire to understand the speech of our ancient forefathers.

IKEDA: Genghis Khan, for example? I was interested by what you attempt in your *The White Cloud of Genghis-Khan*.

AITMATOV: Yes. Although, with the passing of time they become legends, in real life, figures like Genghis Khan were simple, if outstanding, people sharing ordinary human weaknesses and illnesses. I wanted to present him as he was, or might have been, in fact. To do this, I had to strip his image of legendary, fairy-tale trappings, conventions and metaphoric symbols.

IKEDA: Then you had him encounter ordinary people in perfectly ordinary circumstances?

AITMATOV: Of course. The deepest philosophy arises in the simplest circumstances, when human beings act according to the dictates of their hearts without sly philosophising. A human being becomes a true hero only when in love. In the name of that great emotion, he is ready to challenge any tyranny that tries to foist unnatural rules of life on him. This law always has been in force and always will be. That is what I wanted to consider in *The White Cloud of Genghis-Khan*. It does not surprise me that love is praised above everything in mythological subjects. It is enrapturing. I know of nothing greater; as is said in the Song of Solomon (8:6) ' . . . for love is strong as death.' What can excite the imagination of an artist more than this immortal word-thought? Undoubtedly, when inspired by a Biblical subject, we attain immortality, for a time. What more can we mortals want?

IKEDA: Mortal we certainly all are. Buddhist philosophy explains mortality by means of the concept of impermanence. Nothing, no matter how apparently durable, like a diamond, for instance, is permanent. Ultimate dissolution is the fate of all things. The most affectionate couples may swear eternal love; but, sooner or later, death parts them.

Nonetheless, precisely because of our mortality, we cannot suppress the desire for the eternal. Fated to die, we long for the immortal, the world of the eternal. The limited nature of our term of existence compels us to strive for integration with the universe. We are, as the French philosopher and mathematician Blaise Pascal (1623–62) says, thinking reeds, easily destroyed by a single blow from nature. But our attempts to embrace the universe in our thoughts and speculations bear witness to both our humanity and our will to live up to the best of which we are capable.

Art's greatest function is to bridge the gap between impermanence and the world of eternity and complete integration. This explains why the arts have been put to maximum use in the service of religion. The compelling desire for sublimation to love and immortality is behind many of the great works of European religious art. As the English art historian Jane Ellen Harrison (1850–1928) has said, fundamentally, the same things motivate people to attend church and the theatre.

Lest They be Forever Forgotten

IKEDA: In recent centuries, the armies of two fierce enemies, Napoleon and Hitler, have tramped over Russian soil. From twenty to twenty-five million Soviet citizens lost their lives in the Second World War. Not a single family escaped the loss of loved ones. Partly because of the long borders it shares with European nations, China and Mongolia, Russia has frequently been involved in war. In spite of this, however, the people I meet on my frequent visits to Russia always impress me with their deep longing for peace.

At an international Soka Gakkai Peace festival held twenty years ago, spectators in the stadium stands spelt out *world peace* in various languages, including, to my delight, the Russian *Miru Mir* (Peace on Earth) in cyrillic characters.

Interestingly, the Russian word *mir* can mean both world and peace. In addition, it can stand for a traditional Russian village community. This suggests a close connection in the Russian mind between love for the land and love of peace that is exemplified for me in the honest, hard-working Konstantin Dmitrievich Levin in *War and Peace*.

AITMATOV: Thank you for your kind words about the Russian people. Other peoples, too, demonstrate love for land and peace. But, when all is said and done, none of the many wars, great and small, that have occurred in the past could have been waged without the participation of the people.

Power-holders, kings, dictators, governments and nationalistic political parties start wars: but ordinary people are drawn into them; it is the people who must fight the battles.

The subject is both inexhaustible and truly tragic. While stressing the importance of geopolitical factors, scientific theories, which attempt to prove war to be a normal, necessary part of human development, virtually ignore the ephemeral, irreplaceable, individual human being. Now, as throughout the ages, such theories regard individual suffering and ruin as no more than objects of abstract sympathies.

As a rule, war disregards rational arguments. The impotence of reason before the logic of war accounts for a universal tragedy of the human soul. This has always been true in the past. But, fortunately, in this century, powerful humanistic movements are at last gradually getting the upper hand. I hope they will usher in a historical era in which the general struggle for peace is an accepted part of thought and life and, perhaps, the source of a still-unfounded, universal religion of the spirit.

IKEDA: A universal religion for the people is greatly to be desired. To clarify religion for the people, it must contribute to the values of good, such as peace, and work to polish and forge them. Religion for the people must become the medium of friendship, justice, hope, self-control, effort, courage, trust and love, all of which are the values of good. If religion is to survive in the present day, when our choice of war or peace exerts decisive influence on human history, it must promote these values.

Instead of existing for the sake of the people, many religions have adopted the view that the people exist for the sake of religion. Pre-eminence has been afforded to religious authority in various forms, idols, holy men, dogma and so on, to which human beings have been sacrificed. By promoting belligerence in the form of religious wars, religion has frequently degenerated into a cover-up for evil, an anti-human force, a medium for the growth and spread of hostility, mistrust, injustice, malice, cowardice and meanness. Among the many deep thinkers with whom I have spoken, Aurelio Peccei (1908–84), the Italian businessman and founder of the Club of Rome, and the American scientist and two-time Nobel laureate Linus Pauling (1901–94) were sharply critical of this aspect of the role played by religion. Their attitude is understandable in the light of the misery humankind has suffered in the names of gods. I consistently advocate a revolutionary transition away from religions that serve their own ends to a religion that serves the best interests of humanity.

AITMATOV: What you say is true; but war has a kind of magic allure that unconditional taboos may be insufficient to eliminate altogether. There are more than enough reasons why this is true. Once at an international writers conference, I called attention to a deeply psychological factor: the Freudian danger of war, which we tend to leave out of our discussions of lofty matters. I said to my fellow conferees,

> You all discuss peace. You struggle for peace. You try to influence people to think as you do and to participate actively in the pacifist struggle. But have you ever thought that some green, young general, with no laudable achievements to his credit, may dream of inscribing his name in the annals of military history? There are probably plenty of people ready to work for a modern-day Alexander the Great or Napoleon, no matter what the costs to humanity.
>
> Who today gives a thought to the suffering Alexander's conquests cost humanity? That is all forgotten, and Alexander remains one of the most famous men of his epoch. Nearer to our own time, what about Napoleon? How many human sacrifices were laid on the altar of his military campaigns?
>
> Perhaps the celebrated generals fought for good reasons, perhaps for bad. The point is that, to my despair, the Napoleons of history remain great heroes while the ordinary people who perished in their wars count for nothing; they have been forgotten.

IKEDA: Tolstoy saw Napoleon as a fallible human being and, in *War and Peace*, contrasts him unfavourably with the simple, wise Platon Karatayev. Generals today come by hero worship much less easily than they did in the past because, abandoning geopolitical considerations, pacifists oppose belligerents wherever they may be. This seems to be making room for a general acceptance of philosophies like Tolstoy's.

AITMATOV: After millennia of suffering for the sake of spiritual development, now, for the first time in history, humankind is becoming aware of the possibility of life without war. Failure to follow up on this chance would be too humiliating. It would spell the ruin of all the great ideas we have won, at a tremendous cost in self-knowledge, since we became human.

IKEDA: We must not allow this. As you say, ordinary people are becoming aware of the possibility of life without war. The further development of this awareness, plus a good dose of optimism, is essential to further human progress. This is why I emphasise grass-roots diplomacy over state diplomacy. I know that you, too, favour the idea of grass-roots diplomacy.

AITMATOV: Emphasis on the importance of diplomacy at the grass-roots level is a splendid new phenomenon. It represents, not a pose, but a mighty drive for peace. The process is irreversible. I have the greatest respect for your pacifist work in connection with it.

IKEDA: In the ultimate analysis, the struggle to promote global peace amounts to a struggle to stimulate global awareness of the importance of peace.

CHAPTER THREE

Perspectives on Perestroika

Standing Up for Human Dignity

IKEDA: President Gorbachev says *perestroika* is a revolution. I speculate that his belief is that a new revolution is necessary, as seventy years have passed since the Revolution led by Lenin. Lenin rejected the idea of spontaneity and emphasised the deliberate, purposeful nature of the socialist revolution. He insisted that, because bred of the old propertied classes, the intelligentsia must import class-consciousness, which would not emerge spontaneously from the proletariat. In the making of the revolution, Lenin himself assumed the role of leader of the intelligentsia. While teaching the historical inevitability of the transition from a capitalist to a socialist society, Marxism also insists that class consciousness, the driving force behind the revolution, must be deliberately cultivated. A natural revolutionary and a realist, Lenin's great insight was that he found a sense of purpose indispensable in carrying out revolution, as long as revolution is humane, an all-too-humane affair.

In the 1970s, Premier Aleksey Kosygin (1904–80) attempted economic reforms in the Soviet Union. But, going much farther, Mikhail S. Gorbachev instituted *perestroika*, which he described as a new kind of revolutionary movement. His restructuring extended throughout all aspects, political, economic, educational and cultural, of Soviet society. At first sceptical, the West gradually came to realise what he was trying to do. After observing *perestroika* carefully, I came to the conclusion that it fundamentally depended on the human factor. My fellow believers and I understand this well, since we are convinced that the inner revolution of the individual human being is the only possible basis for enduring broader social revolution.

More than a decade ago, in India, I had the pleasure of meeting and talking with the politician and social reformer Jayaprakash Narayan (1902–79), who was called the conscience of his country. He and I shared a firm belief in 'social revolution through human revolution'. I suspect that Mr. Gorbachev shares it, too. In spite of the sweeping social scale of his undertaking, the intense thought he devoted to human awareness in the Soviet social system surely convinced him that social reform must start with the reformation of the individual.

AITMATOV: The Russian revolutionary and writer Aleksandr I. Herzen (1812–70) perceptively remarked that people are only as free socially and politically as they are within themselves. Certainly, if we can agree with Narayan on social revolution through human revolution, we can agree with Herzen on this point.

IKEDA: Yes. It is startling how the thoughts of great people of various epochs and races coincide.

AITMATOV: That is one of the few things in the world that never fails to astonish. Though no professional historian or philosopher, because of the way I have observed and listened to our people, I can speak with complete authority on this point. In our enormous land, *perestroika* was not the result of the spontaneous kindness of power-holders bent on creating a new revolution. It can, instead, be justifiably called a consciously chosen path for all society to follow. No matter what name it went under, structured, fractured, or real, Soviet socialism had ended up in an economic, social and spiritual, moral dead-end.

Many people, including some very honest party leaders, felt, saw and understood the lamentable condition our country was in. It could not be ignored. But anyone speaking out about it was, as a rule, pensioned off, say for reasons of ill health. Admitting the truth cast doubt on the shining future toward which the party had been ostensibly guiding us for seventy years.

By the way, communism itself is not at fault. Communism is a noble concept expressing primordial human ideals. But any idea can be defiled and sullied and basically misused.

IKEDA: Yes. Even liberty has been misused. Condemned by the Jacobins, the famous Girondist politician Madame Roland (1754–93) on her way to the guillotine, cried out, 'O Liberty! Liberty! How many crimes are committed in thy name!' History is full of examples of people with initially good intentions who, like the Jacobins, were manipulated by the devil to do evil.

The revolution of October 1917 enraptured leading intellectuals all over the world. The French novelist and Nobel laureate Romain Rolland

(1866–1944) was such a person. Virtually idolising Mahatma Gandhi, Rolland staunchly opposed the violence and terrorism associated with Bolshevism. Nonetheless, even in the face of Stalin's purges, he consistently supported the revolution and the Soviet Union. Perhaps, like others, he was eager to create a united front, including the Soviet Union, against fascism, which was already on the rise.

Rolland sharply criticised André Gide for expressing concern about Stalin's actions in his book *Return from the U.S.S.R.* Gide wrote a rebuttal to the criticism that is at once so appropriate and so scathing that I cannot help feeling a little sorry for Rolland. Gide said,

> The publication of my *Retour de l'U.R.S.S.* merited me a number of injuries. The ones from Romain Rolland hurt me. I have never enjoyed his writings; but, at least, I hold his moral character in high esteem. I believe that the author of *Au-dessus de la Mêlée* [Above the battle; pamphlet published by Rolland in 1915 urging France and Germany to act humanely during their conflict] would pass severe judgement on the old Rolland. The eagle has made his nest; he sleeps.[1]

AITMATOV: Many outsiders, including remarkable artists and true humanists among European writers, thought the prototypical human being of the future was being created in the Soviet Union. To their number we must add great Latin American painters like Diego Rivera (1886–1957) and David Alfaro Siqueiros (1896–1974), who personally prepared and carried out terrorist acts in the name of the 'World Revolution'. This is food for serious thought. It cannot be brushed aside with irony.

Only recently, to my amazement, I came across the following statement by the subtle, Russian lyric poet Mikhail Mikhailovich Prishvin (1873–1954): 'Revolution is revenge for a dream.' Since he could not have published this remark when he first formulated it, or even much later, it lay hidden in his diary for many years.

IKEDA: Some people call Prishvin the last Russian sage.

AITMATOV: He was a wise man. But I hope not the last. A people is truly alive as long as it brings forth wise men. The people are too sagacious to be deceived. The words of deceivers may awaken euphoria in the masses, and the deceivers may act as if the euphoric reactions represent a true outpouring of the popular will. But this is nonsense. Though they may not express it as a well-formulated philosophy, the people, in their own vernacular, make it known when their situation is no longer tolerable. The important thing is for them to recognise the intolerable state when it has been reached.

IKEDA: If I am not mistaken, a character in your story *The Executioner's Block* shows his own recognition of the intolerable state by saying, 'I cannot go on living this way.'

AITMATOV: Yes, his name is Boston. He conveys the mood of the people. At any rate, that is what I wanted him to do. The Soviet people knew they had reached a dead-end. Their existence had become so senseless that protest ripened among them. Some way out had to be found. The choice was between liberty and death.

In my story, Boston is incapable of coming to terms with humiliation. He cannot shrug it off with, 'You can't fight city hall'. His well-developed sense of human worth demands heroic action. From the legal standpoint, of course, his persona is unjustifiable. But from the higher, the human viewpoint, who could cast the first stone at him?

Here I am using Boston only as an example. In the Soviet Union, the people had come to sense their insulted and humiliated national dignity and to feel the urge to dispute what was being done to them.

IKEDA: The character Sasha in Rybakov's *The Children of the Arbat* is an example of the same kind of thing. Faced with exile, this mettlesome young man experiences a great eternal truth, in comparison with which he finds his own suffering and unhappiness insignificant: 'They can exile us, but they can't crush us. They might think they can, but they can't. People can be killed, but not crushed.' Sasha and Boston represent indomitable determination to guard human dignity. *Perestroika* had to face criticism and setbacks. But it bore great fruit because it, too, embodies determination to stand up for the dignity of humanity.

The Role of the People

IKEDA: Like any sweeping reform movement, *perestroika* required the confidence of the ordinary people. When it lagged, President Gorbachev cited as causes both resistance from conservative bureaucrats and insufficient awareness on the part of the people. The reason for their lack of interest is not far to seek. For seventy years, the Soviet system stifled interest and participation in politics with the result that the people inevitably turned away from public life in favour of their own private spheres of concern.

Lenin was ambivalent toward the rank and file of the people. Cheering crowds greeted him when, after his long journey on the famous sealed train, he arrived at Finland Station in Petrograd. In his *Sternstunden der Menschheit: Zwölf historische Miniaturen* (*Decisive Moments in History: Twelve Historical Miniatures*), the Austrian writer Stefan Zweig vividly describes the event, while commenting on the difficulty of Lenin's position.

Initially well disposed toward the people, Lenin soon found himself plunged into a maelstrom of energy and action compelling him to rely heavily on an avant-garde leadership of which he himself assumed control. The Japanese writer Ryūnosuke Akutagawa (1892–1927) poetically describes Lenin's combined concern and scorn for the people:

> You who love the people most, despise the people most. You who gave birth to our Orient are an electric locomotive smelling of the grass of the fields.[2]

Lenin's pre-revolutionary organisational and national theories were tinged with anarcho-syndicalism. After the revolution, he ceased relying on spontaneous popular energy because he felt the revolution was doomed without an elite leadership firmly under his own control.

It has been said, though recently doubts have surfaced, that Lenin's superior personality helped him maintain contacts with the ordinary people. Whether or not this is true, certainly his sudden illness and death seem all the more lamentable in the light of Stalin's subsequent cruelty.

One of the most outstanding Japanese writers of popular literature, Eiji Yoshikawa (1892–1962), astutely remarked that the ordinary people are a source of great guidance and learning. Both Soka Gakkai and I are guided by the same belief. In Russia, however, relations between the masses and the intelligentsia have been a subject of lively disagreement ever since the populist *narodnik* movement of the nineteenth century. What is your interpretation of the role of the masses in *perestroika*?

AITMATOV: Even today, we still hear muffled echoes (the more naïve, the more fervent) of the argument over whether the revolution was necessary at all. Whether it was worth what it cost. The argument is naïve because history must not be considered in the subjunctive mood; that is, from the standpoint of what might have been. The unthinking search for the guilty, those whose dreams of making humanity happy drove them to revolution, is foolish.

IKEDA: Still, dreams of equality, justice and friendship, the objects of age-old longings, may have consoled people who willingly laid down their lives for the Soviet regime.

AITMATOV: Such people were willing to give their lives to ensure that power was in the hands of the people; that is, in the hands of the councils called soviets. But then, the party that toppled the old regime came to delude itself into thinking that it alone knew what the people wanted and what path they ought to follow into the future.

The great cause of the revolution became a bone, which the winners in the struggle tossed out to pacify a people who had risen up against the slavery of an outdated, stinking system. Interestingly, the name of the sinister character Smerdyakov in Dostoyevsky's *The Brothers Karamazov* is etymologically related to the word *smerdet*, which means to stink.

The inevitable outcome of arbitrary rule is humiliation and oppression of human and national worth and individual dignity – the ultimate meaning of what Eiji Yoshikawa meant by the guidance and learning of the masses. The people suffocate in the oppressive atmosphere of totalitarianism.

IKEDA: In the early years of Soviet power, when the Communists arrogantly appropriated to themselves the role of a dominant avant-garde, signs of a split between the people and the party were already apparent. In a sense, the Communists were parading what might be called the arrogance of rationalism.

Even the most enlightened reason is incapable of grasping human nature in its full, ineffable depth and complexity. Utopian attempts to force humanity into the mould of human reason are dangerous. The haughty, governing, Communist avant-garde gradually degenerated into the self-righteousness and privilege of the so-called Red Aristocrats, who scorned the ordinary people.

In connection with your interesting comment about the name Smerdyakov in *The Brothers Karamazov*, the homophonic relation between the verb *smerdet*, to stink, and an old word, *smerd*, meaning a peasant farmer has led some scholars to suspect an early tendency to scorn workers of the land. In their awareness of privilege, the Bolshevik avant-garde, blind to their own rationalistic arrogance, came to think of the masses as *smerd*. Lenin relied on the avant-garde as emergency guards against counter-revolutionary forces, as a source of the leaders necessary to guide a popular uprising and as compilers of a general plan clearly setting forth the people's advantages and hopes.

AITMATOV: The leading party, or the party that assumes the leadership role, also assumes a tremendous historical responsibility not to use the people as means to the attainment of its own aims. The people must not be held hostage to the so-called 'best and most progressive' ideas set forth in the party program. Nor must the party presume that its program necessarily sets forth precisely what the people want. The people may indeed refuse to support or even oppose the program – with slogans like 'The Soviets without the Communists!' Should this happen, the party might dragoon the people into communism with the iron hand of force. I have always been troubled by the idea that some people are convinced they know better than I what will make me happy. How can they know? Why must I trust them as prophets?

IKEDA: Usually arrogant, narrow-minded and fanatical, such people never lend an ear to what others have to say. Their obsessive, incessant parroting of words and slogans is no more than counterfeit confidence. They do not use words; words use them. With excessive confidence, they seem to believe in the possibility of defining actuality in verbal form.

Shakyamuni Buddha was far less trustful of the possibility of conveying deep meaning through words alone. At first, he hesitated to undertake a teaching mission because of grave doubts that unaided words could make the difficult concepts of his enlightenment comprehensible. But the god Brahma, who descended from his heaven for the purpose, urged Shakyamuni to overcome his misgivings and take his message to the world. Shakyamuni's compunctions about relying on facile verbalisation characterise Buddhism in general.

About five hundred years after Shakyamuni's time, the pivotally important Mahayana Buddhist philosopher and scholar Nāgārjuna (active in about 200 AD) keenly analysed the pros and cons of verbal expression of great truths and roundly criticised contemporary philosophers for being excessively fond of word play. In the opening passages of his *Madhyamika-kārikā* (*Verses on the Middle Way*), he expresses his wish to attain the happiness of one who has transcended the fictions of words.

Of course, to an extent, verbalisation is essential. But we must be aware of the impossibility of giving verbal expression to everything within us. The riches of the world of action and experience transcend words. This is why, instead of relying on hackneyed phrases, we must strive to discover inner meanings through action. Reliance on stereotypical words leads to spiritual petrifaction. Spiritual resilience and constant awareness of the struggle with reality keep our words alive and vivid. Your own receptivity to words reminds me of the Buddhist approach.

AITMATOV: Perhaps I was a Buddhist in a former life. In any case, I have always regarded authorities with suspicion, although it has frequently been dangerous to make a show of my feelings.

IKEDA: *Perestroika* reduced the danger. For a long time, political authority, especially in the form of the state secret police, gagged the Russian people, causing, as one Russian writer has put it, 'fear and malice to ferment'. A large bronze statue of Felix E. Dzerzhinsky (1877–1926), the notorious first head of the secret police, stood for many years in front of KGB headquarters on Lyublyanka Square in Moscow. After the failed coup d'état of 1991, the people pulled it down with their own hands, symbolically expressing the eagerness to begin thinking and acting freely for themselves.

AITMATOV: Russian society has long been, and remains, controlled by people with unjustifiably high opinions of themselves. I find this offensive. *Perestroika* was an historically inevitable movement on the part of the people to make their lives better, more complete and freer. It represents a striving for parliamentary government based on law.

The biggest threat to the success of the *perestroika* process is a jealous power struggle among different factions, all of whom are convinced that they know what the people want. Mutual enmity arises when, carried away by the appeals and promises of politicians, these factions refuse to listen to each other. As long as they remain 'the people', the people are wise. But the rioting mob is fearsome. Pushkin knew this and fruitlessly foresaw danger. The peril became apparent when the revolutionary democrat and materialist Nikolai G. Chernyshevski (1828–89) summoned the Russian people to take up their axes.

Democracy, with which we in Russia have insignificant experience, demands patience. Government by the ignorant mob is nothing but the passion of the political demonstration. Nor is this truth so simple that everyone takes it for granted. Ignorance of its importance is the source of muffled talk about the need for a 'strong hand' to establish order. But we have already been through all that. The wounds of the Stalinist inquisition are still fresh. It is scarcely necessary to recall what Bismarck said about fools who learn from their own mistakes while wise people learn from the mistakes of others.

One of the major tasks of *perestroika* was restoration of dignity to society. No one can do it for us. The people themselves must understand this. Of course it would be splendid if the people who are struggling for the authority of the party and for the attainment of the leading positions of the party, no matter what they call themselves, would inspire the other people to carry out the task. But the people must neither allow themselves to be deceived nor deceive themselves by entrusting their fate to the popular leader of the moment.

IKEDA: Some power-holders would like the spirit of the people to remain always dormant. And the people do sometimes lethargically abandon their rights to the powers that be. There are occasions, however, when the popular soul erupts in mighty, even chaotic, activity. As the French social philosopher Alexis de Tocqueville (1805–59) says in *De la Démocratie en Amérique* (Democracy in America), 'In the democratic age, in the midst of the movement of all things, the thing that moves most is the human heart.'[3] The dynamism and diversity of this motion make the people seem wise or foolish depending on the instance. In countries where the democratic tradition is undeveloped, as I think can be said of Russia, the wisdom–folly contrast can be drastically apparent. Because, as Russia today indicates, suddenly acquired liberty can degenerate into license, the degree of maturity attained by the ordinary population is of the greatest importance.

AITMATOV: The Russian people should heed the words of the painter and philosopher Nikolai K. Rerikh (1874–1947), who defines human existence as both living and being better. As originally conceived, *perestroika* was intended to help people live and be better.

IKEDA: Rerikh's formulation has a decidedly Socratic ring.

Literature Worthy of its High Destiny

IKEDA: At the beginning of his *Kusamakura* (*The Three Cornered World*), the Japanese author Sōseki Natsume says,

If you work by reason, you grow rough-edged; if you choose to dip your oar into sentiment's stream, it will sweep you away. Demanding your own way only serves to constrain you. However you look at it, the human world is not an easy place to live. And when its difficulties intensify, you find yourself longing to leave that world and dwell in some easier one – and then, when you understand at last that difficulties will dog you wherever you may live, this is when poetry and art are born . . . Yes, a poem, a painting, can draw the sting of troubles from a troubled world and lay in its place a blessed realm before our grateful eyes. Music and sculpture will do likewise.[4]

This passage symbolically represents the struggle with, and flight from, reality experienced by modern Japanese authors. As is epitomised by the suicide of the celebrated writer Ryūnosuke Akutagawa, in the process of Westernisation and modernisation that started in Japan in the latter half of the nineteenth century, writers found themselves frustrated and sought ultimate meaning in resignation.

In their pursuit of eternal values, art and literature generally remain aloof from the vortex of greed, machination and involvements of the actual world. Japanese writers and artists have traditionally concerned themselves more with traditional elegance, otherworldliness and the beauties of nature than with politics. Perhaps they are right to do so. Excessive involvement in political and social issues can lead to factionalism and degeneration. Still, fated to be the children of their times, writers cannot isolate themselves entirely from such concerns.

Because of the immense influence politics exerts in our age, we must carefully re-examine relations between literature and political thought and activity. Jean-Paul Sartre, who adopted social *engagement* as a literary theory, believed that, since we cannot extract ourselves from the world we live in, we must accept responsibility for our lives. According to his philosophy, writers must keep an eye on the eternal but must address their contemporaries and compatriots in an engaged fashion. In this sense, his *engagement* was also a kind of self-restraint. In fact, Sartre eagerly made his opinions public and participated in political protests.

With your experiences as a flag-bearer for *perestroika*, you no doubt have your own ideas about the relations between politics and literature.

AITMATOV: The extent to which the writer and the scientist share things in common is surprising. In his autobiography, Albert Einstein says,

I believe with Schopenhauer that one of the strongest motives that leads men to art and science is escape from everyday life with its painful crudity and hopeless dreariness, from the fetters of one's own ever shifting desires. A finely tempered nature longs to escape from personal life into the world of objective perception and thought; this desire may be compared with the townsman's irresistible longing to escape from his noisy, cramped surroundings into the silence of high mountains, where the eye ranges freely through the still, pure air and fondly traces out the restful contours apparently built for eternity.

With this negative motive there goes a positive one. Man tries to make for himself, in the fashion that suits him best, a simplified and intelligible picture of the world; he then tries to some extent to substitute this cosmos of his for the world of experience, and thus to overcome it. This is what the painter, the poet, the speculative philosopher and the natural scientist do, each in his own fashion. Each makes this cosmos and its construction the pivot of his emotional life, in order to find in this way the peace and security which he cannot find in the narrow whirlpool of personal experience.[5]

Of course, certain reservations must be made because of Einstein's famous 'atheism' and particularly his insistence on 'the world of objective perception and thought'. But, in their inner essentials, the viewpoints of the artist and the scientist seem to coincide and, what is more, to enrich each other.

In a later part of the speech, Einstein compares the artist and the non-artist urbanite who, in spite of their different natures, experience the same irresistible longing for another world. I think I am not mistaken in interpreting this equivalent longing as a manifestation, albeit perhaps an accidental one, of the nature of Buddhist philosophy in that it refuses to allow the artist to adopt a haughty attitude toward the non-artist.

IKEDA: Your interpretation is quite correct. Because the essential equality of all humanity is fundamental to its philosophy, Buddhism does not condone ranking people on the basis of such considerations as talent or its lack. The poet, whose role is a distinctive one, must be neither employed by nor subservient to political interests.

AITMATOV: In a discussion of the poem *Attis* by the Roman poet Catullus (*c.*85–54BC), the Russian poet Aleksandr Blok (1880–1921) makes comments pertinent to this discussion:

I think the subject of this poem is not entirely Catullus' personal passion, as is generally thought. On the contrary, we must say, that the personal fate of Catullus, like the passion of every poet, was saturated with the spirit of his epoch. Its fate, rhythms and scale too, like the rhythm and scales of a poet's verses, were inspired in him by his time, for in the poet's understanding of the world there is no split between the personal and the general. The more sensitive the poet, the more seamless his understanding of what is and is not his own. For this reason, in an age of *Sturm und Drang*, the tenderest and most intimate attempts of the poet's soul overflow with storm and alarm.[6]

Although he did not know it himself, Catullus – like Publius Ovidius Naso (43BC–AD17*c*.), author of the brilliant *Metamorphoses* – was, in a sense, a Buddhist. Ovid, of course, was exiled to the Scythians – that is, to the shore of the Black Sea – by Augustus, perhaps for having corrupted the youth of Rome with his poem *Ars amatoria* (The art of love).

IKEDA: Ovid's fate is a vivid illustration of a clash between politics and art.

AITMATOV: Yes. Apparently, politicians like Augustus find singing the praises of love, as Ovid did, harmful. But then, cruel dictatorship and lyrical poetry are essentially incompatible.

I am a politician in spite of myself. And, forgive me, but I do not imagine myself flagbearer of anything at all. *Perestroika* is a relative term. I accept and understand *perestroika* as a chance for us to humanise our way of life. Fate saw fit for me to head certain cultural undertakings, including political activity, for the sake of achieving that end. Do I have the right to disregard the voice summoning me to such a task? In trying to wake society up, I am always a writer. And, though I may use the pen as a sword, I will never abandon the pen for the sword. Personally, I dream of a time when no one will need to pose and answer questions about relations between literature and politics.

IKEDA: You must envision a Utopia where literature and the other arts can be free of social, philosophical and political affairs. Plato expelled poets from his ideal Republic for several reasons. First, he says that art is only imitation (*mimesis*). Furthermore, by stimulating the operations of the baser aspects of the soul, it hampers the intellect. It excites the emotions, which therefore more readily gain control over us. As a great poet himself, Plato was not, of course, rejecting art as such. But he strictly banished poets because, like you, he was in search of an ideal society. Far older than philosophy, in its descriptions of war and heroes, literature provided models for an ideal way of life and paradigms for the universe, gods, politics and military affairs. Plato wished to transfer this role from literature to philosophy and to build an ideal republic in which literature would not need to stain its hands with such realities.

He strove to found national justice on the justice inherent in the human soul. For him, happiness and the noblest ideals consisted of the union of the inner soul with the outer political system. Humanity must pursue the supreme value, which is the *Idea* or Form of the good.

Taken as a whole, Plato's ideal Republic and supreme value constitute one vast poem. Understandably, in a beautiful, noble society in which politics and ideals are integrated, there would be little need to debate the role of poetry and literature. But beautiful, noble societies are Utopias in the literal sense of the Greek word, which means nowhere. Integration of the ideal and the real does not occur in modern politics. Today, the writer must deal with practical affairs as an artist and, more importantly, as a thinking, feeling human being. Given the nature of our world, the words of the English poet and critic Matthew Arnold (1822–88) become ever more convincing:

> The future of poetry is immense, because in poetry, where it is worthy of its high destinies, our race, as time goes on, will find an ever surer and surer stay.[7]

Distrust of Words is Distrust of Humanity

IKEDA: Earlier I discussed the need to be wary of excessively confident verbalisation. Nonetheless, articulate speech, a distinctive human ability, is our most reliable means of practical communication. Specialist in United States and Soviet affairs and professor at Princeton University, Stephen F. Cohen, has described President Gorbachev as a man who trusts the power of words. His faith in words arises from a trust in humanity, which is the guiding principle behind *perestroika*.

In the *Phaedo*, Plato calls aversion to argument and discussion (*misologos*) an illness that can become hatred of humanity (*misanthropos*):

'But first let us take care that we avoid a danger.'

'Of what nature?' I said.

'Lest we become misologists,' he replied, 'no worse thing can happen to a man than this. For as there are misanthropists or haters of men, there are also misologists or haters of ideas, and both spring from the same cause, which is ignorance of the world.'[8]

Plato acutely observes that aversion for words and aversion for human beings share a common origin. Indeed the intimate relation between speech and action emerges clearly in domineering attempts to suppress freedom of speech, in dehumanisation of opponents, and in the rudeness often attributed to heartless bureaucrats.

As was true in the cases of the American, French and Russian revolutions, vigorous drives in the name of freedom of expression often accompany major historical turning points. In his report *Ten Days That Shook the World*, written during the Revolution of 1917, the American journalist John Silas Reed (1887–1920) described the situation:

From Smolny Institute alone, the first six months, went out everyday tons, car-loads, train-loads of literature, saturating the land. Russia absorbed reading matter like hot sand drinks water, insatiable.[9]

In addition to reading material such as newspapers, brochures, scholarly works and literally writings, they demonstrated a burning desire for the spoken word by flocking to countless lecture meetings all over the country.

Today, as in the past, freedom of expression is a driving force for reform. In its first phase, because of the trust in humanity it represented, *perestroika* stimulated a volcanic eruption of critical speaking and writing that, coming after years of misanthropic silence, was essential to further reform. Freedom of expression can justly be called the cornerstone of *perestroika*. I believe Mr. Gorbachev's endowment to believe in the power of words is nothing but his trust in humanity. It seems to me that the significance of *perestroika* lies in the fact that it cannot be carried out without the burst of free expression replacing the huge silent space of misanthropy.

AITMATOV: If you and I had met before *perestroika*, I would have found the invitation to participate in this part of our discussion burdensome but pleasant at the same time. I would have been like a prisoner behind bars who is offered a chance to talk about the principles of freedom with a passerby off the street. Even so, at a time when a word could be worth a life, I would have unburdened my soul fully, complaining and raging against my lot. Nor would it have been surprising. After all, the word is as mighty as it is both vulnerable and insignificant. But, isolated of itself, the word is guiltless in what happened to us. In fact, we human beings are responsible for what happened to the word. The extent to which a society believes in the word is a measure of its moral and political condition. 'You can't make the word fit the deed.' In other words, when words are valueless, no one can guarantee that the speaker will keep his word. *A priori*, the devaluation of the word means a devaluation of the human personality.

At this point, I catch myself thinking how negative our Russian experience in all matters – from ecological to national – is, and how it always serves the purposes of negative analysis. Can this truly be our fate?

No past epoch has been as intolerant of the word as our socialist totalitarianism. My generation spent the better part of their lives in almost mystical subordination to verbal hierarchy. As worthless as the word was the human being behind it. The impossibility of making the word consonant with the deed became the accepted norm. At the same time, however, a virtually military discipline governed relations between the word of the command-issuer and the deeds of the subordinate. The former represented absolute authority; the latter obedience and submission. Perhaps it was no accident that, when it broke free, Russian speech became volcanically destructive. We have now become so carried away with freedom of speech that we have lost sight of its price; the word has become an end in itself.

Still, I believe the current seizure will pass. The word will return to its moral and creative course. I believe this because we now have at our disposal freedom of speech, the principle achievement of contemporary humanity. We will recover; we will regain our health. We cannot afford to forget so quickly how impossible normal life is without freedom of speech.

IKEDA: Even when politically guaranteed, the freedoms of speech and religious belief do not invariably evolve further by themselves. Law is the minimal morality. Everything depends on human effort to elevate laws and the system they support from a minimal to a maximal level. History teaches bitter lessons about the results of failures to succeed in this effort. The Weimar Republic in Germany began with a solid, legally democratic foundation but degenerated into the Third Reich.

As it is hard for people to always dress appropriately, it is difficult for people to make use of the words at their command. People seem to use words, but, in reality, they are used by them. However, escaping into a lonely prison of silence without trust in humanity will not solve anything. In order to be human, we have to train ourselves to be able to use words freely. In other words, we are not human beings as we are; it is when we are trained in the ocean of words that we become truly human beings.

AITMATOV: Inevitably, if forced on pain of death to remain silent and hide his thoughts and feelings, the human being becomes morally deformed. I think it was Chiang Ching-kuo (1910–85), the son of Chiang Kai-shek (1887–1975), who told the people of mainland China that they live in a country where even remaining silent is forbidden. Clearly he was thinking of the absolute obligation to praise 'The Great Helmsman', as Mao Zedong was called. Not to take part in the exulting choruses and thunderous adulation of the leader was suspicious, a flout punishable with the full severity of a dictatorial regime. 'Either you join in, or else . . .'

Mao Zedong invented nothing. He learned it all from us in the Soviet Union. But who knows where suppression of the freedom of expression originated? Perhaps it has always been a part of human behaviour. There is no need to delve into hoary history to resurrect blood-curdling scenes in which so-called 'searchers of the truth' ripped out the tongues or sewed up the mouths of interrogation victims. A little over a century ago, such was the fate of a poet of the Caucasus, Anchil Mari, who dared to speak out in his verses. In the Soviet era, the process was simpler: poets – and not only poets – were destroyed.

Life itself is the price of free speech. That is how it was; that is how it is. By nature, the human being thirsts after truth. Although we interpret the word *truth* as heroic, our longing for it is no sign of heroism. We cannot help longing for it. We can live no other way. As Tolstoy put it: 'I cannot keep silent.'

You are right. *Perestroika* was first and foremost an attempt to break out of the deadening dumbness – the 'darkness of base truths' pawned off as lofty ones that reduced the people to slavery. But there are limits. We are dealing with more than concrete social issues, because what occurred in the Soviet Union was an uprising of human nature – of the primordial and legal striving for freedom, which is unthinkable without self-respect. At the deepest level, spiritual rebirth arises from the need to converse in human language.

Not surprisingly, to cleanse the word from monstrous demagoguery and falsehood, we in Russia must now relearn how to speak heart-to-heart – and how to listen to and understand each other, if we want to begin living according to the truth.

Incomprehension – deafness – is a sad situation. I recall how Soviet parliamentarians, deliberating state issues, refused – were unable or did not wish – to hear words spoken in a low, muffled, slightly hesitant voice by a man who, not long afterwards (alas, after his sudden death) became known as the conscience of the people. I am referring, of course, to treatment afforded the nuclear physicist and Nobel Peace Prize laureate, Andrey Dmitriyevich Sakharov (1921–89).

The parliamentarians' behaviour on that occasion was a stunning, patent example of *misanthropos* and *misologos*. People long accustomed to living lies cannot easily recognise or accept the word of truth.

The incident shocked me. Of course, it is easy to accuse the parliamentarians of practically anything – frenzied aggression, savage ignorance and basic coarseness completely alien to the accepted parliamentary code of behaviour. But I think it is more important to discover why they behaved as they did, to learn the source of their intolerance. Perhaps its fundamental cause, one that is not immediately easy to account for, is inability to accept Sakharov as a type, as a man who, though no orator, expressed the most profound ideas without a hint of histrionics or platform pathos. He invited us to look into the very depths of ourselves and to find there, to our horror, that we, too, are not without sin. The horrendous, still inadequately explained things that happened in the Soviet Union did not occur without our silent consent, if not encouragement. Still, I think the long-standing totalitarian regime is the true cause of everything.

IKEDA: The French Roman Catholic philosopher and dramatist Gabriel Marcel (1889–1973) identified the principal cause of war as a process of abstraction. By this he meant the dehumanisation and de-individualisation of opponents.

> From the moment when something (the State, a cause, a faction, a religious sect, etc.) claims to require me to engage in a hostile action against other beings whom I, consequently, must be prepared to destroy, it is essential that I lose awareness of the individual reality of the being that I may be brought to abolish. To transform that being into a scapegoat, it is indispensable that I convert him into an abstraction: he becomes the Communist, the Antifascist or the Fascist, and so on.[10]

Once this is done, fanatic adherents on one side advance abstract, self-justifying slogans and, with an aversion to objective truth, refuse to heed the ideas of others. Stereotyped jargon, or what, in *1984*, George Orwell called 'Newspeak', takes over. And communication – one of the things that sets humans apart from the other animals – ceases. This failure of words to fulfill their intrinsic role of meaning, communication, results in a distrustful society that readily becomes prey to unanswerable terror, violence and war. According to Marcel, the philosopher is duty-bound to warn against the spirit of abstraction, which poisons not only communist and fascist states, but global society as well.

AITMATOV: Or, perhaps, they were simply blinded by too sudden an exposure to knowledge about the truth, the world and the self. A famous Russian surgeon named S. N. Fyodorov told me that daylight can blind an eye-surgery patient whose bandages are removed too soon.

IKEDA: You remind me of Plato's celebrated cave. People imprisoned in a dark place for a long time are blinded by sudden sunlight. That is part of what Mr. Gorbachev meant when he said that *perestroika* gave the people liberty. The next question is how they will use it.

People Power

IKEDA: *Perestroika* enabled the peoples of the former Soviet Union to complain aloud about government actions clearly detrimental to their own interests. For instance, to irrigate deserts in southern regions, the Soviet government once planned to divert the courses of north Siberian rivers that empty into the Arctic Sea. But the policies of *perestroika* left the door open for an opposition movement to object to the plan and the great threat it posed to the Siberian ecological system. A large number of writers, scholars and representatives of the mass-media took part in the ensuing debate. The Siberian author Valentin G. Rasputin denounced the plan as criminal and forecast the tragic effects it would have for northern and central Russian and their cultures.

In your own writing, you point out the damage human arrogance does to ecosystems. People in other parts of the Union, including Kyrgyzstan, Kazakhstan and Armenia, complained of the peril. In response to the force of public opinion, on 15 August 1986, the Soviet government terminated the project. In the mid 1980s, with leadership from the intellectuals, the

Soviet peoples were already acquiring enough power to stand up against the might of conservative officialdom.

AITMATOV: To avoid being incomplete – or worse, superficial – I must go beyond the mere facts of the case and examine the background of this development. The current, widely accepted, starry-eyed illusion has created a contemporary social myth to the effect that Soviet and then Russian political powers somehow suddenly grew wise. Not long ago, those same powers ignored public opinion and, according to some unwritten law, pretending to have only the best interests of the people at heart, demanded total popular approval of everything that came from the hands of the leadership. I must not allow myself to fall victim to this illusion.

This relation between political authority and the ordinary people did not evolve yesterday. Nor did it begin with the October 1917 revolution, which did, however, put an end to Russian democracy, as the following quotation from a totally authoritative document attests. An article by the theorist and revolutionary Leon Trotsky (1879–1940) in the 20 April 1924 edition of *Pravda* includes the following:

> In connection with the dissolution of the Constituent Assembly, Lenin told me this: Of course not postponing the convocation was a big risk from our viewpoint; it was very, very imprudent. Still, when all's said and done, it worked out better. The dispersal of the Constituent Assembly by Soviet power is a complete and open liquidation of formal democracy in the name of the revolutionary dictatorship. Now the lesson will be binding.

Records of old – and not-so-old – Soviet assemblies provide too many instances of power usurped while the people either stood by silently looking on – as they do in a celebrated scene in Pushkin's drama *Boris Godunov* – or, in hackneyed Soviet journalese, 'broke out in stormy exclamations and unremitting applause.'

On principle, I never condescendingly call any people innately slavish. It is true, however, that at certain periods in their histories, some peoples do appear to be gripped by a kind of torpor and to be too fear-bound to speak out for themselves. Although it may last a long time, such a condition must sooner or later end.

Undeniably, it was the will of the masses of the people, not of the occupiers of the political-structure pinnacle, that brought *perestroika* about.

For long years, an inhuman regime trampled down the people's sense of national dignity and self-esteem. With the passing of that regime, the people ceased to remain silent.

IKEDA: The fate of the attempted coup d'état of 1991 made that perfectly plain. Relying on an ingrained Russian preference for firm, even harsh, leadership, the eight coup leaders continued to believe that, as long as they maintained control over the military, the KGB and the Ministry of Internal Affairs, they could do as they liked with the people. For over a thousand years, the Russian people have slavishly tolerated despotic government. The Soviet writer Vasily Grossman, who wondered when, or if, his people would ever shed servility and find true freedom, equated Lenin's triumph in the revolution with defeat in the face of a slave mentality that necessitated reliance on the military, the KGB and the interior ministry. Ironically, in 1991, all three supported the power of the people against hard-line conservatives.

The frustration of the 1991 coup had epoch-making significance. The effects of the wide dissemination of information made possible by the *glasnost* policy far exceeded general expectations. Gorbachev set all this in motion. And, if the collapse of the Soviet Union and subsequent developments looked like a defeat for him, we must remember that they, too, were all the outcome of his earlier triumph.

Conditions in Russia are too fluid to permit optimism. Still, the emergence of people power capable of influencing the course of history inspires hope that the nation will develop along wholesome lines in the years to come.

Global Union Through Dialogue

IKEDA: Believing in the importance to *perestroika* of person-to-person dialogue, Mr. Gorbachev made extensive use of television, newspapers and the other media to maximise contacts with the people. I advocate the same emphasis on exchange. Face-to-face dialogue can dispel unnecessary prejudices and doubt and bring the sense of relief and certainty. It breaks through false stereotypes and prompts lively human exchanges and inspiration. Because I am certain direct contact and communication deepen mutual understanding, I consistently urge world leaders to meet face-to-face at every possible opportunity.

Teachers like Socrates, Shakyamuni Buddha and Confucius relied on dialogue to disseminate their ideas and beliefs. Some of their dialogues survive in written form to influence the thinking of people today. The great Japanese Buddhist leader Nichiren (1222–82), whom we members of Soka Gakkai revere, employed the dialogue form to carry the light of Buddhism to the people. One of his most important writings, *Risshō Ankoku Ron* (On Establishing the Correct Teaching for the Peace of the Land), a remonstrance with the autocratic political regime of his time, is cast in dialogue form. Soka Gakkai International (SGI) membership today extends to 115 nations [192 countries and regions as of August, 2008] partly because, since the founding of Soka Gakkai in 1930, we have stressed dialogue.

We Japanese have a proverb, 'Hurrying makes detours', or, as Friar Laurence says in *Romeo and Juliet*, 'They stumble that run fast.' Dialogue, the highway to peace, may seem roundabout but is undeniably the surest way.

Your friend and mine, the late American journalist and pacifist Norman Cousins (1915–90) said, 'NO ONE NEED FEAR DEATH. We need fear only that we may die without having known our greatest power – the power of our free will to give our life for others. If something comes to life in others because of us, then we have made an approach to immortality.'[11] My conviction that this is true and my faith in the value of person-to-person dialogue have inspired me to travel all over the world meeting and talking with leaders in many fields.

AITMATOV: Speaking largely from personal experience and observation, I would say that dialogue – what among the Kirghiz people is called conversation with uncovered faces and honest words – as well as improvisatory poetry and singing contests, occupy a recognised place in the life of the simple people, especially in times of conflicts. Dialogue is the most universal form of interaction among human beings and between humanity and the environment. In its lively dialectic, each participant must demonstrate patience, respect, attention, the ability to listen and willingness to compromise in the name of mutual interests.

Monologue, not dialogue, characterised the Soviet society in which I grew up. The politics of dialogue was alien to Soviet reality. The authorities openly and unambiguously cultivated a direct, fundamental monologue in their own interests, especially in all matters connected with ideology, socio-political debate, proletarian slogans and propaganda clichés. The Soviet Union was no place for dialogue.

The spiritual blossoming that accompanied *perestroika* opened the way for euphoric social dialogue, free speech and untrammeled exchange of opinions. But, as life teaches, balance and moderation are essential in all things.

Sometimes in Russia today, a fad for pseudo-dialogue takes the place of an older dialectic culture. The plethora of symposia, roundtable discussions, seminars and teleconferences that has emerged in Russia since the early 1990s reminds me of a kind of marine spawning, a hurried hullabaloo in which everybody wants to say as much as possible and to load the air with as many words as possible. Nonetheless, I have faith that mature forms of dialogue culture will sooner or later replace this infantile dialogue sickness. If it does, it will signal yet another achievement of free speech.

On the global scale, dialogue between East and West, homes of the two main currents of human culture, is being activated. Their fusion – that is, their dialectic integration – signifies the harmony of life, the essence of the universe. Preoccupation with a search for God inside the self has defined Western achievements in knowledge of the exterior world. The East, on the other hand, has been engrossed in contemplating the secrets of the conscious and the subconscious and in searches for God within the spirit. And this has defined its unique achievements in knowledge of the cosmic essence and the substance of humankind. Interchange between these two would represent the supreme world-cultural dialogue.

IKEDA: As you imply, in the West, conjecture about the nature of divinity led to the discovery of natural laws and structures and ultimately to the development of science. Regarding the world as an external object of investigation, Western philosophy has centred its attention on discovery – in the sense of unveiling or uncovering. Generally regarded as an alien world by Westerners, the East has concentrated on the search for fundamental inner ruling principles – for instance, the Buddhist *dharma* and the Daoist Way or *dao* – and unity with the world. Instead of objectifying in the Western way, the Eastern approach has been to perceive the whole, intuitively, through acts intended to promote union with the world.

Western-style objectification relies on words to isolate concepts, which must then be reassembled to form a world construct. At an early date, however, Goethe indicated the danger of reliance on verbalisation when, in *Faust*, he transcended the traditional Western logo-centric approach.

> 'Tis written: In the beginning was the Word!
> Here now I'm balked! Who'll put me in accord?
> It is impossible, the word so high to prize,
> I must translate it otherwise
> If I am rightly by the Spirit taught.

'Tis written: In the beginning was the Thought!
Consider well that line, the first you see,
That your pen may not write too hastily!
Is it then Thought that works, creative, hour by hour?
Thus should it stand: In the beginning was the Power!
Yet even while I write this word, I falter,
For something warns me, this too I shall alter,
The Spirit's helping me! I see now what I need
And write assured: In the beginning was the Deed![12]

As you say, East–West dialogues open prospects for dialectic integration into an inclusive worldwide civilisation, a concept that is no longer Utopian.

AITMATOV: *Perestroika* stripped the veil from ideological demagogy, revealing an arrangement that, by giving supremacy to monologue and rejecting the culture of the dialogue as a servant of bourgeois compromise, caused us great spiritual and scientific loss. Monologue can be called hard-power. During the Cold War, the supremacy of the monologue was completely apparent. True, the monologue approach has certain advantages – negative or positive depending on the goal – especially when the masses must be stimulated to sudden spurts of action.

But compromise always represents reason at work on a higher level, since it is possible only when the interests of both sides of an issue are taken into consideration. For me, personally, compromise occurs when I regard your interests as if they were my own and agree on the need to act for the good of life in general.

The basic art of elementary dialogue is the ability to listen and to discover rational agreement with the other party. Those who have the upper hand must always remember this, since, as the Buddha himself taught, the conquered always harbours the concealed desire for revenge against his conqueror.

I am happy to be living in an era in which a new kind of historic dialogue has begun to triumph. The culture of dialogue is alien to barbarism as a stage in human development, which recognises only one kind of supremacy: absolute domination through power – a monologue relation – under conditions permitting one person to hold sway over many and compelling them to obey commands on fear of punishment.

Dialogue is a study of the world's inner spaces. It is no coincidence that the Buddha and Christ often made use of dialogue in their sermons. Dialogue is flexibility of thought and world-perception. Laozi – again, not by accident

– said that an infant is born soft and tender. That is, the infant is ready to enter into dialogue with the world around him. Whereas, at the time of death, an old man is rigid and inflexible; he is without the ability to participate in dialogue.

Sages of the past left us many teachings on the importance of conversation. History attributes to Socrates the statement – addressed to a young philosopher named Callicles – 'Say only one word, so that I can see you.' In my interpretation, this means that a human being is invisible as long as he remains silent. Unfortunately, meetings among politicians or between politicians and the masses of the people are usually not true dialogues, since politicians notoriously use words to conceal their true intentions.

IKEDA: Trust is a prerequisite of mutual understanding, especially in politics. Today, however, coeval with the degradation of politics itself, political words rarely deserve trust.

In the past, humaneness was the primary condition for a fine politician. Aristotle defined the human being as, first, a political and, second, a speaking animal. Confined within the family and home, man differs little from non-human animals. But, in a community setting like that of the Greek *polis* or city state, where verbal activity is required, he becomes truly human. Verbally achieved consensus, not naked power and violence, governed the political life of the *polis*. Because they were the people best trained and able to achieve such consensus, Plato considered philosophers the only people fit to conduct politics.

Differences in both size and fundamental nature between the Greek city state and modern societies invalidate facile analogies. Nonetheless, in the modern setting, in which politicians are enslaved to their own lusts for power, fame and wealth, the glory of the word and of dialogue has faded from view. You point out the prevalence of a monologue approach in the former Soviet Union. One-way thinking of the same kind sometimes also afflicts democratic societies, resulting in the emergence of what has been called the 'lonely crowd' – to borrow the title of a book by the American sociologist David Riesman (1909–2002) in collaboration with Nathan Glazer (1924–) and Reuel Denney (1913–95).

In spite of the difficulty of the task, we must try to restore dialogue to its former place of dignity and efficacy. As a first step toward this goal, politics must do an about-face and work to unite, not sunder, the peoples of the Earth.

AITMATOV: We must hope that politics can be converted from an immoral art, or game, into a dialogue of sages open-heartedly deliberating problems related to all humanity on the basis of truly noble, humanistic principles.

IKEDA: I agree entirely. Our dialogue has helped me, personally, get to know the people you represent better and to grow fonder of them.

In the Interest of All Humanity

IKEDA: Russia is by no means free of the ethnic clashes that plagued the Soviet Union – for instance, the Armenians against the Azeri – and demands for autonomy on the part of, for example, the three Baltic states. Ethnic problems, like those afflicting Georgia, result from Stalin's policy of relocation and of denying independence to oppressed peoples. The communist argument that international union of the world's proletariats would eliminate ethnic disagreement has proved illusory. As the Russian philosopher Nikolay A. Berdyayev (1874–1948) pointed out, though it enjoyed enthusiastic support among young people for a while, the idea of the international proletariat is actually no more than a variation on Russian Messianism expressed in the tradition that 'There was a first Rome, then a second (Byzantium), then a third (Moscow) but there will be no fourth.' With great perspicacity, Berdyayev said:

> Into the young people's enthusiasm for the Soviet regime the Russian people's religious energy has entered. If this religious energy becomes exhausted, so will the enthusiasm, and self-interestedness will make its appearance, which is quite possible even in communism.[13]

Sadly, what Berdyayev had pointed out proved right with surprising accuracy.

The Soviet Union embraces a variety of ethnic groups, each of which has its own history and culture, making it a multicultural state. But if conflicts and contradictions occur and become escalated, as cancer cells impair our health, the state's good functioning will not fail to be lost. The Swiss cultural historian Werner Kaegi (1901–79) has said that, no matter what form it assumes, our future world will survive only as long as the cell colony called 'home' remains healthy.[14] 'The cell colony called home' refers to ethnic cultures, which stay in good condition by simultaneously evolving independently and interacting with other cultures. Achieving a balance between respect for traditional ethnic culture and membership in a larger inter-ethnic, international association is an extremely difficult task. The Soviet Union failed in it. Conflict between supporters of powerful, centralised control and democratisation ultimately helped bring down the Soviet Union. The process was abetted by ethnic animosities – all that remained of the Union's once vaunted cultural diversity.

AITMATOV: Suppose the entire human race suddenly found itself exiled to the moon. Maybe then we would come to understand and regret the evil bred in us by indulging in rampant nationalism, which degrades the soul and reduces us to the level of mob psychology.

IKEDA: Perhaps we can understand the evil of unbridled nationalism without being sent to the moon. An attack from without might do the trick. The Chinese philosopher Mencius (Meng Zi; fourth century BC) said, 'If abroad there are not hostile States or other external calamities, his kingdom will gradually come to ruin.' If suddenly attacked by, say, Martians, the peoples of the Earth might abandon ethnic rivalries in order to fight off the common enemy. But, probably, once the outside danger was gone, narrow nationalistic prejudices would re-emerge.

AITMATOV: This is an issue each of us must deal with. That is why there are likely to be few specialists in the field of nationalist conflicts. Horrified, I conclude that, in the face of the howling mob, whipped to a frenzy by nationalists, all philosophical discussions, political doctrines and admonitions from sage individuals are impotent. I have seen this with my own eyes. Solving the nationalism problem requires an all-embracing, international, national-relations programme specifying the status of the individual and the nation and endowed with the binding power of a sacred vow. In short, we require a rigorous law, observed everywhere, especially in multinational associations. Maybe we should impose harsh punishments on national-fascist ideologues who stir up nationalistic passions in the masses. After all, repressive regimes use fear of punishment to keep their peoples obedient.

Such controls may be necessary. Certainly the idea occurs to everyone. Perhaps everything will burn up or fall to ashes of itself. But at what price? Consideration of costs has probably not occurred to our ultra-nationalist contemporaries, nor will it occur to nationalists of the future.

But this by no means obviates the need to do something. It would be blasphemous merely to stand by waiting for the crisis that will determine death or recovery for the patient. Blood is spilt. People perish. Children born in the hate of the times will grow up swathed in evil. We must do something. But what?

Many advocate an immediate presidential *ukase* forbidding some things and punishing others. I do not doubt the sincerity of such demands for several reasons. But, the kind of order they posit must be established with an iron hand. And that is terrifying. Such an approach fails to get at the heart of the problem: it merely aggravates the illness.

Folk wisdom says we ourselves – not doctors – cure illnesses. Each nation, each individual, should heed this advice. But, before taking it, we must understand the causes of the so-called nationalistic eruptions that explode here and there with staggering effect. What are their sources? What is behind them?

Whatever it is, it has been going on throughout the history of humanity. Why? Obviously attempts to explain the phenomenon solely on the basis of social categories, like cultural and linguistic differences, will get us nowhere. Everything of this kind – including the struggle for *Lebensraum*, or living space – is a new result of some other, older, result.

IKEDA: If memory serves, it was the ardent French nationalist Charles de Gaulle (1880–1970) who said that social class is insignificant in comparison with nationalism. The Russian empire was called the prison of nationalities. The Soviet regime swept the issue under the carpet, cavalierly proclaiming all nationalist problems *ipso facto* solved. With the fall of the Soviet Union, however, a series of bloody nationalist struggles proved the proclamation to have been premature and added weight to de Gaulle's words.

National pride is a fundamental right and a mainstay of respect for the dignity of humanity. Nationalist struggles have always been fierce. But, as the nation state has evolved in our century, the violence, fanaticism and brutality of these struggles have intensified, reflecting the emotional aspect of what Marcel described as the process of abstraction whereby modern man renders his neighbour an anonymous entity. In the Soviet Union, the process of abstraction exacerbated racial and class conflict. I consider this a peculiarly modern, pathological condition.

AITMATOV: Ideas of racial superiority are primordial and remain alive and well today. Even the racism on which fascism fed was not an original invention of Hitler's theoretician Baron Alfred Rosenberg (1893–1946). We struggle with the same kind of thing now. From time to time, humanity closes ranks to expel it, but it turns up again to challenge us. In our epoch, the theory of class superiority contends with that of racial superiority. Its genesis is not apparent. But this is only because we overlooked the question for a long time.

The consequences of a dictatorship of the proletariat occupied some minds long ago. One such was the anarchist Mikhail Aleksandrovich Bakunin (1814–76). Alas, his works were long shut away from the people in restricted archives and are only now becoming available to us. This is his forecast about the way socialist rulers would conduct themselves in power:

> They would try to impose communism on the peasants. They would stir up and arm the entire peasant mass against themselves. Then, in order to put down the peasant uprising, they would be forced to resort to immense, well-disciplined, well-organised, armed forces. They would entrust the army to the forces of reaction and would cultivate the reactionary military and the ambitious generals in their own milieu. With the aid of this stable state machine, they would have soon found a state engine driver – a dictator or emperor.

In this apparent digression, I am actually trying to examine the problem from the viewpoint of an attempt to create what Soviet leaders called a 'new world', a 'new homeland', phrases that, while not completely amoral, were part of a blind force destroying the structure of our way of life. They wiped out the spiritual echelon that, like a plankton layer, subsumed the ancient popular culture, including all those forms of art evolved over the millennia during which our structure of life evolved. With this destruction, darkness and chaos came to reign in place of the 'old' world.

In his picture of future collectivisation *Anarkhiya po Prudonu* (Anarchy according to Proudhon), Bakunin foresaw this development too:

> The communist government will replace free agricultural associations and will undertake centralised administration of agricultural labour. It will charge its bureaucracy with the task of cultivating the land and paying wages to the peasants. This will lead to the most horrible disorders, the most deplorable plundering and the vilest despotism.

This, indeed, was what happened in the Soviet Union. Interestingly, forecasts of people whom it was considered useful to number among the 'enemy' often come true.

Although we cannot live 'by bread alone', we must eat. And no interests
– not even the so-called noblest – justify the criminal policy of cynically
using food – or its lack – to win political support. According to the anarchist
Bakunin, in a socialist state, such a policy would lead to moral and intellectual
degradation.

> Such would be a society not of people but of beasts. It would be a
> new edition of the unfortunate Republic of Paraguay, which for a long
> time allowed itself to be governed by the Jesuits. In short order, such
> a society would inevitably descend to the lowest level of idiocy.

Man is the measure of all things. And the measure of man is an irrepressible
will to be free. But the longing for liberty can lead to international war.

What then? No matter what organisational structures the unified society
of the future assumes, all peoples of all nations must prize their freedom
and the freedom of others above all else. Is such a thing possible? Is it
merely an ideal? Only time will tell.

IKEDA: In short, we must break with narrow, fanatical nationalism. Education
is the only way to do this. Participation in SGI's work to broaden children's
horizons through such things as the World Textbook Exhibition, exchange
programs for primary and middle-school pupils, exhibitions of children's art
and the UNICEF exhibition has convinced me that children are innate
cosmopolitans. Sadly, as they grow older, they all too often fall under the
influence of the prejudices of the adults around them. Something is drastically
wrong in educational and social environments that permit this to happen.
Norman Cousins put his finger on the crux of the issue when he said,

> *The great failure of education* – not just in the United States but throughout
> most of the world – is that it has made people tribe-conscious rather
> than species-conscious.[15]

In the years to come, our major task will be to cultivate globalism devoted
to the best interests of the entire human race – what Mr. Cousins meant
by 'species-consciousness'. In spite of its tremendous importance, educators
today pay too little attention to this duty.

The question of tribe and racial consciousness was a major theme in a
discussion I had in 1991 with the philosopher/politician Richard von
Weizsäcker, who was formerly president of West Germany and, after

unification, president of Germany from 1990 to 1994. Both Germany and Japan have been led down the tragic path to destruction by fanatical nationalism. This common experience inspired President von Weizsäcker and me to agree on the need for social openness of the kind that SGI consistently promotes. This is why I think true religion, or world religion, needs to be linked with, and supportive of, educational movements intended to foster global citizenship.

Planned History and Sullied Knights

IKEDA: The English diplomat and international-political historian Edward Hallett Carr (1892–1982) said the Russian Revolution of 1917 was the first in history to have been deliberately and purposefully planned and executed. Neither the politicians engaged in the English Glorious Revolution of 1688 nor the crowds storming the Bastille in 1789 were aware of taking part in a revolution. They were merely carried away by the impetus of their own actions, which later came to be called revolutionary. Carr says that Lenin's annotations of Marxism reveal a conviction that efficacious force is the product, not of the spontaneous actions on the part of a few individuals, but of a consciously developed political plan.

Lenin said there can be no revolutionary movement without revolutionary theory. And indeed, certain theories – equation of the masses with the avant-garde, the dictatorship of the proletariat and the demise of the nation state – helped set the course of the Bolshevik revolution. To what extent these theories were realised is another question.

Carr's assertions were strongly influenced by two concepts prevalent in eighteenth – and nineteenth – century Europe: belief in progress and belief in the power of reason. History was generally regarded as a process of progress extending from the past into the future. The problem-solving powers of reason were thought to increase with evolving enlightenment. Humanity played the leading role in this rationalist and optimistic view of history. It is not surprising, therefore, that, since Marx-Leninist philosophy belongs in this general current, the leaders of the Russian Revolution were both optimistic and confident about their abilities to control events.

Unfortunately, things did not go according to their plan. The elimination of classes failed to produce equality. Far from fading away, the state grew hypertrophic. I feel that these developments indicated a breakdown of optimism and belief in progress in all schools of thought – not merely socialism – with only superficial interpretations of history and humanity.

AITMATOV: The important issue is not whether the Russian revolution was the first planned revolution but whether it is possible to plan history at all. Even with the supremely noble aim of making all humanity happy, can we plan history? Striving for lofty ideals is all very well. But history evolves according to its own rules, of which we are ignorant.

It is not hard to understand this. The planners of the 1917 revolution believed they had discovered all the answers. Some of them may have entertained doubts, but they had no time to think about them: the revolution itself was just around the corner. Had I been one of them, I too would have been certain of my own vocation to raze the 'old' to its foundations.

We all have perfect hindsight. Passing judgement is easy now. And it is still easier to pose questions like, 'Was there any need for a revolution?' 'Suppose 1917 had never happened?' But, as I have said, history does not take place in the subjunctive mood.

As far as progress goes, I can say with conviction that I am against so-called forward leaps or going up the ladder of history several rungs at a time. I am on the side of the Great Evolution, in the words of the prominent Russian writer Evgeni Zamyatin (1884–1937), author of the novel *My* (We). Pure politics – politics as a profession – is not in my line.

Alexandr Herzen, publisher of the famous journal *Kolokol* (Bell), was being more a philosopher and literary man than a politician when he expressed his thoughts about the French revolution in the following words, which may have greater meaning today than they had at the time of their writing.

> The attempt of the French to establish sacred human rights and win liberty revealed complete human impotence . . . What did we find? Coarse anarchical instincts that, breaking free, with animal self-satisfaction, destroyed all social connections . . . But some strong man will come along to seize the reins of control firmly in his fist.

Napoleon himself said, 'What caused the revolution? Ambition. What put an end to it? Again, ambition. And for us all, liberty was a superb pretext for duping the mob!' My quotations are from the book *Okayannie dni* (The Accursed Days) by Ivan Alekseyevich Bunin (1870 – 1953), who witnessed the Bolshevik revolution as it took place in Odessa.

IKEDA: The people who made the Russian revolution were called 'blameless, fearless knights'.

AITMATOV: Yes, and that described them accurately. That is what hurts most. But in the wake of 'knights' always come pretenders and brutes who set the gory terror machine in motion to frighten the very masses whose hands created the revolution. Then the machine chews up everything – first the knights, next the ordinary people, and finally the hangmen themselves. Alas, this is a law of history. Of course, it is noble to overturn a rotten regime; but how can we be sure of success? Already too well-known Soviet experiences reveal the inevitable outcome of using living human beings as experimental materials.

IKEDA: Nikolay Ivanovich Bukharin (1888–1935), journalist, revolutionary and one-time member of the Politburo, was one of the knights who fell victim to the Stalinist purges of the 1930s. The apologia he wrote in prison gives an idea of the way the bloody terror machine you mention worked. We know now that Bukharin's so-called confession was a trumped-up affair. Nonetheless, afraid of being swept into nameless oblivion, he wrote it in the hope of preserving his association with the glory of the Soviet regime.

> For three months I refused to say anything. Then I began to testify. Why? Because while in prison I made a reevaluation of my entire past. For when you ask yourself: 'If you must die, what are you dying for?' an absolutely black vacuity suddenly arises before you with startling vividness. There was nothing to die for, if one wanted to die un-repented. And, on the contrary, everything positive that glistens in the Soviet Union acquires new dimensions in a man's mind. This in the end disarmed me completely and led me to bend my knees before the Party and the country.[16]

For Bukharin, the party and the state assumed an absolute, religious significance before which everything else, including his own death, was nothing. Many other outstanding revolutionaries were compelled to make false confessions by the para-religious, Soviet ideology of party and state, the fearsomeness of which the Hungarian-born writer Arthur Koestler (1905 – 83) describes in an ominous fashion in his novel *Darkness at Noon*. Although they must have seen through the myth of the system's infallibility and absoluteness, Bukharin and the others more or less quietly allowed themselves to be victimised by it. Do you think many of the old Bolsheviks died ignorant of their own tragic historical mistakes?

AITMATOV: I believe Lenin saw the mistakes first and that they tormented him and hastened his death. Perhaps he wondered whether he might have lived longer had he followed a different path. There must have been many questions. Will there be any answers? Is it possible to answer?

As early as the end of the nineteenth century, the German philosopher Friedrich Nietzsche (1844–1900) prophetically wrote that the means for achieving socialism were near at hand, and he powerfully prophesied the horrors that would accompany it. His unforgettable words corroborate the history through which we in the Soviet Union lived.

> *Socialism in respect to its means.* Socialism is the visionary younger brother of an almost decrepit despotism, whose heir it wants to be. Thus its efforts are reactionary in the deepest sense. For it desires a wealth of executive power, as only despotism had it; indeed, it outdoes everything in the past by striving for the downright destruction of the indicidual, which it sees as an unjustified luxury of nature, and which it intends to improve into an expedient *organ of the community*.[17]

IKEDA: Nietzsche perceptively points out how, under a socialist regime, instead of withering away as Lenin predicted, the state and its power actually grow hypertrophic. As we might expect from the man who announced the death of God, his perception arose from his profound contemplation of the atheism to which modern society has been fated. Socialist ideology appeared in a godless society, trailing clouds of messianism. Nietzsche attempted to discover how it would be accepted by a humanity already thirsting for some meaning to take God's place.

If Tolstoy is the mirror of the Russian revolution, Dostoyevsky can be called its prophet. With depth equal to Nietzsche's, Dostoyevsky examines the question of atheism as the first principle of socialism and, in his novel *Besy* (*The Possessed*), delivers his classic forecast of the fate of the revolution. Interestingly, Nietzsche felt an extremely strong affinity for, and interest in, the character Kirilov in *The Possessed*.

CHAPTER FOUR

A New Way of Thinking

All in the Same Basket

IKEDA: The atomic bombings of Hiroshima and Nagasaki, in August 1945, changed the nature of warfare. Because their mega-death power threatens the annihilation of both attacker and retaliator, for a while nuclear weapons were considered unusable. However, with later reduction in size and dramatic technological improvements in accuracy, their pre-emptive application came to be seen as an accepted possibility. Regarding them in this light is a mistake, because even their pre-emptive use could set off a bedlam of attack and response that might engulf the whole world, with consequences too horrible to contemplate.

The very threat of nuclear war casts a dark shadow on the human mind. Psychologically undermined by eschatological portents, carpe-diem hedonism and an indefinable impotence lead to hopelessness, which in turn creates a climate ripe for warfare.

These situations make nonsense of Karl von Clausewitz's (1780–1831) often quoted definition of war as the continuation of politics by other means. Einstein said,

The unleashed power of the atom has changed everything save our modes of thinking and we thus drift toward unparalleled catastrophe.[1]

The time has come to adopt a new way of thinking and to abandon confrontational attitudes for the sake of international cooperation. In the late 1980s and early 1990s, Russian leaders seemed to adopt this new way of thinking.

AITMATOV: With this topic, we come to the universal theme of surviving in the new historical circumstances in which we find ourselves. Are we to continue relying on the cult of power, bowing to Mars and sacrificing our bones in struggles in the name of nationalist, totalitarian and class ideologies? Or shall we try to work out a generally acceptable way of peaceful, democratic development of life with a human face, as it were? These questions are fundamental for both the present and the future and can only be answered with the aid of all human experience, the idea of survival and the establishment of a new personal status for the individual, whose rights must constitute the foundation of all society.

Is such a perspective realisable? The way humanity has waged a long struggle of self-control to break through the dark mazes of history and advance toward the light of humanism, civilised attitudes and a global form of communal life may help us answer this question. Living as we do in the shadow of thermonuclear weapons, we find it hard to realise that, after the First World War, the League of Nations debated forbidding 'weapons of mass destruction': the ordinary machine-gun.

Our paradoxical position of having to struggle against a monster we ourselves have created suggests an apparent rule of history, before which we are impotent: humanity is doomed to create obstacles for itself, overcome them for the sake of temporary enlightenment, and then start the whole process all over again. If this law does in fact exist, our world assumes a different colouration. We must re-examine ourselves with a completely different interpretation of humanity.

Is humanity serious about surviving? If the answer is yes, why do we engulf ourselves in the unheard-of, horrifying threat of self-destruction? To find our way out of our monstrous situation, must we undergo a new kind of suffering in the form of a 'trial by atom bomb'? Surely humanity has already had too much experience with suffering.

If such a trial is our fated lot, why beat about the bush, why, as the Russian saying goes, build a fence round a fenced-in garden? Would it not be better to hurl ourselves into the waves of destruction without further ado?

I am impelled along this line of thought, not by the ideas of a professional philosopher, but by the words of a certain old woman, who, observing the folly of some rampaging young people, said, 'Too bad you don't know what war's like!' Her words struck me as sinister. Can we not be normal, well-behaved human beings without experiencing war – the worst thing there is? Such has indeed been the case throughout history. Are we, therefore, the victims of pathological juvenility? If so, how long is the sickness going to last? The Kirghiz people speak of fate in terms of the play of celestial horses. Do human beings lack the power to bridle those horses?

IKEDA: History would seem to suggest that war is built into human fate. The Austrian zoologist, ethologist and Nobel Prize laureate Konrad Lorenz (1903–89) said that few vertebrates are cannibalistic. According to him, among powerful animals, instinctive codes prevent squabbles from turning bloody and deadly. For instance, a weaker wolf mollifies the threatening anger of a stronger one by submissively presenting the nape of its neck. To minimise aggressiveness among themselves, wolves instinctively conceal their potentially deadly fangs. The situation is quite different, however, with puny pigeons that, because they lack outstandingly powerful organs, also lack instinctive brakes on their aggressiveness. Consequently, unlike wolves, they sometimes fight to the death. Human beings are more like pigeons than wolves in this respect. Incidentally, Ivan Karamazov in Dostoyevsky's celebrated novel says calling cruel human beings beastly is an insult to the beasts.

Still, we can keep our aggressive instincts under control by constantly striving to improve and implement moral codes. And, when codes prove ineffectual, we can try sublimation. The American philosopher and psychologist William James (1842–1910) proposed replacing war with moral equivalents like sports events and public festivals. Fair competition in games sublimates individual aggressiveness and stimulates person-to-person and nation-to-nation goodwill. The ancient Greek city states were known to halt hostilities so as not to interfere with the holding of events like the Olympic Games.

AITMATOV: Certain of its traits suggest that our race is still mentally in its teens. It is adolescent to be fond of war games and to believe in the possibility of victory as vanity gratification. Saddam Hussein illustrates my point. But the thing that worries me most is the size of the crowds ready to participate in any kind of war, even a nuclear war. Atavism is insurmountable, even in our scientific–technological age.

IKEDA: Only people ignorant of the nature of war are ready to take part in one. Inability to imagine the horror of war is perilous in a nuclear age like ours. On the other side of the coin, understanding of war-caused suffering cultivates compassion, a Buddhist goal and trait indispensable in peace as well as in war. Nichiren set a model for us all when he said, 'Nichiren declares that the sufferings that all living beings undergo, all springing from this one cause – all these are Nichiren's own sufferings.'[2] Here is the acme of the spirit of Buddhist compassion, which I think should be the foundation of humanity's moral standards. You mentioned the frenzied crowds ready to participate in nuclear wars, but the reality is that nuclear wars are in the hands of a very few people, not the crowds. Even people living in seemingly peaceful regions are at peril; they live in deathlike peace. We often forget to ask at what price we seek satisfaction or seldom think that the price is our life, that which can never be artificially created.

AITMATOV: The Polish Roman Catholic primate Jozef Cardinal Glemp (1929–) has said that peace is more than a state free of war: it is a gift of God. His words reflect a new conception of the unity of human life and fate.

The essence of the 'new way of thinking' is the hope that humanity will discover a great, illuminating purpose, teaching us how to live according to the rules of friendship and brotherhood. Attaining this goal will be a supremely inspiring, truly holy achievement and will demand an unprecedented exertion of all humankind's best spiritual powers and reason.

IKEDA: Animosity is a humiliating form of spiritual slavery. Liberating ourselves from it means breaking free of everyday stereotypes and seeing ourselves honestly and clearly on a higher moral level, as if with the eyes of an outsider.

Buddhism seeks this function in the introspective and reflective self called 'two vehicles': the *shrāvaka* or voice-hearer (*shōmon* in Japanese) and the *pratyekabuddha* or cause-awakened one (*engaku* in Japanese). The voice-hearers try to improve themselves through the search for knowledge or Buddhist teachings. The cause-awakened ones are those who awaken to the truth on their own by observing natural phenomena, such as the scattering of blossoms or of the falling of leaves, and who perceive the truth intuitively. Both of them are the state of trying to be free from the limitations of ordinary existence and to enter into a truly humane life. Because Buddhism seeks dramatic progress or a leap in the individual life, it stresses the concept of the introspective and reflective self.

AITMATOV: Liberty for the strong means liberty for the weak. As long as the idea of general liberty and prosperity takes root in our minds – we want to believe that it will – the fate of humanity will become more foreseeable than it has been in the past. My assumption arises from what is called realistic actuality.

At present, however, we are far from free. Nor is war the only threat we confront. The Chernobyl tragedy demonstrated with textbook clarity that human lives can be destroyed and ruined without war. There is no doubt that weapons of mass destruction are an absolute evil that humanity itself created only to destroy itself. All attempts to control the evil of nuclear power must take into consideration, not merely international belligerence, but also human efforts to subjugate the world of nature – a basic principle of the currently dominant Judaeo–Greco–Roman civilisation. Contemporary super-technology, its derivative achievements and, the more complicated it grows, contemporary technology are becoming more and more susceptible to human ill will. The vulnerability of super-technology to malice is apparent from aircraft hijackings and bombings and from the very idea of, say, a terrorist break-in at a nuclear power station.

As a rule, each new discovery brings as much danger and evil as it adds new might. Many examples could be cited. The super-speeds at which we travel today exert pernicious effects on the human organism. The discovery of superconductivity promises concentrated energy of unprecedented power in small containers. But, at the same time, any accident involving superconductivity could produce consequences comparable to those of nuclear war.

The Hindu–Buddhist civilisation – I include traditional Japanese civilisation – might restore balance by applying its teachings of inner reflection in order to counter Western obsession with the eternal world. Unfortunately, the narrow interests of Western intellectuals restrict its ability to do so. Furthermore, the Hindu–Buddhist civilisation is advancing, with considerable success, along the way of technological progress.

IKEDA: Desire in many guises inspires hunger for new scientific discoveries. The French poet Paul Valéry (1871–1945) once said,

> Wherever the European spirit dominates, one witnesses the appearance of the maximum of needs, the maximum of labour, the maximum of capital, the maximum of yield, the maximum of ambition, the maximum of power, the maximum of modification of exterior nature, the maximum of relations and barter.
> This ensemble of *maxima* is Europe, or the image of Europe.[3]

According to Valéry, European civilisation has come to dominate because it is characterised by the enormous power of desire and will.

Since, in its efforts to reveal the nature of God, it has concerned itself with the superhuman, Western science has assumed an independent, ostensibly objective validity, apart from the interests of humanity. Its vast technology has escaped human control, leaving us estranged and threatened by self-annihilation. Realising this, some scientists have begun re-examining their responsibilities in connection with society and world peace. The 1955 Russell–Einstein Declaration, in which British philosopher and mathematician Bertrand Russell (1872–1970) joined Albert Einstein in advocating the abolition of nuclear weapons and of warfare in general, symbolises their attitude. The physicist Hideki Yukawa (1907–81), Japan's first Nobel laureate in physics, advocated pruning scientific research in the hope of preventing it from getting out of control.

In generally pragmatic oriental cultures, science is considered good only in so far as it benefits humankind; instead of existing for itself alone, as it has come to do in the West. The British biochemist and science-historian Joseph Needham (1900–95) pointed this out when he said,

> Many years later, when I had learned a lot more about these things, I realised that there was a second question hiding behind the first one: namely, how could it be that the Chinese civilisation had been much more effective than the European in finding out about Nature and using natural knowledge for the benefit of mankind for fourteen centuries or so before the scientific revolution?[4]

In spite of the many advantages it has given us, Western science has palpably gone too far. The oriental policy of reducing science to human scale can serve as an antidote to its excesses. Other people seem to feel the same way. For instance, representatives of the Newly Industrialising Economies (NIES) seek to enlist the aid of indigenous traditions in the hope of countering Western cultural influences.

AITMATOV: In another area, Muslim civilisation is also moving to the forefront, as it regains the dynamism of its first centuries. This new vigour is mixed with a concealed sense of enmity and strengthened by enormous material wealth accumulated as a consequence of Western dependence on Eastern petroleum. In accordance with a time-tried reaction, the new rich remember injuries suffered in the days of their poverty.

Consequently, while continuing the struggle against the proliferation of weapons of mass destruction, we must at the same time wage battle with factors that could incite blocs, nations or even individual people to make use of those weapons.

In the face of all weapons of mass destruction – not just nuclear ones – human beings experience a spiritually corroding impotence. We must remember that nationalism and doctrines of national interests inspire belief in one's own power and the right to make use of it. What could be worse?

At one time, it seemed as if the so-called new way of thinking would give us a chance to catch our breath. But that did not happen. We now face a real threat that the Cold War will be replaced by a Hot Peace. During their long stand-off, each of the two superpowers policed its own bloc. Things have changed. Nuclear weapons are more widespread than before. A whole roll of nations is now suspected of possessing them. All of this makes it hard to put faith in measures intended to halt their further proliferation.

Specialists divide the causes of recent military conflicts into the following three categories: economic inequality, ethnic tensions and the interests of state sovereignty. Of course, all those reasons are interwoven to form a kind of basket in which we all find ourselves.

Belief in Bellona

IKEDA: Politicians, who not uncommonly worship power, have made nuclear weapons tutelary deities protecting national authority. They kowtow before these gods in the hope of bathing in their reflected glory. As might be expected, the new nuclear religion depends on mistrust and on the desire to subjugate others. Sadly, too many of its devotees fail to see that, in worshipping nuclear power, they sacrifice their own humanity and, in trying to subjugate others, stifle their own better traits.

Thus far, the new nuclear religion has been able to succeed because older established religions have lost the ability to fulfill their traditional roles; that is, to provide believers with absolute values and behaviour models. Their decline and the advance of secularisation have made former absolutes relative and have tempted us to judge things, not qualitatively, but quantitatively. Power, for instance, whether political, financial or military, is easily measured in terms of greater or smaller. Inner, spiritual values do not lend themselves to quantification.

Nuclear weapons are the summit of military power. The fear of, or trust in, the power of nuclear weapons can be considered a kind of religion. But this religion is the complete opposite to humanity and based on the mistrust in humanity. It has spread all over the world, and paradoxically, human beings are controlled and deadlocked by nuclear weapons they themselves have created. This is why I have stressed the importance of religion that can restore humanity for the sake of peace. In your view, how are we to deal with the alienation of humanity by nuclear weapons and the worship of deified nuclear weapons?

AITMATOV: The worship of military might as a new religion represents the wickedest kind of profanation. However, realising the profanity does not make things better. By 'new religion', I mean ideological deification of state military might; priority given to military over all other problems; unconditional, limitless and even uncontrolled military budgets; and justification of any and all outrageous, excessive programs beginning with atomic aircraft carriers and including things like the Strategic Defense Initiative (Star Wars). This religion poeticises and adulates everything military, including spies – or intelligence officers, as they are called. It demands total submission and unconditional obedience to everything connected with war.

But, it goes hand in hand with technical progress. In industrialised nations, immense appropriations for constantly escalating military needs – virtually religious sacrifices – cannot really be considered wasted because they stimulate research in various fields of knowledge, which, otherwise, would hardly be financed on such a scale. But, in the form of arms races, this religion demands unaffordable sacrifices of under-developed nations, thus widening the economic gap between the North and the South. The former president of Pakistan, Zulfikar Ali Bhutto (1928–79), remarked that, even if forced to eat grass, his people would produce an Islamic nuclear bomb.

Given this kind of attitude, it is difficult to require all nations to adhere to high standards of moral behaviour. Violations will occur. And state-sovereignty interests will always tempt violators to lay the blame on somebody else.

In the meantime, how are we to keep from being driven mad with fear? The only answer is to reinforce our belief in reason and conscience, which, I hope, will lead us to good and compel us to choose life over death, even if only for our children's sake.

I disagree that senility in the older religions has caused the emergence of this new one. The venerable moral bases of all the religious beliefs, by which people have governed themselves for many millennia, cannot have grown old and outworn. Of course, the new epoch of triumphant scientific-technological progress (in the realm of ideas also) demands completely different kinds of people – enterprising, passionless adventurers who stop at nothing, least of all the elimination of whole 'aboriginal' peoples whom these new people consider, at best, fit only for slavery. But that is another matter altogether. Such people have no time for a religion of universal values. This is all the more true now that religion itself has become – or has been compelled to become – a handmaiden of politics. Quite naturally, without realising it, people have drastically altered the way they think about religion.

God – whose nature, patently, is unknown – had to be overthrown. Otherwise, how could we poison drinking water by building chemical plants at its sources? I believe that, in the Far East, such an act is regarded as a mortal sin. But because the chemical plants seemed necessary, they were built; and the damage they did was rationalised away. Traditional religions were powerless to hinder the rationalisation.

Insatiable human extremism has led to atheism or absolute belief in the might of military potential. This, in turn, has led us to regard those people as superior who discovered nuclear power and to look on everybody else as somehow retarded.

The desire to subjugate others arises from primitive ideas of life that corrupt and, in the final count, dehumanise power-holders. The desire to overcome nuclear estrangement seems to reflect man's striving to become, once again, God's creature. This, in turn, reflects the need for new feelings that will certainly arise in us if we manage to free ourselves and others from fear.

Do we need a new religion? Maybe we do, as long as that religion takes into consideration human laws and institutions that have existed since time immemorial but that we have ignored while idolising our nuclear god. Tolerance is one of those long-established laws. Today intolerance is a major threat.

IKEDA: I agree that not all aspects of established religions have become outworn. For example, the teachings of such great Christian figures as Saint Francis of Assisi (1181/1182–1226) preserve their validity.

In some areas, Buddhism too may be faulted. Its Hinayanist form is frequently and justly criticised for promoting excessive introspection and escapist longings for release from the delusions and sufferings of the world. Buddhism has, however, demonstrated consistent tolerance. In contrast, throughout its history, Christianity, like Marxism, one of its derivatives, has manifested virulent intolerance not only of non-Christian religions, but also of diversity within its own fold. To see this, one has only to recall the horrors of the sixteenth-century wars of religion between Catholics and Protestants in France. Christianity has often proved a breeding ground for wars. Perhaps this is why, in our discussions together, the American chemist, pacifist and two-time Nobel laureate Linus Pauling (1901–94) and the Italian founder of the Club of Rome Aurelio Peccei (1908–84), while aware of the importance of religion, demonstrated great scepticism about a religious role in the building of a global peace structure.

Christians have been notoriously intolerant of the needs of the world of non-human nature. Modern Western science evolved within the Judaeo–Christian tradition that Man, created in the image of God, has full dominion over all other creatures. Magnifying the glory of God was the motivating force behind the achievements of great thinkers like Johannes Kepler (1571–1630), Galileo Galilei (1564–1642) and Sir Isaac Newton (1642–1727). Francis Bacon (1562–1626) called scientific experimentation mechanical torture with which Nature could be forced to confess its truths. Running through Western history, from the seventeenth-century witch hunts to the nuclear threat and environmental pollution of our own times, this attitude is related to fundamental Christian intolerance.

Generally speaking, religion is related not only to individual salvation or inner purification but also to our view of the world in a broad sense, such as our views of society, nature and the cosmos. Because of that, the merits and demerits of each religion's world views and ethical foundations need to be examined strictly in the context of history. You comment on intolerance as a great modern peril. Undeniably, this is true. Coping with it requires a sound and accurate understanding of the nature of tolerance itself. Tolerance does not mean the exclusion of disagreement, nor does it necessarily lead to unprincipled ecumenicalism. It must not be equated with collusion or compromise. What the American sociologist P. L. Berger (1929–) calls the formation of mutually protective religious cartels, deprives individual religions of their independence. During the earlier part of the twentieth-century, the Japanese government enforced sweeping mergers among religious sects, which were too dominated by the militarist establishment to do anything to halt the course of events that led to the Second World War.

On the other hand, tolerance does not imply apathy. Religions must demonstrate interest in all aspects of life. They must strive to contribute to the good of humanity and, through full application of pacifist ideas and free speech, engage in ever-widening inter-religious debate and competition. They must constantly prove their moral qualities in actual practice, especially in educational work aimed at cultivating true citizens of the world. Activities of these kinds manifest true religious tolerance and demonstrate that religion is for the sake of humanity.

We Must All Live Together

IKEDA: President Gorbachev once said that we must expand our thinking beyond the interests of single nations. I agree. To solve fateful problems like peace, the environment, natural resources and the economy, we must assume a global – transnational – view of the nation state itself. As all parts of the world are densely interrelated, global affairs are immediately reflected in the domestic affairs of each country. On the other hand, the affairs of each country inescapably influence those of all others. Just as the pursuit of completely selfish aims on the part of an individual is inimical to social life, so nations that overlook the interests of their neighbours in single-minded pursuit of their own aims risk international ostracism. At the very least, such an attitude works to the detriment of those who assume it. Obviously the transnational approach is the only practical one to take.

Venerable traditions of national sovereignty deserve respect. But obsession with them leads to trouble. Likewise, it is only natural for an independent nation to be concerned about its own best interests. Harm, however, arises from intolerant nationalism. In a nuclear world, the unbridled exercise of nation-state rights can lead to the annihilation of humanity. As Norman Cousins said, 'THE PRIME FACT of our time is that the sovereign nations have gone berserk, pursuing measures that are leading to a hideous assault on human life.'[5]

We must fundamentally revise our approach to this issue. National interests must give way to the interests of humanity as a whole.

AITMATOV: Defining state sovereignty is one of today's most glaring difficulties. Contemporary technology has reduced whole numbers of former sovereign-state functions to mere fictions. Aerial photography now reveals literally everything – from harvests to troop movements – occurring within the territory of any state. The Soviet Union tried desperately, but in vain, to keep its borders closed to the streams of information criss-crossing the globe. Inescapably, the spheres of action of all kinds of regional and global organisations, one way or another, regulate and coordinate the actions of separate governments. Humanity has already built global structures and is going to continue building them. For their own good, governments are compelled to limit their sovereignty – in the old meaning of the word. The European Union and the Common Market – which afford the same conditions to mighty Germany and to miniature Luxembourg – eloquently testify to the truth of this.

A colossal stream of information, money, goods and people constitutes the circulatory system of the contemporary world. Although, conceivably it can be regulated and perfected sensibly, it cannot be stemmed. The time has come to realise that state sovereignty no longer exists in its former absolute sense. Increasingly state-government functions are being limited to choosing organs of power, adopting laws and defending property and boundaries.

The Iraq–Kuwait incident of 1991 showed that, even in connection with the especially ticklish issue of boundaries, only decisions reached by political, not military, means are stable. I still remember with horror the evil 'act of state sovereignty' perpetrated by the Soviet military in shooting down over Sakhalin a South Korean airliner carrying 269 passengers in September 1983. The only reason given was violation of Soviet air space. Had a military craft – and not a Boeing airliner – been involved, the action might have been more understandable. Nonetheless, even if, as the Soviet military claimed in self-justification, it had been a reconnaissance plane, downing it would have been criminal and unthinkable. Then and later, I tried as hard as I could to speak out on this topic in the press. But there was no breaching the logic of ferro-concrete state sovereignty. Our inability even to apologise for the military's crime still rests heavy on my mind.

National egoism is costlier than it is worth. In the Soviet Union, it led to painful results, including, as is well known, the sacrificing of human lives. Amity among people is certainly the only way to go. True, 'You can't make somebody love you', as the old Russian proverb has it. Still, official demagogy aside, sincere friendship among peoples ought to be possible. Surely not everything is pretence. The radiant smile of friendship does not necessarily turn into the scowl of ill will at the first opportunity that presents itself. We must not allow ourselves to be deprived of the common sense truth: even a bad peace is better than a fight.

IKEDA: It seems to take a grave, universal threat to unite humanity. The petroleum crisis of the 1970s inspired interest in husbanding the planet's finite natural resources because it seemed to affect everyone. The threat of total annihilation posed by the existence of nuclear weapons has stimulated many people to see that we must cooperate in the name of peace if we are to survive.

But threats represent negative powers. If future human history is to be peaceful and prosperous, we must find positive forces to educate all human beings to the oneness of our fate. In other words, we must cultivate true citizens of the world who regard the entire planet as their home. As one aspect of the education process, I recommend that the United Nations establish a United Nations Decade of Education for World Citizens, which could perform the kind of guiding and stimulating role that the UN Development Decade and UN Decade for Women offered. Of course, training for peace must play a prominent part in world-citizen education.

Soka Gakkai International strives to promote global, peaceful, grassroots solidarity based on universal Buddhist teachings. We take modest pride in the contributions we have made to various countries in this connection and in the knowledge that our exhibition 'Nuclear Arms: Threat to Our World' (compiled and managed in cooperation with the United Nations and the cities of Hiroshima and Nagasaki) significantly pioneered pacifist, world-citizen education. The task now is to discover still more positive forces for inspiring a sense of the oneness of human fate.

AITMATOV: Though each individual person dies alone, we must all live together. Perhaps learning how to do this is the most useful of all sciences for contemporary humanity. But it is so difficult that no one has ever completed the course.

Sometimes, on the grounds of no more than differences of nationality, people who have lived side by side for centuries suddenly become implacable, mortal enemies. How are we to account for this? Purely moral explanations fail to take into consideration the biological nature of such phenomena. Perhaps in attempting to deal with apparently inescapable conflicts, we ought to bypass economic and materialistic issues and think in terms of a hostility gene or of incompatibility in blood groups, lifestyles, languages and so on. Does atavism explain all this?

The apparent parallel between nationalism and the disparate economic conditions of the developed nations of the North and the developing countries of the South does not hold. The truth is that, instead of eliminating them, as was foreseen, technological progress has only aggravated ethnic conflicts. By destroying traditional ways of life, progress has left the individual adrift in an unfamiliar world where he must seek solace and support from compatriots and fellow believers.

It is easy to explain nationalistic antagonism in terms of either bad politics, obviously, or faulty education, equally obviously. Giving priority to the shared values of all humankind is the way out of our impasse and the way to unify our race. But, once again, force will produce no good results. For the union of humankind to become more than a noble ideal, we must feel a spiritual need for it. For this to happen, the general moral climate of society must change. If the sovereignty of the individual was recognised as inviolate, people would gradually – perhaps unawares – come to see how necessary we all are to each other. Then the general sovereignty of humanity would triumph. The well-being of all humankind would get the priority it deserves. The more people become attracted to it, the more realisable this noble ideal will become. I am sure it will find adherents: people have grown weary of enmity, suffering and blood.

Cosmopolitanism had a highly dramatic fate in the Soviet Union. In the name of the many fine people who gave their lives for it, I consider it an important duty to promote the realisation of the truly cosmopolitan view.

To cultivate citizens of the world, we must overcome nationalistic egoism by rectifying economic inequalities. The new economic order is taking form in a haphazard way along the lines on which Western civilisation was propagated. While undeniably demonstrating material superiority, the civilisation of the West has spawned an ecological crisis urgently demanding the search for alternative variants, which will most probably be found at the confluence of all civilisational currents. By contributing to the further development of ethnic traits and by calling on the accumulated experience of peoples outside the circle of Western civilisation, such alternative variants might help reduce nationalistic friction.

Western Christian civilisation attained a position of pre-eminence, not through inherent excellence, but through colonialism. Clearly, the future is going to favour cultural and civilisational pluralism. And, in the opinions of many specialists, this orientation will block the emergence of a universal religion, which must inevitably be synthesising in nature and lack emotional content. For my own part, I long for the kind of spiritual union a universal religion could provide.

Even in the face of these opinions, all reasonable people must energetically promote the emergence and development of ecumenicalism, in the sense of the expression of common traits which undeniably exist among all the world's religions, and work to prevent religion from being converted into a new kind of weaponry.

With conflicts breaking out everywhere like purulent eruptions, talking of ecumenicalism may sound simple-minded. But I cannot help that. Humanity must unite if it wants to survive; as surely it does. Life is to be loved. That is the highest happiness, although many people seem both to have forgotten it and – as bitter and frightening as it is – to have lost the self-preservation instinct. We seem to be willing to sacrifice ourselves and our progeny even though the greatest happiness can be found in extinguishing malice or despair and in loving life. Let us remember to love life now so that a later, wiser humanity will not be able to rebuke us for having concealed simple, ancient truth. Let not the spirit of a single one of us have to ask regretfully, 'Why was I so blind?'

All Children of Humanity

IKEDA: Known in the West as the Brezhnev Doctrine, the Soviet theory of limited sovereignty came into being as an attempt to rationalise military intervention in Czechoslovakia in 1968. In brief, it argued that socialist nations were justified in interfering in each other's internal affairs if the foundation of the socialist system seemed in jeopardy as the result of some domestic anti-socialist movement. In other words, the doctrine impinged on the sovereignty and ethnic self-determination of all Soviet satellite states. In 1988, in what is called the New Belgrade Declaration, in keeping with the novel way of thinking he embodied, President Gorbachev pronounced the Brezhnev Doctrine defunct.

Four months after the New Belgrade Declaration, the Soviet Union reached an agreement with Poland, recognising the equality of the two states and stressing respect for the rights of each to make its own independent political decisions. This same agreement held that, owing to diverse national characteristics and historical conditions forming the basis of socialist reform, there was no one absolute social truth. Its significance was especially great since, unlike unaligned Yugoslavia, Poland was a member of the Warsaw Treaty Organisation.

A whole series of Mr. Gorbachev's initiatives seem to have arisen from the realisation that, for better or worse, ethnic problems – in the Soviet Union relegated to secondary significance, after questions of class difference – are in fact very deep-rooted. Nonetheless, while ethnic interests must not be eclipsed, intense international inter-dependence now makes the survival of isolated nationalists groups impossible.

AITMATOV: Ironically, your own nation made a long and determined effort to remain aloof from the affairs of the rest of the world. In the first half of the nineteenth century, Japan was a closed country jealously guarding its isolation, or its sovereignty, as we would say today. This protection was considered supremely important. As you suggest, however, such a policy could hardly be maintained today. Apparently, the Japanese of that time wanted for nothing. Why, then, did they open their boundaries, and themselves, to the rest of the world?

IKEDA: Under no circumstances would Japan today adopt the isolationist policies of the Edo period (1603–1867). For a variety of reasons, by the latter half of the nineteenth century, the opening of Japan was inevitable. Domestic industry and commerce had already reached a fairly high level of development. The Tokugawa shogunate, which had controlled the nation for two and a half centuries, was enfeebled. And neighbouring countries near and far were pressing for greater openness in Japanese policies.

Both Russia and the United States were urging Japan to open ports. Indeed, in 1853, within a month of each other, the American Commodore Matthew C. Perry (1794–1858) and the Russian Vice-admiral Evfimi V. Putyatin (1803–83) called at Edo (Tokyo) and Nagasaki with requests to this end. It must be said that, respecting Japanese customs and selecting Nagasaki instead of the shogunal capital as his port of call, Putyatin behaved in a more gentlemanly fashion than high-handed Perry, who sailed into Edo Harbour with his notorious, intimidating Black Ships. Nonetheless, ironically, it was Perry's gunboat diplomacy that proved the decisive, direct factor in opening Japan to the world.

At the time, the Japanese people paid greater allegiance to local ruling clans than to the central shogunal government. Allegiance to the Japanese state as a whole evolved gradually after the opening of the country.

In April 1955, at the Bandung Conference, held in Bandung, Indonesia, nearly a decade after the end of the war, representatives from 29 Asian and African nations mapped out a course for harmonious international relations in the form of five principles: mutual respect for territory and sovereignty, mutual non-aggression, mutual non-interference in domestic affairs, equality and mutual respect and peaceful coexistence.

The praiseworthy Soviet rejection of the doctrine of limited sovereignty, and of its own hegemony, is in keeping with the pacific spirit of the Bandung Conference. Events subsequent to it proved worldwide fear of the so-called Soviet threat to have been exaggerated and often no more than political publicity. First the abandonment of the Brezhnev Doctrine and then the collapse of the Soviet Union pulled the ground out from under the feet of western hawks who had used fear of the Soviet threat to justify burgeoning military budgets. In this sense, throwing out the idea of limited sovereignty performed a great service in the name of global peace.

AITMATOV: I am grateful to you for reminding me of Bandung and its principles of peaceful coexistence. The Bandung spirit was a revelation to me as a young man. Its universality and clarity intoxicated me. I adored the phrase 'the Bandung spirit'.

Many of the contemporary problems of our long-suffering world appear much clearer in its light.

To be sure, the colonialism under which the Bandung nations suffered for many years is not yet completely dead. Its philosophy and psychology survive, albeit under new names and in new guises and concealments of sly demagogy and political babble. But people all over the world sense the deception. Former colonial populations realise they are still looked down on by some as 'brainless sheep' (words spoken by Stalin from the Lenin Mausoleum on Red Square) or as slaves now euphemistically called 'labour resources'.

Soviet policies for dealing with nationalities were founded on total contempt for all national interests, including Russian. The ideology of the world proletariat took precedence over everything and everyone. As you point out, the socialists paid significantly less attention to nationalities than to social classes. In some instances, they disdained the nationalities question altogether. What time they had for it was devoted to the demagogy of the question itself and not to its human aspects. They were interested in creating a new kind of human being – *homo-sovieticus* – who would transcend nationality.

Nothing remains of their efforts now but the anger of the simple man who has discovered that, all his life, he has been insolently deceived and used for the selfish aims of flattering hypocrites stoking his smoldering rage. The bloodbath that followed the collapse of the Soviet Union was the final outcome of Soviet policies for dealing with nationalities. Still unaware that we were being manipulated, we failed to come together as brothers. And, all the while, wraiths in another world ridiculed us, just as they had always done.

Instead of becoming the officially touted new *homo-sovieticus*, we went on being Ukrainian, Kirghiz, Russian, Jewish and so on. In the light of this, I find something prophetic in the words of my unforgettable teacher Mukhtar Auezov, who said, 'I am proud to be, not the son of a Kazakh, but a son of humanity.' Still, who listened to him then? Who would listen to him now? In a fight, everyone demonstrates his nationality. Few can honestly call themselves sons of humanity.

It is disheartening to see innocent people divided by dissension. But, upon closer examination, perhaps the innocent were not all that blameless after all. Perhaps they allowed their passions to blind them to our common humanity. We peoples of the former Soviet Union have been given a great opportunity. If we waste it by using our new freedom slavishly instead of in the name of good, the full blame will rest solely on us.

IKEDA: In spite of the idiosyncratic predispositions common to all ethnic groups, I believe the sense of being a 'child of humanity', in the words of your revered teacher, is widespread and deeply rooted and can help us overcome even apparently insuperable barriers. As an example of the depth to which the sense of common humanity crosses nationality boundaries, I might cite an incident that the Japanese writer Shin Hasegawa relates as having occurred during the Russo–Japanese War of 1904–05. Some Russian prisoners of war were being held at a Japanese regimental headquarters. When a Japanese company commander invited his men to take a look at the prisoners, to his surprise, only about half expressed interest. One soldier offered this explanation for the general reluctance:

> I used to be an ordinary workman. A uniform made a soldier out of me. I don't know where these guys come from. But they've had the hard luck to be taken prisoner, and I feel sorry for them. Being dragged around for people to gawk at must be tough on them. That's why I don't want to go over there and embarrass them.[6]

Struck by this soldier's words, the commander called the tour off.

The recalcitrant soldier knew in his heart that he and the Russian prisoners shared the same humanity. Political units, not individual human beings, wage wars. As Jean Jacques Rousseau said, the state cannot make people enemies. Sheer accident pits people against each other in battle. We can promote the unification of the peoples of the Earth by letting our common, innate hatred of war show us the way to mutual trust and amity.

At one level, travel, international conferences and communications technology are already bringing the world together, thus deepening ties of friendship among the ordinary people. I prefer to put my trust in large-scale popular exchanges that expand spiritual people-to-people contacts, not in inherently jingoistic, exclusivist nationalist policies. I intend to do all within my power to promote such positive exchanges.

From Isolation to Unity

IKEDA: In 1988, after returning home from a meeting we had in Tokyo, you wrote to me, 'In the years to come, a new world religion – new religious cultural teachings – will become necessary. Throughout the long history of our race, people have been spiritually and mentally isolated from each other. We must unite them all in a single harmony. If we fail to accomplish this now, the human race will cease to exist . . . Until I visited Japan, my philosophy had been based on the European spirit. On this occasion, through Soka Gakkai, I have learned much from the philosophy of the Orient. If they fail to achieve harmony, the present generation will be passing the task on to our successors.'

Current generations must strive to create a single harmony out of the spiritual and mental isolation that, as you point out, has characterised past human history. Isolation can be found everywhere in today's society: from disunity between thoughts and actions, the imbalance between reason and emotion at the individual level, the generation gap between people, hostility and conflicts between nations to the separation between human beings and nature. Whereas evil disrupts harmony and order, good is born of uniting sundered elements in an orderly fashion. I express this as 'isolation is evil; unity, good'. Therefore, we must make our thoughts and actions consonant with each other, bridge generation gaps, cultivate international bonds of amity and harmonise human civilisation with the natural environment. To fail in this is to choose the path to the annihilation of our own race.

The new approaches evident in the *perestroika* period were attempts to switch away from conflict and strife in the direction of mutual dependence and cooperation. Propagating these new approaches throughout all aspects of life will enable us to re-examine civilisation as a whole, to reunify the human heart and in this way to build a new and harmonious world.

AITMATOV: As you imply, for many of us, the mind and the heart are out of harmony. Internal discord reflects the external discord that rends contemporary society. To your list of splits affecting our world, I would add the split between contemporary humanity and the past, history. No one now wants to accept the responsibility for the past of his own people, let alone that of the whole world. People tend to think, 'What's that past of some off-the-wall ethnic group or extinct civilisation got to do with me?' But if everyone felt this way, nobody would have anything to do with anybody else. We would all be cut off from the cosmos and condemned to a narrow-minded existence in limited, confined space and time. Such an existence is fraught with the inexpressible, but completely real, suffering of a prisoner incarcerated for reasons of which he is totally ignorant. In our instance, the prisoner has turned the key on himself.

As you say, the world has shrunk to an extraordinary degree. At one time, we sensed the shrinkage only intuitively. Later, through cosmonauts' eyes, we actually saw our Earth like a cradle – a small blue star – hung in the limitless spaces of the universe. But, as our world has dwindled in size, our understanding of it has expanded to an equal, if not to a greater, extent. Formerly, we believed we all lived apart with no need to know or associate with each other. Like our forebears, we believed we could shut ourselves off by means of some kind of wall, military or ideological. We now see that all are ineffective. We are compelled to find a new way to understand each other. Are we capable of it?

IKEDA: Realising our shared humanity at once reveals the error of being callous and incommunicative. As political borders grow less and less significant, isolation becomes more and more difficult. I operate always on my belief in the possibility of profound interpersonal communication. As Nichiren said, 'Here a single individual has been used as an example, but the same thing applies equally to all living beings.'[7] At the most basic level, all earthlings are compatriots, all inevitably confronted with birth, ageing, illness and death. No matter what our social or ethnic backgrounds, we all want the peace to devote ourselves to the happiness of our families, rejoice in our children's growth and mourn lost loved ones. As the American philosopher and poet Ralph Waldo Emerson (1803–82) said, 'We live in succession, in division, in parts, in particles. Meanwhile within man is the soul of the whole; . . . the universal beauty, to which every part and particle is equally related: the eternal One.' Though our actions are separate, each of us is part of the universal beauty: 'the eternal One'. I term the fundamental equality of all humankind the 'inner universal'. If we want to do so earnestly enough, we can use the inner universal as a basis for spreading an awareness of the solidarity of humanity. Originally, we all have commonality to understand each other as inseparable comrades on the earth. The reason for our isolation or separation is all artificially created.

AITMATOV: That is a very important viewpoint. Today's tragedy befalling humanity results from disregarding this point. To attain the noble goal of soul-cleansing, harmonious unity among all peoples on Earth, we must rise to the level of lofty thoughts. We disdain this task at our peril. As Confucius said, 'The person who fails to take far-reaching precautions is sure to encounter near-at-hand woes.'[8]

This does not mean that we can disregard mundane, everyday needs. Aleksandr I. Solzhenitsyn (1918–2008) said: 'The spiritual level of life determines the spiritual strength or impotence of a society – the level of industrial development comes second.' There is some truth in this statement. Nonetheless, a hungry man cannot be expected to forget his hunger. Nor can philosophical considerations of the vanity of things help the poor ignore their poverty. Perhaps Solzhenitsyn would have come closer to the mark if he had insisted that spiritual and material levels, instead of being assigned precedence, should be ensured simultaneously and harmoniously.

CHAPTER FIVE

Literature in Life

Russian Literature: Tradition and Traits

IKEDA: Like most Russian literature, your work is permeated with the sincere, relentless search for a higher way of life and for answers to such great questions as why the good must suffer in this world and whether might is truly right. Transcending mere narrative interest and literary artistic merit, Tolstoy and Dostoyevsky sought to establish guideposts for living life better. When Herzen called Russian literature a martyrs' history, he meant that Russian writers are destined to record the sufferings and fate of the masses. The vigorous rejection of art by the critic Dmitry I. Pisarev (1840–68) and by Tolstoy himself in his last years, emerges almost inevitably from this destiny. You seem to have inherited the mantle of these great writers and their artistic and philosophical tradition.

AITMATOV: You are perfectly correct in identifying the hunger for truth and justice as a salient characteristic identifying Russian literature with suffering and the search for, and discovery of, humanity. Moreover, this hunger orients our literature toward discovery of, in Dostoyevsky's words, 'the maximum possible humanity in the human being'. Of course, the impetus for this kind of thinking predates Dostoyevsky. The eighteenth-century philosopher and poet Aleksandr N. Radishchev (1749–1802) put it concisely when he said, 'I looked around, and my soul was wounded by human suffering.'

In his book *Poor Liza*, the historian and novelist Nikolai M. Karamzin (1766–1826) declared, 'Even a peasant woman knows how to suffer.' Obviously a literature that can make such a declaration is engrossed in the human problem. People today find it hard to understand how much courage it took to make such a comment in the world in which Karamzin lived. When courageous art began treating serfs – 'talking bellies', as the ancient Greeks called slaves – as human beings, it removed the keystone from the institution of serfdom on which nineteenth-century Russian society depended. An interesting contrast, by the way, is that the English were moving in the direction of democracy as early as the thirteenth century, but serfdom persisted in Russia until 1861.

The struggle for the assertion of individuality and human worth, which generated and propelled nineteenth-century Russian literature, is the work of the human mind inspired by the concept of liberty. One of Alexander Herzen's books is entitled *Who's To Blame? (Kto Vinovat?)*. Somewhat later than Herzen's time, Russian writers began trying to find an answer to that question by dealing with the theme of the downtrodden – 'the insulted and the injured'. One of Dostoyevsky's novels is actually entitled *The Insulted and the Injured*. The issue is an eternal one, in the face of which truth and conscience forbid us to remain silent. Tolstoy, who considered making readers love life in all its diversity to be literary art's highest mission, was compelled by his own conscience to speak out about the society he lived in. This drove him into unyielding opposition to the official church and the inhumanity of the totalitarian government. He insisted on 'mercilessly tearing away all masks of all kinds'. Only a spiritual giant like Tolstoy could have both survived and ultimately won a duel with the ruling political and social machinery of his day.

IKEDA: Yes, Tolstoy was a giant. After visiting him during the Crimean War, Chekov (1860–1904) described him as a Jupiter, an eagle soaring high above the heads of other men. Aside from his towering literary achievements, he was extraordinary in many respects. As a youth, he displayed extraordinary ambition, passion and hedonism. Later, with astonishing willpower and energy, he reined in all these youthful drives to return to a simple way of life. Certainly, as you point out, his unyielding struggle against political and religious authoritarianism was out of the ordinary; as was his decision, at the advanced age of eighty-two, to leave home and seek the Way. In an age like the present, when human beings seem to have dwindled in scale, Tolstoy's magnificent image startles and shocks but eternally points the way to human revival.

AITMATOV: He is unique, and not accidentally. His time was dominated by stifling oppression and suppression of the slightest hint of free expression, and he was the kind of man needed to overcome such conditions. His mission was the one Russian writers are always fated to fulfill. In our day, it has become the destiny of Aleksandr I. Solzhenitsyn.

Because, when subjected to penal servitude, they experience a double portion, on their own part and on the part of the whole people, Russian writers deserve places of honour among the persecuted Herzen had in mind when he called Russian history a chronicle of martyrs. The writer must stand up for his right to speak out about individual freedom and the people's pain, which he shares. He must ignore personal risk. The word of truth is equivalent to the act. And the act requires civil courage.

Courage brings us back to Solzhenitsyn, whom apocalyptic circumstances put in a position where he had to oppose both totalitarianism and Stalin himself. The evil of the Soviet empire was all-embracing and mighty. But Solzhenitsyn stood up to it resolutely because the power of the word was just as mighty.

A powerful literary figure in the twentieth century, Solzhenitsyn has a distant precursor in the seventeenth-century. As the leader of the dissenting religious group called the *Raskolniki*, the archpriest and seeker of purity and fanatic faith, Avvakum (1620–82) symbolised unyielding opposition to officialdom, especially the Orthodox Church. The great respect Tolstoy had for him is understandable. Avvakum symbolises the kind of profoundly felt and actually experienced spirituality that is the foundation of the Russian literary tradition. By his own example, he proved the word of truth to be more precious than life itself. Indeed, he showed that life without truth is no kind of life at all. Herein is to be found the value of the word, the value of life.

IKEDA: Articulate speech being a characteristic of our humanness, we human beings could be called *Homo loquens*. In our age, however, devotion to the scientific spirit has obscured the vast semantic universe behind verbal communications. And this, in turn, has made it hard for many people to understand why our forebears considered freedom of oral and written expression worth dying for.

Freedom of speech is humanising. Buddhists consider fruitful use of words an aspect of the Buddha's mission. Generally speaking, to be trustworthy, verbal expressions must be unrestricted. Realising this, Mikhail Gorbachev has said that the orientation of a whole life depends on whether that person puts faith in spoken and written words.

However, for all the desirability of freedom of expression, oppression and adversity can strengthen and refine a writer's work, as in the case of Solzhenitsyn and of Victor Hugo. After Napoleon III seized power, Hugo went into exile. He once said that this experience plus his other encounters with oppression made his own words as hard and durable as granite.

You are bilingual in Kirghiz and Russian. To what literary tradition do you assign your own work?

AITMATOV: My position is perhaps a novel one. I write in Russian, therefore my work belongs with Russian literature; my background is Kirghiz. In everything I write, the way I express myself reflects the Kirghiz language and world outlook. My having two native tongues is like having had two mothers who raised and enriched me. This is a matter of fate.

The Mutable and Immutable in Religion

IKEDA: The heretic in your story *Executioner's Block* eagerly publicises his belief in the historical evolution of the concept of God. According to him, the post-industrial age strains human powers greatly enough to necessitate investigations of relations with God, who consequently is deluged with questions about his significance for humanity. A religion that is unwilling to answer justifiable questioning of this kind atrophies and sooner or later ends up in the dustbin of time.

Religions consist of two elements: an immutable, essential philosophical core dealing with eternals and peripheral aspects in which mutability is not only possible, but indeed essential if the religion is to respond to changing human emotions and needs.

AITMATOV: The topic you have touched upon, inescapable in any consideration of man as a spiritual being, is all the more worthy of notice in the light of the intellectual crisis we are now experiencing in the Soviet Union.

In Soviet society, all elements potentially critical of the regime were explained away as 'hangovers from the past'. Religion was primary among them. Though the idea seems ludicrous now, the power of ideology made it serious and conveniently simple at the time. The monopolistic official ideology either refashioned or destroyed everything outside the sphere of what was called 'materialist awareness'.

Religions were uprooted. Places of worship of all faiths were razed. A single world view, imposed on all classes, extinguished spiritual life and led to the moral degeneration of individuals, generations and nations. Evil and violence became our daily way of life.

Intolerance, violence and manipulation of the masses are common to atheistic as well as religious fundamentalisms, which generate political and sectarian stimuli that fan the flames of terrorism, an especially distressing phenomenon in our time.

IKEDA: The United States suffered under a virulent kind of political fundamentalism in the mid-1950s. It was named 'McCarthyism', after Senator Joseph McCarthy (1908–57), who stirred up a furore by accusing people in many walks of life of un-American and communist activities, often on the slenderest of grounds. Ultimately, after McCarthy was reprimanded by the Senate, the matter was closed, leaving many Americans wondering what it had all been about. Actually, it had been about the kind of blind rage that stimulates most fundamentalists to reject diversity of values and to condemn everyone who does not share their beliefs.

In his book *Power Shift*, Alvin Toffler (1928–) cites fundamentalism as one of the gravest impediments to a society's wholesome development. And, in *The Idea of a Christian Society*, T. S. Eliot (1888–1965) describes, albeit without actually using the word, something like fundamentalism as the trap into which secular reformers and revolutionaries are most likely to fall. Incorporating Eliot's observations, I suggest that the following two traits characterise fundamentalism: seeing only the evil without, never the evil within and refusing to recognise the dignity of the individual; a dignity advocated by all the higher religions.

The evil outside the self, which Eliot calls impersonal, is the source of the intolerance and violence characteristic of fundamentalism. Any society wishing to avoid malicious fundamentalism must be willing to look for the evil within itself and guarantee respect for the dignity of the individual.

Buddhism divides life into ten aspects, called the 'Ten Worlds'. Put simply, this doctrine means that a single human life is composed of good and evil elements and can reach great heights of nobility or sink to abysmal depths of depravity depending on which element predominates. The human revolution that I strongly advocate is a way of subduing the evil and activating the good aspects of life. In Eliot's opinion, the individual turns to religion when he realises the need for self-reform as well as social reform. The noble heights we can reach by activating the good aspects of life provide a solid basis for respecting the individual. Conversely, any movement that ignores these things grows more evil as it grows more radical.

AITMATOV: I must ask your indulgence for the exclusively personal, empirical, and non-professional nature of my comments on religion. I think about such matters only to the extent that I am able; and, to a degree, my efforts represent an attempt to become acquainted with new and unfamiliar worlds and ways of thinking and feeling that excite and attract me.

Perhaps beauty is the primary attraction. I do not mean material beauty, but the kind of ancient, primordial spirituality and greatness of soul that I experienced, for example, while listening for the first time to canticles being sung in the Church of Alexander Nevsky, in Bulgaria. I remember thinking at the time how wonderful must have been the lives of the people of those distant, unknown times if celestial music of the kind I was hearing could be born in their hearts, or perhaps it would be better to say, if such music descended on them from heaven. God is truly love. And music is the loftiest, most mystical expression of love.

Inevitably and reluctantly, I must ask myself whether I am a believer. The question constantly pursues me. But I realise fully that the answer I give today may not satisfy me under altered circumstances. It is said that we must grow accustomed to religion from our earliest childhood. I did not have this opportunity. When I was growing up, we were taught that there is no god, that God is a fabrication, and that religion is the 'opium of the people'. Ten years before I was born, Soviet society put God on trial and, as was all too commonly the case then, sentenced Him to death. Guns were actually fired heavenward, and everyone went home, apparently completely satisfied with their endeavours. In general, under such conditions, all members of my generation should have grown up convinced atheists. Many of them did, but far from all. This would seem to be the most convincing proof of the impossibility of destroying whatever concerns the primordial secret of the human soul; those things that inspire people, plunge them into doubt, and at the same time elevate them, apparently giving them the strength to withstand incredible trials.

Each of us is a beginner in the comprehension of eternity. But we are responsible before the gods of our forefathers. Religion is hereditary. And only the individual can decide whether God is necessary and whether to sever the hereditary line.

You mention the character Avdyi in my story *Executioner's Block*. In a sense, he is I. Some critics, who apparently consider themselves experienced experts in Orthodox canons, refer to him disparagingly as a 'naïve juvenile'. Maybe such people are sincere Christians, though I have my doubts. Nonetheless, I wonder how Christian it was of some of them to attempt to dissuade me from dealing with the theme because I am a Muslim. What difference can that make? Since all of us in the Soviet Union grew up

Marxists, we are all world-sullied in the same way. It is good to remember that, although there is only one God, there are many prophets. For my part, I would be immeasurably delighted to find a Russian Orthodox believer who wanted to ponder the teachings of 'my' Mohammed. I wish him God's help. I believe that a man can simultaneously believe in all religions, Christianity, Islam, Buddhism and so on, to the extent that they are available to him and in those areas where they demonstrate values, morality and culture shared by all humankind. I suspect that I am not the only who feels this way.

My contact with the fundamental source of Christianity, the Bible, enriched me and presented life to me in a new light. The cold, soulless, even hypocritical exhortations of the so-called truths of the *Codex of the Builder of Communism* are incapable of producing such an effect. Perhaps it was the beauty of the Bible that Dostoyevsky had in mind when he made the puzzling statement 'Beauty will save the world.'

Having been moved in this way, I suddenly grew frightened. Why had so divine a source been kept from us Soviet citizens? How had we lived without it? How had we presumed to write books and consider ourselves, as some did, instructors in living? But terrifying backwardness and ignorance are abundant always and everywhere. Having lived through the scientific-technological revolution, we today consider ourselves wiser than our poor forebears, for whom such, to us, commonplace activities as air travel would have been unimaginable. However, in adopting such an attitude, we demonstrate ignorance, dangerous naïveté and the arrogance of the slave.

Some so-called twentieth-century supermen and heirs to the great achievements of the scientific-technological revolution imagine themselves enlightened and free of all prejudice and pride. Before making such self-serving assessments they should remember Saint Paul's 'archaic' insistence on the need for charity:

Though I speak with the tongues of men and of angels, and have not charity, I am become [as] a sounding brass, or a tinkling cymbal.
And though I have [the gift of] prophecy, and understand all mysteries, and all knowledge; and though I have all faith, so that I could remove mountains, and have not charity, I am nothing. And though I bestow all my goods to feed [the poor], and though I give my body to be burned, and have not charity, it profiteth me nothing. (Corinthians-I, 13:1–3)

These words should teach the self-proclaimed modern superman that, in the face of death, everything is weighed in the scales of good and evil. When we have learned this lesson, we can feel ourselves part of the universal, eternal mission of humanity of all faiths. This sense of participation bestows a happiness in comparison with which all other happinesses are mere illusions.

In Soviet society, religions were compelled to tread a true *via dolorosa*. A certain modern preacher has said, 'Once religion was a banner going on before its followers. Now it is transport to pick up the wounded.' There is much truth in this statement.

Fortunately, in recent years, the situation in our country seems to have improved. A law on freedom of religion has been passed. But we must still exercise restraint, if not skepticism, in prognosticating speedy normalisation. Although I hope everything will turn out well, we must learn patience and tolerance both in daily life and in the Church itself. We can do it, if we have love in our hearts.

IKEDA: I must admit to ignorance about the childish shooting into the sky to carry out a sentence of death on God. Silly though it is, as an indication of raging anti-religious propaganda, this prank is no laughing matter. At the end of the twentieth century, as we awaken from the nightmare of the intolerance of ersatz-religious ideologies like fascism and communism, tolerance is more important than ever before.

All of the finest human beings I have met in my extensive travels and experience have shared two characteristics: tolerance and humility. This does not mean that they are irresolute or lacking in self-confidence. Indeed, unshakable conviction in religion and all other areas is the source of their tolerance, just as recognition of the merits of others is the heart of their humility. Great spiritual tolerance like theirs strengthens self-confidence and convictions.

Avoiding fanaticism and blind faith, religions must be open to outside ideas and views. No matter how heated they may become, true religious dialogues always foster and encourage tolerance, humility and other good aspects of human relations like love, friendship, trust and hope. These are the things that contribute to the cultivation of spirituality and of the 'values, morality and culture shared by all humankind' of which you speak.

Tolstoy said the kingdom of God is located in our hearts. I feel certain that his 'kingdom of God' is a blanket term for all the good traits he hoped for and sought with extraordinary honesty. He must have believed that a person with the kingdom of God in his heart is truly righteous, good, complete, estimable and strong. This is the kind of person religions must cultivate.

Religions engrossed in superficial considerations like doctrines, ceremonies and buildings, on the other hand, inevitably lapse into cliquish formalism. Obsession with formalities constitutes a hotbed for dogmatic fanaticism, which in turn generates intolerance and arrogance. Such a religion does only harm and is incapable even of serving as a truck to pick up the wounded, as you said.

Once again, in this connection, Mahatma Gandhi says the right thing:

> Hence the necessity of tolerance, which does not mean indifference to one's own faith, but a more intelligent and purer love for it. Tolerance gives us spiritual insight, which is as far from fanaticism as the North Pole from the south. True knowledge of religion breaks down the barriers between faith and faith.[1]

Myths and Folk Tales

IKEDA: Several of your works, including *The White Steamship* (*Bely Parakhod*) are popular with Japanese children. As the author of books for children myself, I know that to appeal to innocent, emotionally sensitive young people, juvenile literature must be unsophisticated but at the same time must be filled with meaningful messages.

As exemplars of the kind of writing children need, the folk-oriented tales, especially *Ivan Durak* (Ivan the fool), that Tolstoy wrote in his old age come immediately to mind. These stories, which Romain Rolland praised highly, satisfy Tolstoy's own requirements for true art: it must be clear, simple and concise in form; it must contribute to human well-being; and it must be universal and easy to understand.

Among the many other writers who have understood the value of juvenile literature, the Russian national poet Aleksandr Pushkin (1799–1837) derived both material and inspiration from the folk stories and songs recited to him by his beloved nanny Arina Rodionovna.

AITMATOV: No sphere in Soviet reality, not even juvenile literature for which only the noblest thoughts and serenest inferences are appropriate, was free of tension or unscarred by the political system. As far as mythology is concerned, Soviet critics tended to regard interest in it as a mortal sin, an infringement against and profanation of Soviet realism. I was listed among the profaners. That a considerable number of readers eagerly supported this pseudo-belle-lettrist criticism was the most offensive part of the whole thing.

IKEDA: Why is that?

AITMATOV: In part, the deeply didactic and trivially moralising nature of Soviet prose formed stereotyped literary tastes and standards. Everything people read set forth and canonised the image of the acceptable hero, both his psychology and behaviour from the standpoint of secular expedience or, in more precise terms, the standpoint of ideological purity. This kind of literature is irrelevant to the underlying culture common to humanity. It is equally unrelated to nineteenth-century Russian literature, with its vigorously developed psychological definitions of the profound and passionate search for truth in human existence as a whole.

Standard Soviet critics believed they detected passion for myths, legends, miscellanies and ornamental orientalism everywhere in contemporary writing. This surprised them and aroused their righteous wrath, though it is difficult to understand why. 'What's all this?' the scowling critic would ask. 'Where did this kind of thing come from? Aha! Folklore is at fault. That's what makes myth-making so attractive. That's what leads our writers from the true path, the path of realism.'

IKEDA: Only an impoverished imagination could blame folklore for the poverty of Soviet realism. It is folly to expect high imaginative powers from people who think literature can be created by industrial production systems. The Soviet regime claimed that economic reforms would make everything right, even in fields unrelated to economy. This claim proved illusory. Presumably, the critics you mention reject fantasy, allegory and folk literature as irrational. But fantasy is found in many of the great literary masterpieces, which surely cannot be described as childish and primitive.

AITMATOV: Certainly not. Myths and folk stories represent the very real lives and aspirations for justice, goodness and truth of the societies that create them. By no means sunny, pastoral escapism, legends embody dramatic, often tragic, social-moral experiences and, more often than not, record misfortune and struggle.

IKEDA: That is certainly true. Folk tales in Japan, as elsewhere, frequently recount the harshness of life. But equally often they reveal the wisdom with which ordinary people coped with their predicaments. One famous example of both aspects of folklore is the story of *Uba-sute Yama*. This *yama*, or mountain, was the place where feeble old women incapable of performing useful labour went, or were carried, to die alone. The story reflects the tragedies of rural life in a society where it was impossible to maintain people incapable of pulling their own weight.

In one version, an affectionate son conceals his old, infirm mother instead of sending her to her death in remote mountains. One day, for some reason, the local lord demands that the villagers send him a rope made of ashes. No one can figure out how to satisfy this apparently impossible demand until, with the accumulated experience of the elderly, the old woman in hiding instructs her son to make a stout rope and then to burn it. Thus the old woman proves that the elderly are far from useless. And the local lord is so pleased that he abolishes the practice of sending the old to die in the mountains.

It seems absurd and unjustifiable to attack mythology by comparing it to literary classics, as, I have heard, was done in the Soviet Union.

AITMATOV: Self-professed lovers of the excellent and eternal use the classics as a Procrustean bed to judge contemporary literature and to lop off what they find incompatible with Soviet realism. Such people usually treat the classics as classroom textbooks. To judge by their lights, we would be forced to deny the title of realist to Nikolai V. Gogol (1809–52), whose writing is the most tempestuous, audacious and indomitable fantasy. For example, *Dead Souls*, the very cornerstone of Russian realism, is a celestial feast of symbolism and hyperbole, an all-engulfing fire of poetic imagination. One of his most famous images is that of the flying troika, with which *Dead Souls* concludes. Gogol's magical realism hypnotically compels the reader to believe in its engrossing spirit.

His fantasy materialises ideas, thoughts and feelings in living, actual characters and in a complete, imaginary world developed in its entirety to infinity. A true writer creates his own artistic reality on the basis of spiritual – that is to say philosophical, moral and aesthetic – experience, his own and that of the whole human race. He employs all the necessary inventive means at his disposal. Since each does it in his own way, it is absurd to try to impose modes for expressing exciting ideas on artists as varied as, to name a few, Dostoyevsky, Hoffmann, Balzac, Bulgakov, Thomas Mann,

Tvardovsky in his *Terkin in the Other World*, Hemmingway, Updike and Garcia Marquez.

IKEDA: Many great literary masterpieces employ mythological material. Plato's celebrated mythological references include his discussion of the legendary island of Atlantis and the ring of Gyges, which makes its wearer invisible. They occur in *The Republic*; as does the story of the Arcadian temple of Zeus, where anyone who tastes of the entrails from a human sacrifice is transformed into a wolf, a symbolic illustration of how shedding compatriots' blood turns leaders into tyrants. Towards the end of *The Republic* occurs the story of Er, son of Armeius, who returns from the post-mortem world to relate how the dead are allowed to choose the nature of their subsequent existences.

AITMATOV: Long dormant, apparently extinct myths and legends can come to life with illuminating seismic force, like the earthquake, which a certain scientist once described as a lantern lighting up the bowels of the Earth. Though relative and conditional, my comparison of myth and earthquake is apt. Contrary to the will of time and of scientific-technological progress, myths and legends exploding into new life influence human memory in a volcanic way, naturally and by no means at the caprice or ill-will of writers incapable of writing like Soviet realists.

Why does this happen? What meaning has so called myth-making for artistic thought in contemporary literature? Some critics condescendingly refer to it as frippery. Some readers decide it is only a fad. The same kind of reader would no doubt find it faddish for a son to discourse with his father's ghost, as in *Hamlet*; for a man to talk to a mighty oak, as in Tolstoy; or for an old man to converse with a fish, as in Hemingway's *The Old Man and the Sea*. Contemporary writers have an easy time of it: they need only choose a fad to their own liking and make up their own frippery.

Sometimes people ask why the hero of my story *The Piebald Dog Running along the Seashore* calls a perfectly ordinary boat his brother. It is a little awkward for me to explain that I had to use this device to reveal the hero's innermost nature and thought. To him, his kayak is a brother. He built it with his own hands; into it, he put his whole soul and his hope of triumphing over the elements. All of us sometimes confer animation and affection on purely material objects. No doubt, some people feel brotherly towards their cars.

Sometimes people ask me, with embarrassment, whether I like Hemingway. Their embarrassment arises from the suspicion that I imitate Hemingway, because both the hero of my *Piebald Dog Running Along the Shore* and the hero of his *The Old Man and the Sea* talk with fish. The two are spiritual brothers. Faced with the elements, which they suddenly recognise as their mother, at the threshold of death, they see that, instead of cursing her, they must prove themselves worthy of, or even superior to, her. There is no arrogance in their attitude. In supreme moments of the kind these two experience, unusual emotional powers, always latent within them, suddenly break forth in poetic form. Perhaps poetry is the only way for us to overcome the fear of death.

Anyone who remains unspoiled by contemporary civilisation and its mass culture is essentially a poet by nature. As the Russian-American novelist Vladimir Nabokov (1899–1977) commented, a poet is not a person who writes poetry but one who dies of poetry. For the poet, death is not non-existence but the possibility of reincarnation into this world in a totally different form.

IKEDA: All totalitarian and dictatorial systems regard folklore suspiciously as a threat to their own iron sway. Their fears are well-grounded, because folklore suggests alternate ways of life and alternate approaches to human relations, attractive to the masses but intolerable to dictators.

AITMATOV: In a preface I once wrote for a two-volume collection called *Skazki Narodov SSSR* (Fairy tales of the peoples of the Soviet Union), I dealt with the issue of myths and folk stories in the following way:

> How did the first fairy tale come into being? Who made it up? We can never know. I have no idea what compelled a person in hoary antiquity to express something that, though invisible, moved him deeply, filling him with passionate feelings like ecstasy, fear, a desire to fly, or a sense of blood-relationship with Nature – with the full-antlered deer dashing in the distance, with tumultuously stirring grasses, or with the iridescent stars glittering in the infinities of night space. For this person, Nature breathed and was alive, teaching and forewarning him. Her great secrets attracted him. Attempting to unravel them intensified his humanity by causing him to confront the wonderful vortex of unseen forces and phenomena around him with an artist's mind. He drew a vast and staggering picture of Creation, animating it and populating it with startling creatures, both splendid and horrible, between whom an endless duel took place and is still taking place. The eternal controversy of Good and Evil.

IKEDA: Please allow me to interrupt you to make a comment about the horrible cruelty often found in folk tales. In an attempt to protect children today, harsh elements are frequently bowdlerised from fairy and folk tales. For instance, an ancient Japanese children's story about a raccoon dog (*tanuki*) that kills an old woman, makes miso soup of her and feeds it to her husband, is now considered too gruesome. Either the whole miso-soup episode is left out, or the killing is changed to a mere rap on the head. This may be misguided over-protection. Leading psychologists insist that gory tales do not warp the childish psyche since, instead of taking them as models for action, children tend to analyse and assimilate their contents in ways that actually prevent cruelty.

Probably not limited to Japan, the tendency to sanitise fairy stories possibly arises from unwillingness to confront the inevitability of death. But we may be robbing life itself of depth and weight by consigning death, a natural and inevitable rounding off, to hospital wards.

AITMATOV: That is certainly true. But to return to my preface:

> Folk tales constitute a kind of unending, never-never land history preserved in the heart of the people. It is a guiding thread leading to the light. It is the golden key with which humanity opens the door to that unknown land called the future.
>
> When he said, 'No wonder on Earth can outshine the wonder of human perception,' the great poet Boris Pasternak meant that the human being can always experience wonder at the birth of a world created by human hands and that those capable of such experience are older than creatures that, for thousands of years, have regarded reality with indifference.
>
> Some adults preserve the ability to experience wonder even after childhood. For example, Yanush Korchak (1878–1942), the astonishing Polish educator and author of many stories and the book *Kogda ya snova stanu malen'kim* (When I become a little child again). In a certain sense, becoming a child again is tantamount to becoming a giant. The child is master of the elements. To save someone in trouble, he will battle with them like a fearless, blameless knight, and blameless as a knight. The child willingly duels with the unknown and is sure to win, because he fights, not for himself, but for the happiness of the humiliated and oppressed.

Today it is especially important to believe unconditionally in fairy stories. Fantasy is a metaphor enabling us to see life from a new and unsuspected angle. Scientific-technological achievements have invaded the world of what was once considered fantastic. This has increased the importance of metaphor. But so, and to a greater extent, has the fantastic nature of the world we live in.

Long ago, the originators of fairy stories and folk tales foresaw a never-never, future world. To prepare the younger generations for it, they devised extreme situations so demanding in courage and willpower that adults today shudder at them.

Once a fairy story has come true, does it grow old? Do the stars age? In the heart of a child, the world is constantly being renewed and reborn. At a given moment, the folk tale may represent a particular historical phenomenon or stage in the development of the human soul. But, at the same time, it is a manifestation of the eternal spirit of life. Unique, it preserves the blessed memory of wonder itself and the human heart, in which heroes from all epochs and races abide and sometimes, unbeknownst to us, awake into vivid life.

Since we are all members of one humanity, by its very nature, the folk tale is international. As a certain poet from the Caucasus has rightly said, 'All peoples weep and laugh in the same language.'

IKEDA: As you imply, folk tales know no boundaries. They are at once international and even cosmic in subject matter. They illuminate the workings of the human heart and provide an eternal link among the world's peoples.

This is obvious in the mythologies of Greece and Rome and in some Japanese stories. *Kaguya-hime*, the heroine of the celebrated ancient 'Tale of the Bamboo Cutter' (*Taketori-monogatari*), comes from the moon and returns there at the conclusion of the narrative. In the extremely popular *Ginga Tetsudō* (Milky Way railroad), by the Japanese poet and writer of juvenile literature Kenji Miyazawa (1896–1933), a small boy has a ticket to ride a magical train throughout the cosmos. Stories of this kind cultivate faith and stimulate inventive originality of the kind that causes a child to answer 'springtime' and not the more prosaic 'water' when asked what is left when ice melts. A certain Japanese scientist, who realised the importance of applying creative thinking to original scientific work on the inner world, recommended that fledgling physics students read Greek mythology.

The Bitter Companion of Happiness

IKEDA: In speaking of the misery and the elevating power of tragic experiences, like his own exile during the Nazi period, the Austrian writer Stefan Zweig said,

> Has anyone ever composed a hymn to exile? It is the fate-creating power that lifts a man when he is down, that, in the constraint of loneliness, gathers together the shaken strength of the soul into a new and different order. But the rhythm of nature requires enforced caesuras of this kind because only a person who knows it most deeply understands life whole. It is only through setbacks that humanity acquires its full strength to go forward.[2]

You have called the tragic element the driving power behind artistic talent and contemplation throughout history. Several of your own works, for instance, *Executioner's Block* and *The Day Lasts More than a Hundred Years*, involve a struggle between good and evil culminating in the hero's tragic destruction. For all the suffering it causes, tragedy jolts us from our daily rut, making us better aware of our own inner natures and stimulating in us the will to live and the power to trust in the possibility of good.

Ironically, the tragic death of a literary hero can give him, and the work he appears in, life in an expanded form. The tragic strain deepens and vitalises human history. And even death under tragic circumstances can seem a blessing rather than a disaster. Perhaps this, in part, explains the tremendous importance all peoples assign to funereal ritual.

AITMATOV: In spite of universal human strivings for cloudless happiness, our lives are never free of burdens and troubles. Although I should like to see us all protected from such fortuitous, excessive suffering; as the Kirghiz people say, things such as traffic accidents, mutilation, fires, landslides and so on, our paths should not be freed of the spirit of tragedy. We must remember that tragedy is the bitter companion of happiness.

The tragic is the common denominator encountered in the search for truth, righteousness and justice and, in opposition to the negative forces of reality, reveals an individual's true capacities. In attempting to overcome a tragic situation, a person either perishes or rises to full stature.

Life and art sometimes take different views of what constitutes a hopeless dilemma. From the common sense standpoint, Juliet's death in Shakespeare's play amounts to the suicide of a weak spirit incapable of breaking out of a desperate situation. This, at any rate, is the way it would seem in lesser art. But, in Shakespeare's hands, Juliet's desperation generates spiritual strength, unbending resolution, relentlessness, certainty and unwillingness to compromise. In Juliet, despair simultaneously breeds love and hate, challenge and faith, and ultimately the affirmation of an individuality attained at the price of life itself.

In spite of its desperate finale, the death of hero and heroine, *Romeo and Juliet* is unconditionally a life-affirming work. It is high tragedy exposing the evil of its times. True, the hero and heroine suffer defeat in their struggle with negative elements. Nonetheless their story compels us to understand and appreciate the meaning of the right to be free human beings. In sacrificing their lives for that right, Romeo and Juliet achieve beauty, even magnificence, in the eyes of the living.

IKEDA: As you aptly put it, tragedy is the bitter companion of happiness. Each tragic encounter with apparently insuperable odds strengthens and deepens life. How much more precious than the halcyon, commonplace existence is the life made brilliant through triumph over obstacles and hardships. The glorious crown of happiness gleams only above the heads of those who have definitively won the ultimate battle: the battle with self.

Great art, like *Romeo and Juliet*, no matter how tragic its ending, or perhaps because of its tragic ending, purifies and strengthens the spirit as suitable exercise does the body. This is the reason why, from the dramas of ancient Greece, tragedy has attained greater heights than comedy. This also explains tragedy's uncloying appeal.

Your *The White Steamship* tells the story of a boy who indicts the evil and unreasonableness of this world and opposes it with his own death. How did your readers react to this treatment of the situation?

AITMATOV: To judge by my mail, I would say that, apart from a few critics of the kind I mentioned earlier, most understood its ending correctly, not because it is inevitable or because it is foreseen by the pockmarked, crippled old woman, but because good as embodied in the boy is incompatible with evil. Unwilling to compromise, the boy becomes a fish and swims away. And, if he finds a place in the hearts of my readers, it is owing to his strength not to the hopelessness of his predicament.

In 1989, while I was in Beijing, I had a startling experience in connection with that story. I was a member of a group of cultural personnel accompanying President Gorbachev. Our hosts housed us, not in a hotel, but in a government residence in a heavily guarded park. Tired after a long flight and apparently isolated even from my companions, I was feeling depressed and let down. After having wandered aimlessly from room to room, I was getting ready for bed, when, to my great surprise, the telephone suddenly rang. I knew absolutely nobody in Beijing. When I picked up the receiver, a pleasing, ringing, young voice on the other end said, '*Ata! Aksakal*!', which means father in Kirghiz.

'And who might you be, my son?' I asked.

'Me?' The speaker began talking more slowly. 'Don't you know me? I'm the boy in *The White Steamship*. The one who swam away.'

Of course, I saw at once that this was a game and played along with it.

'Well, what happened to you after that? How did you end up here?'

'Well, you see, I swam from one river to another. Swam on and on until I got to China. Now I'm grown up and a student at Beijing University.'

'So that's what happened! Thank God! So you're safe and sound and a college student?'

'That's right. And I'm calling you in the name of all the Kirghiz students in Beijing. I really would like to meet you, *Ata*. We heard you were here on the radio. And my friends asked me to talk to you. After all, I am your son out of *The White Steamship*.'

Deeply touched, I hurriedly agreed to a meeting: 'All right, my son. I'll be there. You can count on it.' And we set the time and place.

Next day I stepped out of a car beside the large, centrally located hotel where we had agreed to meet. A mob was milling about. I was afraid I would miss my students from the Kirghiz countryside in the crowd. Then suddenly I saw them, a group of young people wearing white Kirghiz hats and headed right for me. While we were meeting and getting acquainted, I kept eagerly looking out for one who might be the boy out of *The White Steamship*. And, if you will believe it, I recognised him the instant I saw him. There were about thirty young men and girls, all about the same age, lively and hearty, with radiant eyes. Camera shutters clicked. Someone was taking movies. But one of the young men struck me as especially animated, and I said to him, 'Are you the one who swam from the river Issyk-Kul all the way to China?'

'Yes,' he said, smiling gladly. 'I called you last night. I hope I didn't disturb you.'

'What made you say you're the boy from *The White Steamship?*' I asked.

'Because I didn't want him to die. He can't die. And I decided to take his fate on myself.'

'Maybe that's right from your viewpoint. But, in the story, I was trying to show his tragedy. He has to die as a sign of protest. He has no other way to triumph over evil. His spirit is too pure.'

'I understand. But the only way I could help him was to pretend to be him. I don't want him to drown.'

IKEDA: I sympathise with the student's desire to save the boy. Like the rest of us, he loved the story in spite of its tragic ending. He reacted simply and sincerely to it. Older, more experienced readers no doubt react in a more sophisticated way.

AITMATOV: The sophisticated and experienced critic is convinced he knows how the writer must see and reflect life. Simple readers seek truth, beloved truth. Tragedy requires participation. That is the source of its strength. Undeniably, in Soviet society, most lives were lived in the tragic mode, and not solely on the personal level. All humanity shares this experience. There is no escaping it. We cannot take refuge in literary happy endings. Overcoming the dilemma means putting oneself in the line of fire and sharing the fates of the most honest, the most noble and the purest souls.

As everyone knows, tragedy is high art. And I believe that contemporary literature develops under its sign.

IKEDA: Social good and bad are concrete concepts confined within the framework of a given epoch. The evil of our own age would no doubt seem incredible to peoples from other ages. We ourselves are to a certain extent too accustomed to it to find it as shocking as it really is. What methods must artists employ to depict it in such a way as to jolt twentieth-century humanity out of its complacency?

AITMATOV: Yes, people today are not easily shocked by art. The horrors of the war against the fascists, the tragedies of Hiroshima and Nagasaki and the brutalities occurring daily all over the world have drastically altered our threshold of pain. Not long ago, however, the Book of Revelation could stun the human imagination and inspire holy horror with its depiction of the end of the world as the ancient poet–prophet imagined it:

> And the shapes of the locusts were like unto horses prepared unto battle; and on their heads were as it were crowns like gold, and their faces were as the faces of men.
> And they had hair as the hair of women, and their teeth were as the teeth of lions.
> And they had breastplates, as it were breastplates of iron; and the

sound of their wings was as the sound of chariots of many horses running to battle.

And they had tails like unto scorpions, and there were stings in their tails: and their power was to hurt men five months.' (Revelation IX: 7–10)

Obviously, the aim of the art is not to frighten but to help people overcome fear and despair, to awaken the emotions enabling us to withstand evil in all its forms and aspects. It is in this connection that I see the problem of tragedy as a genre capable of expressing today's dispositions with the greatest fullness.

IKEDA: Do you believe that our age can produce great tragic writers of Shakespeare's calibre?

AITMATOV: I once asked the celebrated Russian composer Dimitri Dimitrievich Shostakovich (1906–75) a similar question. His idea, which surprised and delighted me, was that the chances are greater for the emergence of new Shakespeares because the contemporary universalisation of the human spirit would enable a great artist to express the whole world in himself, as in music. This was only a passing remark. But later, as I pondered it, I came to comprehend its larger meaning. Shostakovich expected literature to produce an all-embracing, 'musical' generalisation of life. The task of expressing everything in one's self may be daunting, but surely no artist could be confronted with a greater challenge.

Evolution instead of Revolution

IKEDA: In your story *Executioner's Block*, a confrontation between the protagonist Boston and the party official raises many interesting questions about the way a revolutionary leader must think and act. I feel filled with pity to imagine that there were many instances of such antagonism, paradoxes and conflicts in the process of Stalin's collectivisation of agriculture.

Our Buddhist movement has no need of professional revolutionaries whose total absorption in their work isolates them from the ordinary people and desiccates their normal human sympathies, thus either tying them to the planning table or compelling them into radicalism, violence and bloodshed. As the French philosopher Simone Weil (1909–43) warned, 'Revolutionary war is the tomb of revolution.'[3]

Life is essentially an unbroken continuum; revolutions create a rupture between past and future. To be truly effective, a revolutionary leader must know how to ensure that the rupture does not harm the continuum of life. Few have made the necessary effort, and even fewer have succeeded in it. Unless revolutionary leaders take the greatest care to prevent alienation from the needs and feelings of the ordinary people, they are certain to cause great suffering, as the party official does in your story.

AITMATOV: As you say, few revolutions have successfully harmonised past and future. I cannot think of a single one. In fact, I doubt that such a thing is possible. Some of the revolutions in East Europe in the late 1980s were described as 'velvet'. On closer consideration, the term seems to have been too hastily applied. We might have been justified to expect better performances in East European nations where democratically inclined, civilised populations had prevented the emergence of full-blown, Stalinist-type totalitarianism of the kind that definitively perverted Soviet ideas of democracy.

From a different viewpoint, perhaps we can say that the three great Russian revolutions of past centuries were intended to help us appreciate what you call the 'continuum of life' and what I shall here refer to as the 'great evolution'. Interestingly, in a letter to Stalin, the Russian novelist Mikhail A. Bulgakov (1891–1940) expressed a similar idea.

Hotheads always demand immediate changes. The trouble is that truly profound changes, accompanied by psychological and moral alterations, take time. In his novel about the nineteenth-century Russian People's Will (*Narodnaya Volya*) movement, Yury Trifonov (1925–81) psychologically accurately characterises such would-be knights of impatience as always ready to start everything over from scratch, as long as they themselves cut a fine figure in the eyes of the rioting masses. But the riots cannot last forever. There is a time for everything: a time for casting stones and a time for gathering them. In the preface to *Der Klassenkampf* (Class Struggle), even Friedrich Engels (1820–95) frankly admitted that he and Marx had been deluded in their definition of the duration of social and political development.

In order to keep power in their own hands, hothead leaders must constantly feed the people on inextinguishable hatred and, in the name of the World Revolution, channel it as they see fit – in the Soviet Union, in the direction of endless struggle. The people became hostages to a fantastic idea, for which they later paid bitterly.

IKEDA: We must be constantly on the lookout for psychological and moral changes precisely because of the slow pace at which they evolve. Vociferous promises to make everything good overnight produce no real improvements. They cannot be achieved in isolation from the people. Consequently, as I have intimated, I doubt the value of the professional revolutionary dwelling in his own ivory tower.

With his usual perspicacity, Goethe said,

> The true liberal tries to do as much good as he can with the means at his disposal. He is wary, however, of wishing to eradicate often inevitable deficiencies with fire and sword. By sensible steps forward, he tries gradually to supersede apparent shortcomings without destroying an equal amount of good by applying forcible penalties. In this far-from-perfect world, he remains content with the good until time and circumstances encourage him to achieve something better.[4]

AITMATOV: Goethe's liberal mind would deplore the attitudes and behaviour of the Russian public of the past few years: addiction to the romance of public demonstrations, extremist speeches, potential violence, fists raised in wrath, demolitions, explosions and so on. The same kind of thing has happened before, and it led only to disturbance, bloodshed, dictatorship and the barbed wire of prison camps. This time, history has given us a chance to live in a human, civilised way, discussing instead of screaming inflammatory slogans, honouring the tender-green buds of democracy, abiding by new and just laws and joyously creating afresh instead of being obsessed by the hazardous redistribution of what already exists.

IKEDA: Surely the relation between leaders and people is important in this connection.

AITMATOV: In terms of relations between the authorities and the people, we are living through the most complicated period in the history of the Soviet Union. The communist leader and theoretician Nikolai Ivanovich Bukharin (1888–1938) was fond of quoting the French revolutionary Saint-Just (Louis Antoine Léon de; 767–94), who said, 'If you cannot rule by law, rule by iron.' Although everyone knows the outcome of Soviet experiments in iron rule, Russia is still incapable of the rule of law. The new leaders, the parliament and the people are learning. And in these circumstances, the special sobriety of mutual evaluation and a new kind of coordination between authority and the people are essential.

The sooner we break with the old simplistic formula 'great leader equals great people', the better it will be for both the authorities and the people.

IKEDA: Undeniably, a paradoxical strain in their national ethos inclines the Russian people to respect, even idolise leaders of forceful will, no matter how cruel and tyrannical their behaviour. Stalin, who could have no respect for anything but political calculation, is only one example of the 'great leader' obeyed during life and mourned after death by the Russian people. Based on exhaustive research, Anatoly Rybakov's novel *Children of the Arbat* convincingly portrays Stalin as callous and Machiavellian in the worst sense of the word.

The already colossal difficulties faced by *perestroika* were aggravated by a national psychology, which not only permits but seems to welcome tyranny. True, Russia lacks a tradition of social order based on law and moderation between the extremes of anarchy and authoritarianism. But to judge so vast a country on the basis of a single criterion is to neglect the possibility of local variations. The former mayor of Moscow, Gavril Kharitonovich Popov, said that the Stavropol region, where Mr. Gorbachev was born and raised, has a long tradition of autonomy and for centuries knew neither bureaucrats nor police. This sheds light on the background of Gorbachev's own liberal and democratic ideas and helps explain what inspired him to 'pull the hot chestnut of *perestroika* from the fire'.

Two Letters
Transcending 'isms' Non-violently
From Chingiz Aitmatov to Daisaku Ikeda

Luxemburg, January 23, 1991

My dear friend Mr. Ikeda,

At present, the world seems to be experiencing a new geopolitical epoch. Post-confrontational tendencies are becoming a stronger, universal force in the development of contemporary social awareness. Our spirits soar as realisations of post-Cold-War spiritual insights arouse hopes of the coming of the long-awaited Kingdom of God. In some learned circles, it is said that history as we have known it is ending or being transformed into something qualitatively different: a new, tranquil world model, a technological era free of conflict. Is such a thing likely to come to pass? Can there be a future without history? The American philosopher Francis Fukuyama thinks so. Still, as brave and innovative as it is, I find it hard to condone his view of social phenomena.

If only circumstances justified such prophesies! Unfortunately, however, they do not. And, even as Fukuyama's theories were being debated, in spite of global efforts to achieve a peaceful solution to the problem, war broke out in the Persian Gulf. People on both sides of the issue ended up destroying each other.

The basic problem might have persisted even had the immediate Iraqi–Kuwait affair been settled. Realising that a local conflict can ignite a global military crisis, although our efforts looked naïve and futile, you and I did what we could to prevent the outburst of war, the absolute evil. We appealed to the common sense and generosity of the president of Iraq and, as we might have foreseen, learned a bitter lesson for our pains.

Still, the realities of the world remain, and we must confront them. I should like to begin by examining the correlation between force and the justification for its application and the way it is applied among nation states. I might have formulated the issue differently before the Iraqi invasion of Kuwait. At that time, the idea of disarmament was taking root. The Gulf War struck a terrible blow to that idea and would have done so no matter how it ended.

You and I are convinced supporters of avoiding force in international and all other relations. Violence cannot solve conflicts: it merely drives them underground for longer or shorter periods. Mutual concessions and reasonable compromises offer the only hope of real solutions. Heretofore, intergovernmental relations have consisted almost entirely of coercion in various forms. Short of the most pressing need, nothing is likely to convince governments to repudiate it now.

I have deliberately avoided the word *non-violence* because I think it requires careful definition. It is often interpreted to mean refraining from the use of military might. But is that sufficient? Does not refusal to cooperate and participate in dialogue also constitute a form of coercion amounting to covert violence?

You say, in our day and time, the old maxim, 'If you want peace, prepare for war,' should be restated, 'If you want peace, prepare for peace.' I am inclined to think that humanity would find preparation for peace much harder than the more familiar readiness for war: at least resistance, if not aggression. Where should we start preparing? With the creation of a new, more just order in inter-people relations? Or with efforts to train humanity to relate to the existing order in a new way?

I, by no means, insist on preserving the existing world order, the injustice and folly of which go without comment. Still, from personal experience, I know the results of even well-intentioned attempts to destroy a social order violently.

Instead of relying on force, we must try to renew the world order by ameliorating it. We must redress the unbalance in development level among nations and peoples. We must coordinate the satisfaction of human needs with the limitations of our planet. In addition, we must create a single world economic system. Can all this be done non-violently?

I am haunted by the notion that the current apparent abandonment of confrontational policies has been to a significant degree unwilling. Compulsory pacifism can hardly be durable. The Russians have a proverb: 'Better a bad peace than a good quarrel.' Undeniably a bad peace is better. Nonetheless, it is better still to support pacifism and attain a good peace. How can we do this?

For some time now, as integrative processes have gained impetus, peoples and nations have tended to want to associate in unions. Though the threat of war persists, the ecological crisis, the reverse face of technological progress, has compelled nations to shelve their disputes. Various other stimulating factors play a role in the desire: the economy, common defence and so on. At the other end of the scale, however, fundamentalism – not merely highly visible Islamic fundamentalism – and the explosive emergence of national self-awareness have exerted a divisive influence.

Fundamentalism reduces religion to a primitive black-and-white level of aggressive pretensions to a monopoly on ultimate truths. It is akin to degraded, Soviet socialism, according to which Marxism ceased being a socio-economy theory and became a totalitarian religion with neither a god nor a morality. We must not tolerate subordinating morality to an ideology whose exclusive system – government – opposes the rest of humanity.

In the Soviet Union, a widespread, deep-rooted totalitarian mindset produced many baleful consequences. For one thing, it retarded the development of ecology-minded thinking and, by hiding them, impeded the adoption of measures to clean up after ecological catastrophes, as was true in the case of Chernobyl. Totalitarianism is always short-sighted. It exists only for the present; it pursues only the goals of the moment. Ironically, however, it has no present because it is always chasing bright dreams of the future, in the name of which the present must be sacrificed. The upper levels of society set policies without feeling responsible for their consequences. The lower levels are trained to do as they are told and hold their tongues. This highly pernicious relationship is inevitable under a totalitarian regime.

Totalitarianism, divisive national egoism and unbridled capitalism all have evil aspects. What we need is a single, world in which the interests of all humanity transcend such 'isms'. At the risk of exaggerating its importance, I recommend an artistic and spiritual culture – although the distinction between the two is almost impossible to define – as a major, non-violent, contributing factor toward the creation of such a single world. In a time when old sovereignty concepts grow meaningless and rigid state boundaries lose their former impenetrability, spiritual culture becomes the supreme bearer of national originality and the fullest expression of the national spirit.

Today, as technology makes the once inaccessible accessible, greater acquaintance with the cultural values of all peoples can invalidate the notion that sovereign states have special regulatory privileges over their component national and ethnic groups. States infringe the common human rights of their citizens and reject as 'interference in internal affairs' international efforts to curb such abuses. Surely there must be a moral limit beyond which non-interference in domestic matters becomes condonation of violence?

Reviving Spirituality

From Daisaku Ikeda to Chingiz Aitmatov

My dear friend Mr. Aitmatov,

I have read excerpts of the article in which Francis Fukuyama claims that history has ended and feel that it contains some elements of truth. The discrediting of communism and the collapse of the Soviet Communist Party brought about the demise of the Western model of historical progress as interpreted by people like Auguste Comte (1798–1857) and Georg F. W. Hegel (1770–1831). To some, the new era threatens to be commonsensical, prosaic, uninteresting and ideal-less. This is, however, only one of the various possible interpretations. According to a view of history that emerged in about 1989, the bicentennial of the French revolution – itself subjected to revisionist criticism – the collapse of the Soviet Union terminated the development of the Jacobin elements of the French and the Bolshevik elements of the Russian Revolution. Actually, the collapse came as no great surprise. What did shock was the speed with which it fell apart.

However, in spite of theories like Fukuyama's, as long as human beings remember, speculate and hope, history cannot end. If it could end, why should we, in our world of fin-de-siècle chaos, try to make sense of things for the sake of the coming century?

As to the question of non-violence, the Institute for Non-violence of the Soviet Union once asked me to write something on this topic, and I append my thoughts as I put them together on that occasion. I deal only with larger principles. The United Nations must work out the pertinent regulations. And it should address the problem promptly since the need for military might is unlikely to evaporate in the near future.

Of course, I do not approve of the United Nations in exactly the form in which it operates today. Unless in the future it behaves more impartially and avoids West-centric attitudes that undervalue the needs of the Third World, we may find ourselves in a quagmire of regional conflicts. This is in line with keen recommendations from such researchers in Third World Peace as the Hindu philosopher Surendranath Dasgupta (1887–1952).

You yourself share ideas with my friend, the Norwegian sociologist and authority in peace research, Dr. Johan Galtung (1930–). According to his concept of structural violence, in many peripheral regions of international society, even in the absence of actual war poverty, discrimination, hunger and violation of human rights compel people to live under warlike conditions. Going far beyond the definition of peace as non-war, he calls internal restrictions necessitating such conditions structural violence and insists that there can be no peace where they exist. In the light of his approach, *violence*, not *war*, is the apt antonym of *peace*.

The very existence of structural violence intensifies the likelihood of war by breeding and even justifying conflict. Good ideas on making peaceful alterations in the global system, so as to eliminate structural violence, are to be found in 'Goals, Processes and Indicators of Development', in the United Nations University's 'Human Social Development Plan', organised by Dr. Galtung in 1977. In the past, developmental goals have concentrated mainly on the interests of sovereign states and on growth. Dr. Galtung's plan is a fundamental rethinking of such policies. It restates goals on a global scale so that they centre on the interests and wellbeing, not of nation states, but of human beings and on the independence of regional communities.

Since, as set forth in its charter, it is an assembly of all humanity, the United Nations is obliged to emphasise deference to the will of the people over that of nation states. In this connection, United Nations non-governmental organisations, of which Soka Gakkai International is one, will play an increasingly important role in the years to come.

To your question about opposing the totalitarian mindset, I recommend the cultivation of spontaneous self-knowledge in the individual human being. Louis XIV, the so-called *Roi de Soleil*, claimed to be the state itself – '*L'État, c'est moi!*' Actually, however, he stood, not for the whole state, but only for the interests of the aristocracy. In a sense, Stalin came closer to standing for the whole state because the power he wielded extended to everything, even the inner thoughts of his subjects.

Mr. Gorbachev's adviser Georgii Shakhnazarov said that, in the Soviet Union, ideology did more than swallow up morality, it erased it from the list of the controls governing social life. The violent and practically unprecedented power of Soviet totalitarianism was uniform, completely externally imposed, and so all-prevailing as to leave no room for individuality. Healing the scars left by seventy years of such a regime is no easy task. There is no foolproof plan. The only way to accomplish the task is for each person to revive his or her spirituality painstakingly and spontaneously from within. Shortcuts lead to peril. Though it may seem long and hard, the thorough way is the only way to attain the goal. Treating symptoms alone aggravates the sickness.

You express doubt about over-emphasising the importance of spiritual and artistic culture in times when old state concepts and boundaries are losing validity. I do not think you over-emphasise. You are making a proud statement appropriate to an outstanding literary artist. Cultural activities sublimate ethnic energies and divert them from potentially violent courses. It is vital to remember, however, that each of the world's diverse spiritual and artistic cultures deserves respect for its own merits.

In this connection, it is apropos to say a few words on the merits of cultural relativism, which helped break down the formerly dominant West-centric view of history. Before the advent of cultural relativism, history was interpreted as progress and culture as absolute, universal and founded on modern-European value criteria. But, after the First World War, when interest in pioneering cultural anthropology increased, Western culture began manifesting a capability for conscientious introspection and self-purification. Relativistic investigations showed that cultures once denigrated as childish or even barbarian possess distinctive values equivalent to those of European civilisation.

A storm of vandalism is sweeping the Soviet Union now. But as one of those who have seen cultural richness rooted in Russia's soil, I am strongly convinced that your country potentially possesses a noble spirit of its own and that you are well aware of such beautiful aspects of your own nationality.

Having said this much in reply to the points you set forth in your letter to me, I shall now turn to the general theme of non-violence by referring to the contents of the paper I submitted in 1990 to the Institute for Non-violence of the Soviet Union.

Observations on Non-violence, Daisaku Ikeda

(Written at the request of the Institute for Non-violence of the Soviet Union, Autumn 1990)

The modern intellectual's anguish over the nature of the self is the theme of *Kōjin*, a representative novel by the celebrated, modern, Japanese writer Sōseki Natsume. Toward the end of the book, the hero, a university professor named Ichirō Nagano, and his perfectly ordinary, practical friend H take a trip to get away from things for a while. After their return home, H writes a letter to Jirō, Ichirō's younger brother, relating an incident that took place during the trip.

One day, during a discussion, H recommended that Ichirō seek liberation from disturbing self-absorption by putting his faith in God and devoting himself to some great cause. Ichirō asked whether H himself were content to live or die trusting in whatever plans God had made. H says,

> It seemed funny that he should press me this way. But I didn't worry about it. After all, we were so carried away with the conversation. Then all of a sudden, he raised his hand and smacked me on the side of the face. 'What's that for?' I asked. And he replied, 'See! That's what I'm talking about.' I didn't understand him and asked him why he had to get rough. 'That's what I mean. You don't trust God at all. You lose your temper. The least little thing upsets you.'⁵

Possibly, when he wrote this passage, Natsume had the following famous passage from the Bible in the back of his mind: 'But I say unto you, That ye resist not evil; but whosoever shall smite thee on thy right cheek, turn to him the other also.' (Matthew V:39) Be that as it may, Ichirō's slap abruptly terminated a debate as futile as medieval Scholastic scholars' arguing over the number of angels that can dance on a pinhead.

Isolating the topic of violence and non-violence from practical affairs and discussing it on the plane of self-contained abstractions is meaningless. In general, articles of faith aside, deciding whether to react violently or non-violently to any given situation must be decided case-by-case. Making generalised abstractions is tantamount to saying nothing at all. Pursuing the issue in terms of formal logic leads only to contradiction, dilemma and antinomy, in short, to answerless questions. Our century's most brilliant advocate of non-violence, Mahatma Gandhi, knew this from his own experience.

In the late twenties, during a political election, a member of the Indian National Congress Party, headed by Gandhi, was insulted and spat upon by a scoundrel from an opposing party. When the injured man asked whether he should react non-violently to such insults, Gandhi replied sternly,

> Every Congressman who is non-violent is so because he cannot be other-wise. My advice therefore emphatically is that no one need refer to me or any other Congressmen for advice in the matter of non-violence. Everyone must act on his own responsibility, and interpret the Congress creed to the best of his ability and belief. I have often noticed that weak

people have taken shelter under the Congress creed or under my advice, when they have simply by reason of their cowardice been unable to defend their own honour or that of those who were entrusted to their care.[6]

For Gandhi, choosing non-violence meant putting the whole self on the line, beliefs, conscience and, if need be, life itself. All believers in non-violence must be willing to follow his example, since, as Gandhi himself said, they are advocates of non-violence because they can be nothing else. Trying to hide behind the counsel of others, whether unawares or in conscious violation of non-violent principles, amounts to grave misconduct. Gandhi said,

> It (non-violence) is not like a garment to be put on and off at will. Its seat is in the heart and it must be an inseparable part of our very being.[7]

Consistency of behaviour transcends pre-established theories and hypotheses. Non-violence permits no facile generalisations and conforms poorly to abstract philosophical speculation. The operations of the imagination project consistent behaviour in inevitable, concentrated forms with an aura of their own.

It must be admitted, however, that non-violence does not attract everyone. Some of the world's great books provide examples of both favourable and unfavourable evaluations. Victor Hugo's *Les Misérables* shows the matter treated negatively. In the early part of the book, the old bishop François Bienvenu Myriel, who inspires the hero, Jean Valjean, to change his way of thinking and living, discusses violence and non-violence with a dying, octogenarian revolutionary and former member of the Revolutionary Tribunal. Proclaimed in the name of *Liberté, Égalité, et Fraternité*, the French Revolution bred the bloody horrors of the Terror, which reached peak frenzy in 1793. In the scene under discussion, the bishop and the old revolutionary are arguing the pros and cons of these events.

From the standpoint of Christian neighbourly love, the pious and meek bishop criticises the bloodbath and all attempts to justify it. The old revolutionary, on the other hand, marshals his last strength to spit out a list of the evils of the *ancien régime*. Then, catching his breath, he goes on:

> 'Let us get back to the explanation that you asked of me. Where were we? What were you saying to me? That 93 was inexorable?'
> 'Inexorable, yes', said the bishop. 'What do you think of Marat clapping his hands at the guillotine?'
> 'What do you think of Bossuet chanting the Te Deum over the dragonnades?'

> The answer was severe, but it reached its aim with the keenness of a
> dagger. The bishop was staggered, no reply presented itself; but it
> shocked him to hear Bossuet spoken of in that manner.[8]

The contrast is drawn between the revolutionary Jean Paul Marat's (1743–
93) applauding the guillotine at its killing work and the Roman Catholic moralist
Jacques Bénigne Bossuet's (1627–1704) conducting prayers of thanksgiving for
official attacks on Protestants. Clearly, by demanding to know how the bishop
can condemn one kind of violence while remaining silent about another, the old
revolutionary puts the principle of non-violence in a weak position.

This episode shows how difficult it is to preserve a non-violent stand during
seasons of madness like the days of conflict between the *ancien régime*, whose
misgovernment made popular uprising inevitable, and the cruelty of the Jacobins,
representing what the novelist Anatole France (1844–1924) called the 'thirst
of the gods'.

If *Les Misérables* offers an example of a negative approach to non-violence,
the Grand Inquisitor segment in Dostoyevsky's *The Brothers Karamazov* contains
the best positive attitude toward it that I can think of. In the scene quoted
below, Ivan Karamazov reads from his drama 'The Grand Inquisitor' to his
younger brother Alyosha.

> . . . and at that moment the cardinal himself, the Grand Inquisitor,
> passes by the cathedral. He is an old man, almost ninety, tall and
> erect, with a withered face and sunken eyes, in which there is still a
> gleam of light.[9]

The inquisitor, who in terms of age and appearance resembles Hugo's old
revolutionary, interrogates Jesus, who insists with impressive eloquence that
the people must love each other freely and that they really long for rule based
on mystery, miracle and religious authority. The inquisitor's dominant theme
is one of combined selflessness and arrogance. He is a kind of human divinity.
Like the revolutionary, he is eloquent. Unlike Bishop Myriel, the silent Jesus
emanates a stronger light the more eloquently the inquisitor criticises him.

> When the Inquisitor ceased speaking he waited some time for the
> Prisoner to answer him. His silence weighed down upon him. He saw
> that the Prisoner had listened intently all the time, looking gently
> into his face and evidently not wishing to reply. The old man longed
> for him to say something, however bitter and terrible. But He suddenly

approached the old man in silence and softly kissed him on his blood-less aged lips. That was all his answer. The old man shuddered. His lips moved. He went to the door, opened it, and said to Him: 'Go, and come no more . . . come not at all, never, never!' And he let Him out into the dark alleys of the town. The Prisoner went away.[10]

Ordinarily, non-violence is considered in terms of people like Jesus and, in this case, his alter-image Alyosha. After having heard the drama through to the end, Alyosha kisses his brother, an act that Ivan calls plagiarism from his own drama. But the approach represented by Jesus in the novel fails to grasp the full issue and cannot germinate productive debate. Personally condemning violence on the basis of non-violent principles is essential but insufficient. It would be naïve to expect it to produce a non-violent society. Without extensive teachings and the kind of organisations human society inevitably relies on, no effective non-violent movement is possible.

Throughout history, most violence has been politically motivated, whereas the true spirit of religion has always stood for non-violence. In this, therefore, politics and religion have consistently been at odds. Building a bridge between the two is the only way to create a non-violent society. It was Gandhi's genius to take the bridge-building process very seriously. He believed that right action depends on thorough spiritual reformation. After a lifetime in the political arena, he came to the conclusion that values transcending politics are the only thing that can save us. The German philosopher Karl Jaspers (1883–1969) sympathised with this conviction.

History proves that power clashes are inevitable as long as we limit ourselves to purely political considerations. Nonetheless, politics, which Aristotle regarded as a fundamental element of human nature, cannot be ignored. As Rousseau deplores in his *Social Contract*,

> Since princes and civil laws continued to exist, the consequence of this dual power has been an endless conflict of jurisdiction, which has made any kind of good polity impossible in Christian states, where men have never known whether they ought to obey the civil ruler or the priest.[11]

Because, in the sacred-secular double power structure, the things that are God's and the things that are Caesar's never converge, Aristotle's political animal cannot act as an undivided whole.

Incompatible value systems sometimes compel human beings to make a deliberate choice between violent and non-violent approaches to action. Perhaps no two figures in history so vividly illustrate this kind of opposition better than Vladimir I. Lenin and Leo N. Tolstoy.

A bottomless abyss separated the two men. Tolstoy ferociously and uncompromisingly attacked the evil and injustice of imperial Russia as embodied in state military and secret police, the legal system, the Orthodox church and private property. Nonetheless, he flatly rejected violent social reform, insisting that everything must be achieved through moral reformation. In this, he wished to put into practice the New Testament exhortation: 'Ye have heard that it hath been said, An eye for an eye, and a tooth for a tooth; But I say unto you, That ye resist not evil.' (Matthew V; 38–39) The Russian writer's devotion to what might seem an impractical program inspired Stefan Zweig to say,

> Owing to his power, determination and tenacity and the tremendous scale of his courage, he outstrips, on the one hand, the most ardent reformers like Luther and Calvin and, on the other hand, in the sociological sense, the most audacious anarchists, like Stirner and his school.[12]

No czar, and no one else for that matter, could stand in Tolstoy's way.

It takes extraordinary spiritual strength to temper initially weak non-resistance to steel-like strength. As Tolstoy himself points out in *The Kreutzer Sonata*, the higher the ideal, the better. Readily attainable ideals do not deserve to be called ideals at all. Once having chosen his path, Tolstoy pursued it single-mindedly, always attempting to convince the people to follow him. But his distrust of institutions made him wary of organised mass non-violence of the kind Gandhi advocated.

Highly critical of the world-famous writer's doctrine of non-resistance, with rapier-like keenness and first-rate powers of persuasiveness, Lenin points out the weak points in Tolstoy's approach. I have chosen the following quotation, from the famous *Lev Tolstoy, As a Mirror of the Russian Revolution*, more for tone than content.

> On the one hand, an artist of genius who has created not only incomparable pictures of Russian life, but also first-class works of world literature. On the other hand, a landowner who behaves like an idiot in Christ. On the one hand, a wonderfully powerful, direct and sincere protest against social lies and falsehood – on the other hand, a Tolstoyan; that is that worn-out, hysterical sniveler called the Russian intellectual who, beating himself publicly on the breast, cries 'I'm nasty! I'm vile.

But I'm morally perfecting myself. I don't eat meat anymore: only rice cutlets.' On the one hand, merciless criticism of capitalist exploitation; exposure of governmental violence, of the farce of the courts, and of state management; disclosure of the full depths of the contradictions between the growth in wealth and the achievements of civilisation and the increasing poverty, brutality and suffering of the working masses. On the other hand, a silly sermon about not opposing evil with violence.[13]

As is often pointed out, Lenin was ruthless in assessing opinions divergent from his own. His ruthlessness allowed Lenin unhesitatingly to use armed force during the revolution and to resort to terror and tyranny to safeguard Bolshevik power. Ironically, Lenin's refusal to compromise sometimes sounds like Tolstoy's uncompromising asceticism.

Essentially, Lenin's violent measures were, as the Polish-born specialist in Soviet affairs Isaac Deutscher (1907–67) pointed out, unavoidable expedients for dealing with temporary crises. Stalinism was guilty of welding them into a governance of fear. Russia is big and diverse enough to have born two men as far apart in fundamental approach as Lenin and Tolstoy. As different as they were, however, both men raged against the oppressive czarist government and the depraved church.

For more than eighty years, Tolstoy devoted himself selflessly and fervently to serving the masses as he rushed headlong down the path of moral reform and regeneration. Himself the author of imperishable masterpieces like *War and Peace* and *Anna Karenina*, he disregarded commonplaces and relentlessly criticised such artists as Shakespeare and Beethoven in the name of the people.

Tolstoy and Lenin shared the single-minded passion and unbending will to carry out their resolutions in spite of all obstacles. I realise that, in the *perestroika*-period Soviet Union, the once deified Lenin has undergone extensive re-evaluation. I myself have no intention of blindly idealising him. Still, Lenin was the driving force behind the immense changes accompanying the Russian revolution. The British novelist and poet D. H. Lawrence (1885–1930), who made a study of his power-related dialectical dynamism of good and evil, said that the blood coursing all the way to Lenin's marrow was saintly. Certainly, Lenin seems to have experienced the pathos for social reform peculiar to other ascetic revolutionaries like Oliver Cromwell and Robespierre. He neither drank nor smoke, was sociable, and enjoyed music, the theatre, literature and walking. He preferred the simple clothing of the ordinary people. But, as D. H. Lawrence could have learned from his own analytical study, Lenin was able to stifle his amiable traits in the interests of the power struggle. The process whereby he did so provides ample material for a profound psychological drama.

The facts of Russian history inspired both Tolstoy and Lenin with sympathy and rage. Their great souls erupted, however, in diametrically opposed directions: one non-violently, the other violently. The tragic gap separating them was too broad and deep for ordinary bridging operations. In this connection, in his *History of Russian Communism*, the Russian philosopher Nikolai Aleksandrovich Berdyaev (1874–1948) made an acute observation when he pointed out the bestial *Rus* – the old word for Russian – that has always existed behind Holy *Rus*. Russia has always wanted either the angelic or the savage and has failed adequately to awaken the human within herself.

It would be a mistake to hasten to identify Tolstoy with the angelic and Lenin with the savage. Such was not Berdyaev's meaning. The point is not that even superior men can be incapable of eradicating the perennial extremes of the Russian soul, but that, as if partly by fate, the greater the genius, the deeper the gap between those two extremities. This would seem to be the traditional tragic paradox of a contradictory and antinomic nation that lacks the moderation indispensable to spiritual balance. Attainment of such moderation, for Russians as for everyone else, depends on self-discipline.

I should like to conclude this discussion with some comments on the power of self-discipline, not specifically in connection with Russia and the Russians, but as a universal topic. At the beginning, I mentioned Sōseki Natsume's novel *Kōjin*, in which Ichirō, the hero, suddenly slaps his friend and then accuses him of losing his temper and getting upset over the least trifle. Ichirō's censure is directed toward the failure of self-control when something unexpected happens. Under sudden provocation, even a pacifist can find non-violence unacceptable. Violence and non-violence then come to seem irreconcilably contradictory. But self-discipline facilitates making the right choice. Buddhism teaches self-discipline as a means of attaining the complete self-knowledge that is part of the enlightenment of the perfect being: a Buddha or Enlightened One. And, given enough people with well-developed powers of self-discipline, non-violence can become the dominating spirit of our age.

This is true because, as the Buddhist doctrine of dependent origination (*engi*) explains, nothing exists in isolation. All things are related by causes (*en*), which are either direct (*jun'en*) or reverse (*gyakuen*). For example, a direct cause can lead an individual straight to belief in Buddhism. A reverse cause, on the other hand, may take the form of an evil perpetuated against Buddhism that has the ironic effect of leading the perpetrator himself to Buddhist teachings. The one cause is pacific and amicable; the other, antagonistic and hostile. Still both produce the desired effect. A person who understands this sees hostility as an impermanent obstacle on the way to the attainment of a larger relationship.

The story of Shakyamuni Buddha's cousin Devadatta symbolically illustrates how this works. Though a disciple, Devadatta rebelled to the extent of making an attempt on Shakyamuni's life. But, his very great evil acted as a reverse cause leading to his being promised the attainment of Buddhahood at some time in the future.

All of this goes to show how Buddhism refuses to recognise Manichaen-style dualisms, like good and bad, light and dark, enemy and ally. Making enemies of opponents, and eradicating them as the Nazis and the Stalinists did, is alien to Buddhist thought. Both direct and reverse causal relations are indispensable.

The Buddhist approach cultivates the power of self-discipline and the ability to see the good in the other and the evil in the self. Refusing to blacken the opposition unilaterally and self-righteously takes courage, the courage Gandhi had in mind when he said that non-violence demands more bravery than being a swordsman.

On the basis of Buddhist teachings, Soka Gakkai International (SGI) strives to promote peace, culture and education by pitting spiritual powers generated from within life itself against the repressive powers of violence, authority and money. As a non-governmental organisation of the Economic and Social Council and the Public Relations Bureau, SGI cooperates with the United Nations in various projects. One of them was the exhibition 'Nuclear Weapons, A Threat to the Modern World', which has been shown in twenty-five cities in sixteen countries. Opening first in New York, in November 1989, the exhibition called 'War and Peace' has also toured many parts of the world. In addition, SGI has participated in fund-raising campaigns for refugee relief. Soka University engages in educational and scholarly exchanges with forty other universities in twenty-seven countries. The musical organisation Min-On and the Tokyo Fuji Art Museum conduct programs of cultural and artistic exchanges. A membership of 1,260,000 in 115 countries and regions [192 countries and regions as of October 2008] is now engaged in creating a cultural network through diverse activities transcending state boundaries. A spiritual movement based on dialogue and mutual understanding forms the bedrock of all these activities. I am confident that, just as drops of water come together one by one to make up a great river, so all of our efforts to stimulate awareness of the importance of peace will bear great fruit in the twenty-first century.

The Summing Up

IKEDA: In your story *The Day Lasts More Than a Hundred Years*, in anger and resentment, the hero Edigei asks about some visitors from the city:

> 'What kind of people are these? What are they?' complained Edigei in his heart. They think everything on Earth, but death, is impor-
> tant . . . And if death means nothing to them, then life has no value.
> What's the sense? Why and for what do they live?[14]

Edigei is angry because modern society treats death negatively, as something outside ordinary experience. He, however, knows that death gives life value. He knows that respectfully keeping death always present, in the background, as the comprehensive summing up, exerts an immense influence on the meaning of life and on the way it is lived.

Buddhism originated with the attempt to come to grips with the fundamental issue of death as one of the four sufferings: Birth; Ageing; Illness and Death, all of which are unavoidable aspects of human existence. Buddhist philosophy treats death and life as the obverse and reverse of the same thing. As a Buddhist, I consider it impossible to elucidate life without shedding light on death as well.

AITMATOV: Ikeda Sensei, I felt certain that, as we sit around your fireside talking on many topics, we would be unable to avoid the unbounded theme of life and death. 'Life and death' is easy to say. But no one has ever surveyed the full limits of the issue, because it embraces everything, even cosmic universal space. Each human being dies alone. But one life, one soul, in its numbered days, contains so much! And an understanding of the phenomenon of death means so much to the individual! Many people struggle to make each day last as long as possible, although they know full well that death will come. Why we make the struggle is another great enigma.

We can deal with the question of life and death only cursorily and partly. We can never formulate a profound answer to it. The burden of dealing with it is beyond my powers. There are, after all, only two ways of representing death: to reason about it and to describe it. The artist most often describes it.

From the rational scientific viewpoint, death is the definitive, normal, ineluctable and expedient result of biological development. But can our souls be satisfied with this view? No, not even at the moment of death, because there is another underlying reality. From the spiritual viewpoint, death is a nagging, undecided philosophical question, as inscrutable as it appears simple. For some reason, the human being persists in thinking about death ceaselessly until his last moment on Earth. Each death is a new tragedy and a new, inexperienced shock, the final boundary and the end of thought, which breaks off with unanswerable, rhetorical questioning of the reason for our mortality. Every person approaches the issue in his own way. I like to think of it in terms of responsibility in the face of death — responsibility both to the self and, even more, to others.

I tried to make the character Edigei illustrate inherent folk consciousness and practical wisdom and philosophy. From these things arise dual attitudes toward death: fear and deference, glorification and despair; with hope of outliving the race and realisation of the futility of the hope itself. Much about a society's history, life philosophy, religious cults, morality, ethics, traditions and rites is revealed in its attitude toward death.

In a totalitarian society, the nature of the prevailing ideology, its politics and seniority system are manifest in its reactions to the death of its members. In some instances, official considerations like rank determine funeral arrangements. Never suspecting this, on the occasion of the funeral of a close friend, Egidei encounters people demonstrating scornful cynicism toward the deceased. And this provided the subject of my story.

Many attitudes toward death are possible. Once people greeted each other with the words '*Memento mori*' (remember that you will die). In doing so, they brought to the forefront a major moral crux. In the Soviet era, since the individual per se amounted to nothing, the worth of a life was measured first and foremost in terms of its necessity to class, ideological and state interests. Death was regarded as no more than sad luck. These attitudes were the source of a nihilistic, deliberately distorted understanding of human life, its value and significance.

For their own purposes, governments sometimes try to romanticise self-sacrifice and glorify it in the interests of the state. I consider this a violation of our very humanity. It is a generally accepted stereotype that the death of an enemy is good — that is, successful — and the destruction of the conquered useful and worthy. The Japanese *kamikaze* of the Second World War epitomises this pathological attitude, the mere thought of which makes me shudder.

IKEDA: It is said that we cannot look directly in the face of the sun or of death. Facing death honestly demands inclusive, religious thinking. This is why all religions, both primitive and sophisticated, include teachings for coping with the phenomenon of mortality as pivotal elements.

Such teachings do not guarantee their believers solutions to the problem of death, since everybody interprets and practises what they are taught in different ways. As the histories of religions in all place, and times eloquently reveal, ignoring these differences and attempting to compel everyone to think and act in the same way breed fanaticism, thoughtless acceptance, superstition, credulity and wrong beliefs.

In one place in the *Analects*, Confucius is reported as having said, 'When you don't yet understand life, how can you understand death?'[15] In another, occurs a disciple's famous comment that Confucius never discusses the supernatural, the violent, the disorderly or the occult. The two statements are generally interpreted as expressing Confucius's lack of interest in the post-mortem world and the irrational, including gods, and to typify the rationalist, practical nature of Confucianism.

They do not, however, indicate indifference to death. On the contrary, they constitute a warning – even a self-admonition – against facile, standardised interpretations of the issue. A person of Confucius's calibre cannot have failed to ponder the meaning death has for life. He must have understood the importance to life of living always in full awareness of death. This is where I see a similarity between his words and your own sincerity and humility. Although I believe firmly in the Buddhist view of life and death, I always eagerly engage in discussions of the issue with sincere people of other faiths – like yourself, because I realise that frank exchanges prevent religious conviction from degenerating into dogmatism.

During the Second World War, as you say, the Japanese militarists spawned a, fortunately, rare group madness that sent young members of the so-called special attack corps (*kamikaze tokkō-tai*) on one-way journeys to death in suicide aircraft and torpedo-boats. To one extent or another, war always violates human rights. Nonetheless, this contempt for human life is totally unjustifiable. Like the Soviet authorities, the wartime Japanese military evaluated the individual solely in relation to state interests.

It must not be thought, however, that all Japanese young people lost themselves entirely in mass madness. Foreseeing premature death, many of them, especially among student conscripts, agonised over the search for something greater than themselves, something to give meaning to both their remaining days and their imminent deaths. At the cost of great psychological strain, some of them did manage to overcome attachment to life; to the extent that, no longer cursing the war, they were able to face their fate on the front with a kind of religious, psychological normality. Reading the numerous surviving testimonials of men compelled to undergo this hell is a heart-rending experience.

The French moralist Sébastien Chamfort (1741–94) said that, whereas preparing for war is always a vice, fighting wars is always virtuous. Certainly the Japanese government wished young people to believe that fighting and destroying the enemy were virtuous. The special-attack philosophy of the government relied on this belief and on the courage and self-sacrifice of its youth. It is not the manipulated young but their manipulating leaders who deserve harsh censure.

Tsunesaburo Makiguchi, first president of Soka Gakkai, consistently urged young men leaving for the front to do everything they could to come home alive. A firm believer in the dignity of life, he absolutely rejected the idea of prettifying attempts to cheat young people of their very lives. His courageous denunciation earned him the animosity of the militarists, who threw him into prison, where he died at the age of seventy-three. His convictions and actions are the source of our organisation's pacifist activities.

The Truth about Ourselves

IKEDA: Your story *The Day Lasts More Than a Hundred Years* contains the thought-provoking legend of the slave (you use the word *mankurt*) who lost his memory as the result of horrifying torture. In her grief, the slave's mother, Naiman-Ana, cries out, 'You can take away land. You can take away wealth. You can even take away life!' she said aloud. 'But who got the idea? Who dared to tamper with a human being's memory?'[16]

Her cry gives voice to a profound truth: human dignity can survive death; but violating the memory is to strike a blow at the very roots of that dignity, since a human being without a memory is virtually a living cadaver.

Reading your story brought to mind the legend of the hero Er, the son of Armenius, in Plato's *Republic*. After ten days in the underworld, Er returns to life to relate his experiences there. One of his final revelations is of the opportunity souls are given to select their fates in their next existences. Once their choices were made,

> They proceeded together to the plain of Lethe through a terrible and stifling heat; for the land was without trees or any vegetation.
> In the evening they encamped by the Forgetful River, whose water no pitcher can hold. And all were compelled to drink a certain measure

of its water, and those who had no wisdom to save them drank more than the measure. And as each man drank, he forgot everything.[17]

One of the things they forgot was their having chosen their own fates. An aspect of this legend concerns the difficulty of grappling with and mastering one's own destiny. Plato stresses the supreme importance of introspection and self-knowledge when he adds at the end of the story,

This at any rate is my advice, that we should believe the soul to be immortal, capable of enduring all evil and all good, and always keep our feet on the upward way and pursue justice with wisdom.[18]

To be without self-knowledge and the power of introspection is to remain unaware of having drunk from Lethe, the Forgetful River. And the upshot of this state is something very close to the slavery of the hapless *mankurt*, who, robbed of the core of his being; that is, his memory, becomes a living corpse.

AITMATOV: A person incapable of self-analysis is a 'voluntary *mankurt*', as one critic remarked about Sabitzhana, one of the characters in *The Day Lasts More Than a Hundred Years*. All too often, people hear only things that neither upset them nor compel them to take an objective, uncompromising look inside themselves. Alas, whereas we lightly and pleasurably judge others, as soon as criticism is turned on ourselves, we hasten to find all kinds of dodges and self-justifications.

IKEDA: That is true. In such cases, the will toward introspection is lacking. Introspection is also a component of human dignity. A person with it cannot consent to live according to outside directives or goals.

AITMATOV: Unfortunately, it never occurs to many people that living according to another's way of thinking is living less than a full life. On the other hand, some people are unaware of inner loss or of their own inability to describe what is wrong with them inside. Theirs is another case entirely.

IKEDA: Certainly. Still, some conditions inevitably compel human beings to think seriously about themselves and about eternal issues.

AITMATOV: Yes. For example, the Indian Muslim politician and philosopher Abul Kalam Azad (1888–1958) confessed that his arrest in 1916 gave him his very first chance to analyse himself. Of course, prison is not the ideal place for philosophical reflection.

IKEDA: Perhaps. Still, since Azad chose a way of life very likely to lead to prison, he must have been prepared. Maybe prison gave him the opportunity to test his ability to preserve his sense of judgement in adversity. It is far sadder to live life thoughtlessly, leaving all decisions up to so-called professionals.

AITMATOV: I am interested in fate as a socio-philosophical problem; that is, in the right to choose. I am frightened by the very idea of fecklessly abandoning one's own fate to others, or of governments that claim to know what is best and legislate their own right to manage the fates of a people. This a blasphemy that converts the human being into a state slave or serf.

IKEDA: Thanks to people, like you, who warn us of the danger, enslaving others is less easy than it once was.

The People

IKEDA: As is indicated by the back-to-the-people (*V-narod*) movement of the nineteenth century, Russian intellectuals have been more concerned about the ordinary people than their counterparts in other countries. Perhaps for this reason, few literatures deal with the people as extensively as Russian literature. My own impression of the Russian people as indomitable, unspoiled and perennially cheerful and good-natured; in spite of the heavy burdens of hardship and sorrow historical experience has imposed on them, derives from literature. In his *The Diary of a Writer*, Dostoyevsky gives a prototypical example of the kind of person I mean in the character of the peasant Marei who calmed the writer when, as a child, he was frightened by the shadow of a wolf. Dostoyevsky perceives the great possibilities of the man's disposition and is surprised to find the spirit of a poor, unsophisticated peasant to be filled with profound, enlightened, human emotions and an almost feminine gentleness. Your own writing reflects the earthy people who raised you. You have said that you come from the lower classes depicted by Maxim Gorky. I should be interested to know what kind of image you have of the masses of the ordinary people.

AITMATOV: Traditionally, the ordinary people are regarded as bearers of truth and justice. Oaths are taken and trials are held in their name. Warnings, thanks and indignation are issued as if in their voice. Still there is room for speculation about the premise on which this assumption is based. Everyone knows it takes all kinds of individuals to make up the people. We thank our lucky stars for the chance to know some of them. Others are so cruel and barbarous that we would go to any extremes to avoid contact with them. The people constitute a major, and generally welcome, subject of literary portrayal. Every writer has his own experiences and convictions on this score.

You mention the child Dostoyevsky and the *muzhik* Marei. In this connection, it is entirely appropriate to share with you an occurrence from my own adolescence. I will relate it in some detail to demonstrate clearly how it came about that, during the hard years of the war, I almost committed murder.

At the beginning of February 1943, a sudden and devastating blow fell on our family. Over and above obvious hardships like hunger, poverty and the war, we were a persecuted family, the children of a man repressed by the Stalinist regime as an 'enemy of the people'. There were four of us children. Mother was ill with chronic arthritis, which, possibly brought on by the shock of father's execution in 1937, lasted until the end of her life. At the time, I was fifteen, the oldest, and had one brother and two sisters, all in primary school.

When the war broke out, to spare us from hunger, mother gave up her work as a book-keeper in a regional centre and took a job as an accountant in a small collective farm. We moved to a village called Dzhiyde, which still has the same name, where we made our home in an ownerless, half-broken-down, daubed hut. Before the war, our relatives had given us a calf that grew up to be our benefactress. I called her, I still remember, Zukhra. Because we had no shed, with the *kolkhoz* director's permission, we kept her in the common barn.

We could not survive without the cow, and we children all knew it. She meant the difference between life and death. We used to spend whole days hanging around the barnyard, feeding her and giving her water. In the winter of 1943, she was about to calve. To keep her in good condition, we scrounged leftovers from neighbours to put in her trough. At home, we talked of nothing but the spring and our dreams of fresh milk, cottage cheese and sour cream.

One dark winter morning, I shall never forget it, I got up earlier than usual and made my way through gusty winds to the barnyard. I got there before all the cowmen. At a glance, I saw that our cow was gone. I could not figure it out. Her stall was empty. Her tether lay near the door. The half-broken gates stayed open, day and night. Had Zukhra been nearby, I would have known it at once. At first sight of any of us, even from a distance, she always started lowing.

First I thought she must have broken free and roamed off somewhere around the barnyard. I searched barn and yard, but in vain. Then I rushed to the night watchman, who was asleep on some straw in a corner of the barn. The old man either knew nothing or pretended not to understand when I asked about our cow's whereabouts. Maybe she drifted out into the fields, he suggested.

Alarm gripped me. I searched high and low. No Zukhra, not in the gullies and not at the river where we generally watered her. She was nowhere to be seen.

Animals do not leave shelter that early in the morning. Suddenly, I realised that somebody must have stolen her. I hurried home to tell Mother. From that hour, our world went black. No doubt about it: thieves had made off with Zukhra. We wept with dismay. What would we do without her? For four small children, an asthmatic mother tortured by polyarthritis, and an equally ill aunt, the loss was a real tragedy. My mother's older sister, our aunt Gul'sha, lived with us. She had been left alone when her husband had been repressed and her eighteen-year-old son had been mobilised to the front.

Neighbouring soldiers' wives sympathised and joined in both our lamenting and our cursing of the villains who had done the evil. We all prayed that God would bring a black day down on their heads. And, as we did so, a passionate decisiveness rose in my soul. As the oldest, I was responsible for protecting the younger children. I had to act. I had to avenge our sorrow. In my frame of mind, this could mean only one thing: to kill the thieves.

I went straight to the local tractor driver Temirbek. In the autumn of 1990, a friend from Talas told me he had died at the age of seventy-seven. May the earth lie light upon him. I had been his helper and water-carrier all the preceding autumn ploughing season. The only tractor driver in our village, Temirbek drove the one tractor, an XT3 as I recall, assigned by the local machinery and tractor station. One tractor with one plough constituted our total mechanisation. Temirbek had been granted the village's one deferment. After all, drafting our one tractor operator would mean letting the fields go unploughed.

My job was to fill the radiator after each turn in the field. I lugged buckets of water from far away and had to be at the right spot by the time the tractor made its turn. It was hard work. But I did my best because both the tractor driver and I got fed. That was the important thing.

On the morning in question, filled with rage, I wanted to borrow Temirbek's rifle, the same one that used to be issued to me to protect the kerosene barrels in the fields at night.

It turned out he was sick in bed, feverish and breathing with difficulty. He had already heard what had happened. And, when I asked for the gun, he said, 'Take it. It's hanging there on the wall. Shot's in the bag hanging on the nail beside it. If I was well, I'd go shoot the rats myself!'

I left Temirbek with the rifle in my hands and a thirst for revenge in my heart. All-engulfing bitterness and anger drove everything else out of my head. I was totally obsessed with the idea of finding and mercilessly punishing the criminals. I knew they could not have got far yet. A cow can't gallop like a horse. To avoid people's eyes, they would travel by night and hide by day. If they slaughtered the animal, they would have to hide the meat before finding some place to sleep.

The notion that the thieves might think nobody from our 'outsider' family would come after them made me all the hotter. But I would descend on them terribly and pitilessly, like an avalanche, and shoot them all – two, three, however many – point blank. Yes! That was the only way it could end.

Tireless, like a madman, I trudged through fields and gullies, up and down foothills. It was cold, but I was hot. To keep myself going, I ate snow, like a wolf. The shoes I had on were a pair my brother, and I took turns wearing. Clambering over rocks and ploughing through deep snow, I would have ruined them completely if, finally, I had not grown too exhausted.

Noon was near, but I had found nobody. All the world seemed empty and spotless. The day had become an agonising burden. Lifeless hills interspersed with empty space surrounded me. There was no trace of the thieves.

Then suddenly I realised that probably, almost certainly, they had made straight for Dzhambul, the nearest town, where they could slaughter the cow and sell the meat at the bazaar.

This idea made me sadder than before. On fire with vengefulness, my heart beat deafeningly in my breast as I hurried towards the town. I knew I could not reach it until morning, even if I walked non-stop all night. Still, I didn't hesitate or look back. Hastening down the hillside, I headed in the direction of the main road to town. All the time, I was imagining how, next morning, I would search out the faces I was looking for. Maybe I would be standing right beside the fresh hide of our cow. But even that wouldn't matter. I didn't need any evidence. I'd recognise them by their eyes. They'd recognise me, too. But by then it would be too late. I'd shoot them down on the spot: right behind the meat counter.

Continuing along the main road, rifle in hand, I was so engrossed by my relentless passion for revenge that I didn't notice a grey-bearded old man in wretched clothes with a worn, though warm-looking hat on his head. He was riding a mule that trotted along like the road was familiar. They were coming from the direction of an old, abandoned cemetery. When our paths crossed, I neglected even to give the customary greetings. My mind was too occupied and overflowing with wrath. I was going to pass by, but the old man stopped me. 'Hey there, my boy, something tells me you've got killing on your mind.'

Oddly indifferent to the remark, I replied, 'That's right. There's somebody I want to kill.'

My eyes met the all-comprehending look in his haggard face. Nodding his head, he said, 'Well, if that's the way it is, hang on a minute. Let's talk it over. What do you want to do such a thing for?'

'Somebody stole our cow. She's about ready to calve. And there's four of us kids. I'm the oldest. And Mama and our aunt are both sick.'

'That so! Well now, you folks are in a spot. But listen a minute. Don't let revenge eat you up. Don't kill. Don't even think about it, not even a low-down thief.'

I stifled a sob and said nothing.

'Believe me, I understand,' he went on. 'I'm so sorry for you. It makes me sick at heart to think about it. But pay attention to what this old traveller says. Get killing off your mind. Go on home. And remember, life punishes wicked people. No two ways about it. You can be sure of that. Punishment will dog them wherever they go. It'll go to bed with them at night and get up with them in the morning. But, if you go back now and stop thinking about killing, life'll bring you happiness. It'll come to you without you realising it. It'll settle in your soul. You may think I'm just gassing. But believe me and go home. And someday you'll remember my words and realise I was right. Go on back, son, and tell your mama all about it. You go your way; I'll go mine. And no matter how bad people treat you, never think about killing again.'

I took the old man's advice. Glancing around, I saw that he and the donkey were already headed in the opposite direction. Passing through deserted fields, I bore on my shoulder the rifle grabbed up in despair but now no longer needed. As sunlight glinted on the snowy fields, without understanding why, I burst out in sobs that shook my whole body. Plodding along in my now ruined shoes, I went on weeping, with the weapon of intended revenge still on my shoulder.

For years, I never so much as thought about that incident. Then, suddenly, something brought it all back, just as it had been – the unknown old traveller and his donkey disappearing in the distance; his words still lodged in my heart.

IKEDA: You mentioned this episode in your speech 'Literature and Life', delivered at Soka University in 1990, when you and your family visited Japan. Although I was away and unable to attend the meeting, many of our members reported it enthusiastically to me. Some correspondence-student housewives in your audience were very moved by what you had to say. After your message, a student said a few words of gratitude in Russian; and the way you embraced and congratulated him brought tears to some eyes.

You concluded your own speech in the following way:

For a long time, I forgot all about the incident of that old man. But a question put to me by Ikeda Sensei reminded me of it and stimulated me to write down my memories. Several factors provided the inspiration I needed. First were my contacts with Ikeda Sensei's thought and writings. Second was my exposure to the great philosophy of Buddhism and its spirit of tolerance.

My youthful meeting with a shabby, raggedy old man riding a donkey was a major turning point in my life. My meeting Ikeda Sensei was another.

The old man you describe in the incident brings to mind Platon Karataev in *War and Peace*. Although he appears in a limited number of scenes, Karataev makes a vivid impression and strikes me as the personification of all that is best in the Russian peasant. His heroism outshines the bravery of Napoleon himself. The encounter between him and Pierre, both prisoners of the French, is described in tellingly realistic detail. For example, Tolstoy uses the quality of roundness to evoke Karataev's generosity and good nature.

Twenty-three soldiers, three officers and two officials were confined in the shed in which Pierre had been placed and where he remained for four weeks.

Later Pierre remembered them all as misty figures, all except Platon Karataev, who always remained in his mind a most vivid and precious memory and the personification of everything Russian, kindly, and round. When Pierre saw his neighbour next morning at dawn, the first impression of him as of something round, was fully confirmed: Platon's whole appearance, French overcoat girdled with a cord, a soldier's cap and bast shoes, was round. His head was quite round, his back, chest, shoulders and even his arms, which he held as if ever ready to embrace something, were rounded. His pleasant smile and his large, gentle brown eyes also were round.[19]

Platon Karataev is a harbinger of Tolstoy's mature philosophy of non-violence and non-resistance to evil. In a sense, he coincides with the old man of your youthful experience. His approach to life corresponds in many respects to Buddhist humanism. I am very happy that I somehow supplied the impetus that helped you recall this figure from your memory.

AITMATOV: Tolstoy said the idea behind *War and Peace* is a history of the people, something that is very difficult to write. In any epoch, a history of the people remains the pinnacle of the possible. The best guide to have in its creation is a hero from the period about which the history is being written.

In *The Day Lasts More Than a Hundred Years*, I attempted to use the image of Buryani Edigei as way of touching upon this theme. His story represents my attitude toward the fundamental principle of realism, the major object of which has been, and remains, the people: the working human being.

For Edigei, work is more than a means of making a living. It is his life goal, his calling and his duty. The choice he makes is freely made but demands courage and nobility. This is why he is a worthy human being, in the full meaning of the words. Cupidity and gain are alien to him. He sees accepting privileges as an insult to his dignity. More important still, his attitude to work is the source of his sense of vital participation in his epoch and in the life of the people. Without these two factors, he would find both himself and his fate inconceivable. For a person like Edigei, thinking is more than vague, idle musings on trivial topics or on no topic at all. The 'last' word he utters is born in his soul at the bitterest moment of his life, at a time when he stands face to face with ineluctable eternity. It is addressed to his dead friend Kazangap and to all the living. Edigei has a duty to tell about the great and wise life of a human being – a worker. Edigei's 'last word' is at the same time his 'first word', aloud at any rate. And I, the writer, consider it my duty to say what Edigei left unsaid.

He will go on living in silence, guarding the land and affirming the power of the spirit. He discovers himself, a participant in the history of the people, through many trials: war, hunger, storms and bitter love. Without cursing his unhappy fate or avenging himself on life, he regards all experiences as unavoidable. He embodies what I might call genetic humaneness.

In discovering himself, he also discovers other people and the future. In a difficult moment, his childlike smile saves him. But his stern silence helps other people live. Edigei has no use for war, nor time to think about it. He lives according to the working man's paramount rule: universal peace. To Edigei, this rule is as important as the law of universal gravity.

Edigei dreams of turning the desiccated Sarozek steppes back into the paradise his friend Elizarov told him they once were. How fascinating, to create a splendid, living paradise in the sands! Given the armament we possess now, it would probably be an easier task to destroy the whole planet. But that is not for Edigei, not for the normal. People like Edigei should live long and have grandchildren, maybe even great-grandchildren, to whom they can impart their spirits.

The writer who, with the best intentions, flatters the so-called simple man, or the people in general, is guilty of a kind of mortal sin. His flattery fools nobody, except perhaps himself. Still more important, the hypocrisy and greedy incentives of flatterers sooner or later must come to the surface in the form of confrontation – maybe with the intelligentsia.

The people do not want to become an icon or object of veneration. They want to hear the truth about themselves. If the people are, as some have said, an ocean, a natural force, then the poet is a wave on endlessly rolling waters. Because they are immortal, comparing the people to nature is apt.

From this standpoint, the cherished desire of the French satirist Jean de La Bruyere (1645–96), *to become the people*, must be understood in a sense different from the accepted one. His statement reflects the desire to participate in eternity; that is, to be able to ignore the limitations imposed by his own personal allotment of time and to live in a space of historical existence with neither beginning nor end. Only when he can do this is the writer justified to claim the right to speak in the name of the people.

As the literary historian Dmitriy Sergeevich Lihachov (1906–99) acutely observed in his discussion of the characteristics of Russian literature, modesty of literary form reveals this ability in a writer.

I am not convinced that the people, and representations of them, can be, or ought to be, the main literary theme. I am apprehensive of the so-called discoveries of the inveterate socialist realists, for whom the people were a mere fetish. Such realists thought in terms of the masses controlled by the iron will of the Party and under its allegedly wise guidance performing heroic deeds like, for example, liquidating the kulaks, constructing the White Sea Canal and so on. In brief, for the socialists, the people were tools stupefied by hysterical slogans and promises of paradise, a mob applauding what was being done to them, easily seduced and bought for trifles.

Epitomising the loathsomeness of flattery, Stalinist ideology started out by distorting the idea of the people. It lavished loud praise on them, in their name mouthed so-called sacred vows, and dispensed punishment and grace.

The writer today must restore the former, true understanding of the nature of the people, the eternal, immutable, spiritual values that the people embody and that proved ineradicable even under the most exquisitely fanatical methods of destruction. At the same time, with profound gratitude to them and their unchanging nature, he must try to develop a worthy, real, not Utopian, way of life for them. Instead of acting like an instructor, he must join them in learning how to live. And he must never despair when he discovers that they want to live according to their own rules, which may not be to the taste of us so-called 'engineers of human souls'.

IKEDA: In the horror that was the former Soviet Union, countless innocent people were condemned and killed by people's courts conducted against enemies of the people for having opposed Stalin, the 'Father of the People'. The Soviet ideological version of the people was a conceptual monster unrelated to the reality of the masses themselves. In your story, Edigei castigates the intellectuals who administered Soviet ideology in ignorance of true popular feelings and needs in this way:

> And what came of what he learned from different courses in different institutions? Maybe they taught him so he could turn out to be just what he has turned out to be.[20]

No matter how grievously abused by political regimes, the masses of the people are the origin of all things. Some time ago, I tried to give my thoughts on this topic the following poetic form.

People!
You alone are reality
Outside of you there is no real world
The age will not forget to wait and pray for the true movement of
    the people
It will not forget that you alone
are the great sea into which all things flow,
the furnace, the crucible in which all things,
emerging from chaos, are refined
for the sake of a new birth
and you are the touchstone
to distinguish truth from falsity in all things
Science, philosophy,
art, religion,
all undertakings
must be directed toward the people

Science without you is cold-hearted
philosophy without you is barren
art without you is empty
religion without you is merciless.[21]

After the funeral of his friend Kazangap, your Edigei, who embodies the
spiritual wholesomeness of the masses, addresses God in a way that reveals
his attitude toward prayer:

> I want to believe that you exist and that you are in my thoughts. And
> when I pray to you I actually address myself through you. At such
> times, I am permitted to think as you the creator might think. That's
> the essence of everything. But those young people don't think about
> it and despise prayers.[22]

The young people he has in mind represent the haughty atheists who
disdain the spiritual wholesomeness of the ordinary people, the wholesomeness
Edigei embodies. Their attitude was a source of the spiritual devastation
that afflicted the Soviet Union.

Their Most Brilliant Attribute

IKEDA: In Japan, the behaviour of certain birds is used to symbolise feminine selflessness. One is the pheasant hen that sacrifices herself to safeguard her chicks when stubble fields are burned in autumn. Another is the mother crane protecting her chicks from the night cold with her own wings. It is true that women are more capable than men of giving deep love. At the time of the disastrous earthquake that hit Armenia in 1988, I recall reading a newspaper article about a mother who, until rescue came, fed her little girl on blood from a self-inflicted wound in her own arm.

I was the fifth of my parents' eight children. Our family made a living processing edible seaweeds. While I was still quite young, my father fell ill, leaving Mother to cope with financial hard times and the difficult task of raising us. No matter how difficult things got, she constantly encouraged us all by her unfailing cheerfulness. She used to joke that, if poor, at least we were champion paupers.

I understand you were a great help to your mother in her struggles to raise four children after the death of your father.

AITMATOV: My *Materinskoe Pole* (*Mother Earth*) deals with this topic. No doubt, by today's standards, it seems slightly sentimental. But it was the result of a sincere desire to say a word about Mother, to add even one stroke to her portrait, which is sacred to me. It embodies the tenderest love, faithfulness and courage. Everything that is finest in the heroines of my works derives from my mother. As you suggest, literatures of all times and peoples sing the praises of the self-sacrificing and selfless nature of maternal love. The great mother image!

IKEDA: Your literary work contains several impressive mothers. There is, of course, your *Mother Earth*. A robust nature, boundless affection for her family and ability to endure sorrow make Akbar in *Executioner's Block* extremely real to the reader.

Other Russian writers, too, have depicted the forgiving spirit, nobility of mind and courage to endure anything for the sake of cherished ideas and people on which maternal selflessness is founded. Through the exigencies of fate, in *War and Peace*, the enchanting young Countess Natasha Rostova evolves into a generous wife and mother who, grown indifferent to her own personal appearance, devotes herself wholeheartedly to bringing up her children, running her home, and guarding family ties. As an evocation of the beauty and nobility of motherhood, she is profoundly moving. In his *Mother*, Maksim Gorky creates a simple, unselfish woman who is always ready to lend a helping hand and who develops her own independence as a result of sympathy for her son's revolutionary ideas. Judging from these works, the characteristics of mothers can be found in their Mother Earth-like nature that displays selfless love and infinite forgiveness. They cherish what comes to their hearts instead of reason, and possess courage and nobleness to bravely confront unjust authority, if necessary.

AITMATOV: Natasha in *War and Peace* is one of those literary characters that always seem alive and present. She is the embodiment of motherhood. Although she is one of his eternal, traditional, female images, it must be pointed out that Tolstoy deliberately contrasted her with the idea of feminine emancipation, which was actually widespread in his time.

IKEDA: An idea that has gained vastly greater depth and impetus in our own time.

AITMATOV: True. But, like a realist acting irreproachably according to the rule of life, Tolstoy understood the extraordinary complexity, and inevitability, of the choice between emancipation and traditional ways. In his view, not only the personal fate of the individual, but also the destiny of society and of the people as a whole depended on this choice. As is customary with Tolstoy's heroes, Pierre experiences a tempest, an emotional heaven and hell, triumphs over a multitude of temptations and seductions and often seems on the verge of hopeless spiritual and physical catastrophe. Natasha, on the other hand, discovers the truth of life. How? In her radiant soul, the impressionable, ardent, young girl survives for the sake of something higher and deeper; that is, she survives for the fulfillment of her true desires and her calling, which she must attain by means of personal suffering.

By conducting his hero along a very difficult path of self-realisation and self-perfection, Tolstoy wants to make us realise the importance of the moral atmosphere of society as a whole and of the enormous part education plays in the life and fate of the individual. Beginning at the cradle, education must guide the soul toward a clear understanding of the role of the intellect and toward the cultivation of gratitude to the continuation of the human race. This is what Tolstoy wants us to understand.

Ultimately, Natasha finds supreme happiness in motherhood. This is no mere illustration of the normal destiny and accomplishment of a woman.

In Natasha, the instinct – natural need – to become a mother is elevated to spiritual heights where the woman realises her innermost essence, motherhood. She becomes one with nature. But then, motherhood is nothing but nature endowed with the power of feeling through her children, thanks to whom she experiences an incomparable sense of immortality.

Unfortunately, in our times, the status of motherhood has been perverted and flouted. I cannot remain silent about what is perhaps one of the most distressing tragedies of our time. Newspaper reports of mothers' abandoning newborn infants, fleeing from obstetrics clinics or, worst of all, killing their babies, make me shudder. Are these only isolated cases? Is this pathological behaviour? All such incidents can hardly be coincidental. Are women losing the instinctive willingness to carry a child full-term? If so, why? Perhaps we can stimulate this willingness by giving all due praise to women, who, in spite of hardships, bear their children and, in the name of the future, devote themselves to rearing them. Abandonment of babies, usually firstborn, by their mothers is becoming so grave a social ill that many cities run institutions for infant orphans. True, social factors are behind this distressing phenomenon, but it is nonetheless a curse of our day.

When I was a child, no woman would have thought of abandoning her infant. She might not take good care of it, she might not nurse it, and in times of famine and harsh weather, she might perish with it. But she would never abandon it. She would never renounce inescapable, God-sent duty.

As a teenager, I spent the summer vacations with my Aunt Karakyz, my father's sister, in a Kirghiz village, where, like the rest of the boys, I drove sheep and lambs to pasture. One summer, my aunt had about ten ewes with their lambs. And, mysteriously, one of the ewes rejected her lamb. She would not let the poor thing come near her. She would kick it, butt it and run anywhere to keep it from nursing.

My aunt considered this a great tragedy, foreboding world destruction and the wrath and punishment of God. Weeping all the while, she struggled to bring the recalcitrant ewe to its senses. She whispered to it and hung charms around its neck. In the evenings, she sat by the fire, engrossed in her own thoughts and asking heaven whether some kind of blasphemy, some injustice, were taking place in the world. Had mountains collapsed? Were rivers running upstream? Had the stars on high gone out? Had the sun gone dark? Was the moon ill? Had the winds been stifled? If none of these things were happening, why did a ewe reject its own lamb? That is the way people thought in those days about sheep; a far cry from the way some of them feel about children today.

Contemporary civilisation is permeated with egoism. Everyone strives to live for the sake of satisfying desires that, alas, ultimately turn out to be questionable. Even in the face of the severest historical conditions, such selfishness must not be overlooked and cannot be condoned.

The mother symbolises unselfish, self-sacrificing love. In self-denial, the mother gains the whole world, in the form of children, who, we hope, embody our finest, albeit often unmanifested, traits. It is not in vain to dream our children will be better than us. We should be encouraged by the very possibility. Surely, it is precisely in our children that we can find supreme happiness.

IKEDA: We human beings can learn much from the behaviour of animals like the wolf Akbara in your short story *Executioner's Block*. Each summer, in the heart of Tokyo, in a pond among the skyscrapers, a spotbill duck makes her nest and hatches and rears her ducklings. One day, when autumn is in the air, she leads her whole family of ten or so across a broad, heavily travelled thoroughfare to the waters of the Imperial Palace moat, where they then grow to maturity. Traffic stops for the procession, and people from all over come to observe, at a distance, this demonstration of parental caring. The eagerness with which the mass-media cover the event suggests that our society may be hungering for the kind of motherly love the duck represents.

You say that, raised to psychological peaks, instinctive mother love enables women to contact the eternal through their children. I agree and find your opinion highly valuable. The diametric opposite of egoism, mother love is the most brilliant of all feminine attributes. At the same time, it is one of the most important of the things our blatantly self-assertive society is losing sight of. It shows us the royal road that has existed since the beginning of human history and that leads us to the greater self while overcoming the lesser self.

It is highly significant that the principal religious emotion, love in Christian and compassion in Buddhist terms, is often compared with mother love of the kind illustrated by the following story from the Nirvana Sutra.

Once a poor, homeless, pregnant, beggar woman, who was ill, hungry and thirsty, took shelter in an inn, where she bore her child. But, when he found her there, the innkeeper drove her away. Though still not recovered from childbirth, she took up her infant and started off for another country. On the way, she encountered violent winds and rains. She was afflicted by cold and tormented by mosquitoes, gadflies and caterpillars. When, still holding her child, she attempted to ford a swollen river, she was swept away by the raging waters. In spite of everything, she clung to her baby. Both of them drowned. Ultimately, however, because of the strength of the poor woman's love for her infant, salvation was forthcoming for both.

The parable reveals the possibilities inherent in mother love, possibilities that today are too often wasted in frivolous living. Self-renunciation, or in Nietzsche's words 'self-conquest', does not mean despising the self. On the contrary, it means, in Buddhist terms, expansion from the lesser to the greater self. Ironically, though women are naturally more responsive to religious emotions, today, in their eagerness to attain equality with men, they underestimate the greatness of motherhood. From the standpoint of their children, this is disastrous.

The Humanity of Children

IKEDA: Walks through parks during my visits to Moscow have shown me how much Russians love and cherish children. I have heard that young men who neglect to give their subway seats to women with children are scolded by fellow passengers. This traditional attitude has deep historical roots, which probably influenced you in creating the impressive scene in the story *Executioner's Block*, in which the female wolf Akbara howls in sorrow because outlaws have stolen her cubs. Your stories *The White Steamship* and *Pervy uchitel* (First Teacher) are indictments of adult deception, fraud and arrogance as seen in the eyes of children. The many maltreated children in your work call to mind an incident related by Ivan Karamazov in Dostoyevsky's celebrated novel.

> This poor child of five was subjected to every possible torture by those cultivated parents. They beat her, thrashed her, kicked her for no reason till her body was one bruise. Then, they shut her up in the cold and frost in a privy.[23]

Incidentally, working notes to *The Brothers Karamazov* say that, after leaving the monastery, Alyosha Karamazov becomes head of a boys' school. Although glimpses of this kind of child abuse occur in literature, I have the impression that modern Russian citizens tend to be more loving and compassionate.

AITMATOV: I should like to agree with you; but, alas, the facts do not substantiate your contention that people invariably 'loved children' in the Soviet Union. Actually, the idea of love of children served ideological interests.

When society as a whole regards – or does not regard – children as what the Russian writer Andrei P. Platonov (1899–1951) called 'jolly little humanity', the issue takes on social and moral–philosophical significance.

I seriously doubt the existence of such a jolly little humanity. One can read in any contemporary paper, accounts that belie the very concept: children who are to all intents and purposes orphans, though their parents are alive, thieves serving as kindergarten trustees and making a living off funds intended to relieve the deprived, cruel treatment of small children or teenagers. Examples are numberless. Are these isolated cases? There are a lot of them. And everyone knows how precious is even a single tear from a child's eye.

Although the task is a painful one, for the sake of our children's future, we must uncompromisingly expose the tragic plight of the juvenile soul in a pathologically abnormal society built on irresponsible Utopian ideas, false promises and enforced affirmation of lies.

I admit that, in the beginning, we all sincerely believed our children were better off, that 'Soviet Children are the Happiest in the World!' and so on. But this turned out to be only another falsehood. Such claims were fundamentally Utopian, idealistic outcries of self-satisfaction and self-consolation. And, I am afraid, in the final count, they were only propaganda for the 'Soviet way of life'.

Most frightening of all was the way ideology regarded children as essential 'human raw material', as minds to be moulded in new ways, starting in nursery school, if not sooner. This amounted to violence against the individual, a crude invasion of the holy of holies – that is, against genetics. At the time we in the Soviet Union rejected genetics as pseudo-science.

I am not sure it is possible fully to represent in literature the suffering of a child forced, unbeknownst to himself, to be a mindless robot imitating adult activities, political rituals and so on. I am sure, however, that an alteration in our attitudes toward childhood is prerequisite to the restoration of a humane society. First, we must understand the nature of children. Then, we must take pity on them! More than anything else, the teenager needs for people to accept him as a human being. Only those who themselves are truly human beings can see a human being in others.

IKEDA: President Gorbachev's aide Georgii Shakhnazarov said that ideology buried the whole Soviet Union in a way history had never witnessed before. Although Soviet Utopianism seems to have held the entire nation under its spell, I seriously doubt that ideological education can recast human nature.

The Soviet system tried to create the appearance of having mass-produced *Homo Sovieticus*, but it could not alter fundamental human nature. The Soviet authorities devoted extraordinary attention to education because they accepted the standard idea that ideology can be inculcated more securely in children. Even so, the results of their efforts seem suspicious. I imagine that the nature of children is more constant than we usually think.

At the end of his book *Return from the USSR*, André Gide describes an encounter in Sevastopol with some *bezprizorniki*, waifs made homeless in the confusion following the Russian revolution. We have already mentioned how Gide's perception of corruption in the Soviet system at an early stage won angry criticism from intellectuals in France, like Romain Rolland, and elsewhere. Not surprisingly, it was unwelcome to the Soviets as well. His lively description of these homeless children recalls the waifs in *Les Misérables*, who preserve sunny, childlike dispositions in the grimmest adversity.

At one point in Gide's story, two plainclothes policemen drag away a boy of about eight who bawls, rages and tries to bite his captors. About an hour later, Gide happens to pass the scene of the incident and sees the child seated on the pavement, smiling and chatting with one of the policemen. Before long, the police wagon pulls up, and the policemen takes the boy in his arms and gently lifts him into the vehicle, which drives off somewhere.

Gide concludes in this way:

I have related this little incident because few things in the USSR moved me as much as the way the man treated that child: the persuasive softness of his voice (Oh, how I wanted to understand what he was saying!), a smile with all the affection he could put into it, the endearing tenderness with which he lifted the child in his arms. I envisioned Dostoyevsky's *muzhik* Marei. It was worth going to the USSR to see that.[24]

CHAPTER SIX

The Long Journey Inward

Dostoyevsky's Religious Views

IKEDA: In 'The Grand Inquisitor' section of *The Brothers Karamazov*, Dostoyevsky contrasts the Roman Catholic practice of using miracles, mystery and power to maintain ecclesiastical authority with the love and inner spiritual teachings advocated by a Christ who has returned to Earth. In another part of the same novel, Dostoyevsky has the venerable Father Zosima, Alyosha Karamazov's mentor, define hell as suffering caused by the inability to love. In his view, hell, like love and spiritual values, is to be found within the human being.

All higher religions must confront the problem of inner values opposed by external pressures. Even the Russian Orthodox Church, whose practices fell short of Dostoyevsky's own idealised religious philosophy, could not escape this issue. The teachings of Christ himself and the thoughts and deeds of primitive Christians reflect concern with it. But, as the church grew larger and stronger, and especially after Constantine I made Christianity the official religion of the Roman Empire, external ecclesiastical power got the upper hand. Subsequent developments have led many thinkers, including the French aesthetician, philosopher and member of the *Académie Française* René Huyghe, with whom I shared a dialogue published in book form as *Dawn After Dark*, to believe that the organised Church, and not Christianity itself, was the ground in which ecclesiastic authoritarianism grew.

As a result of a long journey into his own soul, Avdyi, the hero of your story *Executioner's Block*, discovers a new spiritual church and decides to abandon the seminary studies he had been pursuing. In speaking of his experience, he employs almost Dostoyevskian ideas: '. . . overcoming age-old ossification, liberation from dogmatism and giving the human soul freedom to recognise God as the highest essence of his own being. I am my own Church. I don't recognise temples.'

AITMATOV: No atheist, I am a supporter of free religious alternatives. Presumably, no matter what form it takes, all faith is founded on respect for life and for humanity. I have enormous respect for all religions, since, expressing the venerable spiritual, philosophical and moral experiences of their ethnic groups, they provide the higher ethical codices that help people to live and to find their places in both daily life and in the universe.

Faith constitutes a special kind of interpretation of the world. The person who believes, not blindly, but deeply and consciously, is humane because he senses the presence of a wonderful secret in the world around him. Such a person knows he can only guess about the nature of that secret and is respectfully grateful if it reveals itself to him.

Each individual must determine for himself whether to accept religion. Some will; others will not. Still others remain neutral on the issue. This third group constitutes a buffer zone reconciling polarities and warning of the possibility of bloody conflicts. In spite of past religious wars of the cruellest kind, today the West experiences this kind of mediating process.

However, in other parts of the world, we observe fanatical religious confrontations. This is the case in some Islamic nations. Why? Is it merely that Islam, as a young religion, is still experiencing inevitable growing pains?

IKEDA: Religious fanaticism is by no means limited to Islam. From the eleventh to the thirteenth century, Crusaders tried to recover what Christians considered their Holy Places. From the Muslim viewpoint, however, the Crusades were calamities brought on by fanatic opponents. Ironically, the Crusaders represented a European culture isolated in its own Christian views, whereas the Muslim world they attacked was experiencing a flourishing phase of cultural expansion. The twentieth-century growth of Islamic fundamentalism and its conflicts with the West must be seen against a background of centuries of Western military intrusion and economic domination.

The gap between the Muslims and the modern secularised world is difficult to bridge. For one thing, Westerners cannot condone certain apparently vengeful Muslim practices. Nonetheless, while keeping differences in mind, we must strive to attain mutual understanding in a level-headed fashion. Cultural relativism, of the kind represented by the work of the *Annales* school of historiography, led by French writers and thinkers like Lucien Febvre (1878–1956), Marc Bloch (1886–1944) and Fernand Braudel (1902–85), indicates a growing attempt to attain this end and to modify Eurocentric interpretations of history. Westerners must recognise the important role Islam has played in human history. Muslims must learn about the West. And both sides must engage in open, sincere dialogue, the only way to a peaceful resolution of differences.

AITMATOV: The religious urge and its *Weltanschauung* have inspired humanity to great philosophical heights. At one stage, however, formalised Christianity degenerated into a collection of dead canons and official rituals sharply dividing shepherds from sheep. The shepherds then assumed the role of guides, sanctified and set apart from the followers, who were no longer certain where their priests were leading them. The priests themselves and their way of life were veiled in utmost secrecy.

In such circumstances, the believer is no longer his own man. He is entirely dependent on the interceder, or in Tolstoy's words, the functionary, who is in a position to arrange audiences with God. The real mystery disappears, leaving behind only the kind of secret court intrigues associated with the Escorial of Spanish King Philip II.

In his book *Pererozhdenie idei Dostoevskogo* (Regeneration of the ideas of Dostoyevsky), the Russian existentialist theologian Lev Shestov (1866–1938) speaks of the way stagnant, dead, church teachings kill the soul, enslaving it and depriving it of free will. The person who has tasted true liberty cannot submit to such a thing. He remains essentially what the primitive Christians were.

For the first Christians, caves served as assembly places. They equated asceticism with valour, thus challenging the scandalous, offensive luxury with which imperial Roman state religion attempted to veil its spiritual poverty. But, once it had replaced the old paganism, Christianity too donned golden robes, gradually transforming itself from a faith into an ideology. Ultimately it attained the unshakable status of a political doctrine, or what today we might call a command-administrative system with its own deeply mercenary interests.

In 'The Grand Inquisitor' section of *The Brothers Karamazov*, Christ is amazed to see how people have perverted his teaching. The Inquisitor tells Him not to get involved, or else. The inherent threat is that, if Christ, God made man, dares protest openly against what he sees, he faces a second crucifixion. Actually, he would have been crucified, in secret, long before having a chance to protest. Tragically, no one in Dostoyevsky's book so much as knew about His Second Coming. Perhaps this has already happened time and time again without our being aware.

But there are always people, they seem to arise from the Earth, who refuse to accept official ideologies. They always perceive the interior poverty, the decay and the defilement of spiritual ideals behind the glittering facades. The perception is first instinctive. The soul rebels. It will not accept the effrontery of deception.

Avdyi, the hero of my story *Executioner's Block*, is such a person. He is in search of pure truth, which he is convinced cannot be found in temples, where true spiritual teachers are replaced by hired dogmatists handing out ossified postulates they themselves do not believe and living in ways contrary to the Christian idea of sanctity.

Is he unsophisticated in his protest? Several critics have considered him a naïve adolescent. As I now realise, this evaluation probably arose from his apparent defencelessness in abstract argument with expert demagogues and preceptors armed with what at first seem to be convincing conclusions supporting the status quo in the church. What chance has Avdyi against such people, such co-ordinators? He is a mere lamb. Or, at least, so it would seem.

IKEDA: Unfortunately, though ostensibly promoters of human happiness, priesthoods have historically sought lambs to sacrifice, in the name of God, to their own greed. Soka Gakkai International is now engaged in a battle with religious authoritarianism of this kind. If the masses of the people remain passively silent, ruthless authoritarian clergies may take oppressive advantage of them. When this happens, their own good intentions can drag people of good faith into an abyss of unhappiness. Downright struggle is the only way to avoid this tragedy. When the time to fight comes, indifferent to power, custom or tradition, the ordinary people must guard the justice of their faith. Failure to take a firm stand invites horrendous consequences.

In his *Time of Parting*, the Bulgarian writer Anton Donchev (1930–) teaches the importance of knowing when to fight by illustrating how blind docility leads to tragedy. The setting is Bulgaria under the Ottoman Turks, who are compelling the citizens to convert to Islam under the threat of unspeakable punishment. Seeing that most comply with the order, a Turk sneers,

> One sheep starts off in a certain direction and all the others follow. Have you ever tried to draw one of them out of the flock? It's hard to do. What will the others say? That's where these creatures are happy.[1]

Human beings on the verge of submitting, sheeplike, to ecclesiastical domination desperately need a leader with leonine courage. The emergence of one such guide is certain to inspire the emergence of others who, like members of our organisation, are devoted to cultivating the fundamental inner conversion in each human being that will assure ultimate triumph over religious authoritarianism.

AITMATOV: In the Hans Christian Andersen fairy story *The Emperor's New Clothes*, a little boy announces to all, that the emperor, who is deluded into believing himself decked out in fresh finery, is stark naked. The point of the story is not that adults who saw the truth chose to remain silent about it. There is a deeper meaning. The adults actually did not see. Their sight was so distorted that they accepted nakedness as being clothed. They needed the unprejudiced, unspoiled sight of a child incapable of lying and unwilling to accept falsehood out of cupidity. As the Russian Orthodox Metropolitan Anthony said, being reborn means seeing the world with the surprised eyes with which God himself beheld it on the day of Creation. Avdyi sees with such eyes. Since true wisdom and childishness are inseparable, he is the eternal child. His true worth probably lies in his ability to behold the primordial world and humanity unshadowed by sin.

True, had certain thoughts come into my head earlier, Avdyi might have turned out less naïve. But this hardly would have made life easier for him. It would not have altered his fate. No, because Avdyi thinks with the 'mind of the heart', not the 'mind of the mind'. Dostoyevsky puts words like this in the mouth of the character Aglaya in *The Idiot*, but I feel sure they reflect his own ideas.

I wanted to create a hero who lives according to the mind of the heart. At first he only suspects, but later he comes to see clearly that some people thirst for a higher truth. They are willing to suffer for it, even to the extent of laying down their own lives. They know that knowledge unrelated to the heart is dead; it belongs in the domain of Pharisees theatrically mouthing socially approved homilies.

But a hero like this ends up in a *cul de sac*. He knows that, because it estranges him from other people and the realities of their lives, existence in the world of illusions and self-delusion is alien to his nature. The best the preacher in the 'temple' can do is provide rest and temporary oblivion from burdens left outside the House of God. But this is not the full meaning of church ritual, which ought to wake the soul to an inexhaustible source of spiritual energy and of love and gratitude with which to create relations with the world and the self.

Only a person who has consciously chosen the path of devotion to love of the people can experience this. Never borrowed nor bookish, his words are rich with the gold of personal moral experience. If they were not, they would bring little happiness to himself or to others. True happiness is born of the radiant wonder of liberation from all stagnant dogmas and canons. A boundless heaven opens before people who know this happiness.

IKEDA: Ultimate happiness depends on truth. No tempest can shake it because its roots spread wide and deep in an inner spiritual soil.

Alyosha Karamazov, the youngest of the brothers, seeks and loves truth passionately. He is eager to sacrifice everything to attain it. No gloomy ascetic, he is wholesome, bright, faithful and sincere. He spreads his arms wide to embrace the whole world. His associates call him angelic. In lucid, perfect faith, he evokes a famous passage from the New Testament: 'Jesus said unto him, If thou wilt be perfect, go [and] sell that thou hast, and give it to the poor and come [and] follow me.' (Matthew 19:12) Yet Alyosha deprecates himself because, instead of everything that he has, he can give only two rubles and can only attend mass instead of following Him.

His father and his oldest brother Dmitri wander in the depths of delusion. His second brother, Ivan, is an intellectual atheist. In contrast to them, the 'lovable' Alyosha delves deeper and deeper into his own soul. Gradually, his persistent efforts to answer the problems over which he agonises alter his very appearance. Ultimately, his journey into the soul transforms his personality. The inward-directed search for truth, the internalisation of faith, is an important theme in the novel.

Alyosha's experiences tell us that truth abides even in the actual world of suffering and joy, of love and hate. He embodies the process whereby we temper ourselves, ascertain, rediscover and assimilate truth. Leaving the monastery where he has studied, at the behest of his mentor Father Zosima, Alyosha goes out into the world to be a peacemaker. This new journey leads him to discover profound truth in everyday realities and to find a universal element uniting the worlds of the self and the other.

The sequel Dostoyevsky planned to *The Brothers Karamazov* was to have dealt with Alyosha's subsequent life. It is fascinating to ponder the treatment the author would have given this theme had he completed his plan. How would he have bridged the gap between the tempestuous reality of the lives of the other members of the Karamazov family and Alyosha's inner world of the soul?

The Divinity Within

IKEDA: In his late years, completely absorbed in the inner spirit and opposed to external authority like that of the church, Tolstoy insisted that the realm of God can be found only within us. We must seek it there, for it is to be found nowhere else. Everyone who tries to come to terms honestly and sincerely with the world must share this conviction. The Bulgarian revolutionary poet Hristo Botev (1848–76) put it this way:

> O my God, my righteous God.
> Not you, in heaven apart,
> but you, who are within me, God,
> within my soul and heart . . .[2]

Aside from considering God near and almost equal with humanity, Tolstoy and Botev were fundamentally different. Tolstoy preached love and non-resistance to evil; Botev was a revolutionary ultimately killed by enemy bullets. Nonetheless, both advocated love and the liberation of humanity from bondage to external, in particular, ecclesiastical, authority. Both found human dignity, liberty and equality in the process of discovering divinity within the self. From the idea that God exists within us, it naturally follows that each of us has internal standards; that is, religious convictions. This in turn means that religion exists for the sake of humanity and not the reverse.

Although different from the Protestant idea that each man is his own priest, the concept of the internal divinity leaves interpretation of God up to the individual. Under such a dispensation, interpretations may become highly diverse. Nonetheless, to avoid confusion, basic ideas must be kept clear.

AITMATOV: As the well-known saying has it, 'God is everywhere and nowhere.' How do we relate this idea with Tolstoy's statement to the effect that the kingdom of God is within us? Does not the first contradict the second? Or does not the idea of God within us contain a hidden temptation to consider oneself equal with the divinity? For instance, a person in a pathological state of ecstatic arrogance might convince himself that God abides within him. The notorious Gregori Yefimovich Rasputin (1872–1916) is a striking, comparatively recent example. He convinced members of Russian court society, including the tsar and tsaritsa, that he was a holy man, or *starets*, through whose mouth God spoke.

Hardly anyone would consider Rasputin merely psychologically abnormal. Calling him a mere mercenary confidence man is too simplistic to explain his malevolent persona completely. The particular phenomenon of Rasputin is possible in certain historical conditions and especially in a social atmosphere loaded with signs of impending, global tragedy and mystical harbingers of the end of the world avertible only through miracles and supernatural powers. In his case, the power was manifested in himself as a kind of new miracle worker. The staggering impression he made on people thirsting for improbable wonders is connected with the aura of holiness he deliberately created and ultimately came to believe in himself. Of course, stupendous numbers of well-intentioned people acquiescing in his holiness aided him.

I have chosen Rasputin as an example in order to show what can happen to undoubtedly good intentions and how they can be used for deeply mercenary aims. It is very dangerous to accept the superhuman ambitions and prerogatives assumed by an individual obsessed with the false idea of his own intimacy with God. Had it only been God he was close to!

Sometimes the deck is stacked against us, as when the ecclesiastical authority of an institution turned ideological is used for the totalitarian repression of dissent or opposition. Once it becomes a state institute dictating the, as a rule, conservative codex of communal life, the Church limits all manifestations of spiritual freedom and all scientific–philosophical interpretations of the world that threaten to shake the religiously established cosmology.

Then the Holy Inquisition, or its equivalent, swings into action. The flames of the *auto-da-fé* start blazing, exposing the medieval bigotry that, in the words of Ezh Stansislav Lets, exists in every age. At different times, the Inquisition assumes various forms associated with diverse names – symbols like Torquemada, Hitler, Stalin and so on. It is often said, especially recently, that the inquisitions of the past were better than their successors. Numbers of victims sacrificed on the altar of dissension are advanced to substantiate this assumption. But the logic is impious. No matter what scales they are perpetrated on, all 'inquisitions' represent cruel violence against the individual.

IKEDA: Cruel violence of the kind you describe arises from within life itself. Buddhist philosophy divides human life into stages called the Ten Worlds. In the lowest, the World of Hell, life is crushed to inactivity by suffering. In the second, the World of Hunger, mind and body are dominated by violent desires. In the World of Animality, the third stage, life is characterised by fear of the powerful and contempt for the weak. Life in the fourth state, the World of Anger, is controlled by the selfish desire to get the better of others. These four lowest ways of life are called the Four Evil Paths. But life is capable of attaining higher planes.

Once free of the Four Evil Paths, it rises to a more humane and loftier level. The fifth state is called the World of Humanity, or of Tranquillity. In it, life is capable of calm judgements. In the sixth, the World of Heaven, or Rapture, life is filled with a kind of happiness. Life in the seventh and eighth stages, Voice-Hearers and Cause-Awakened Ones, is concerned exclusively with its own individual enlightenment. However, in the ninth stage, Bodhisattva, it is compassionately devoted to the salvation of others. The tenth state, Buddhahood, represents complete, perfect, harmonious enlightenment.

At any given point, life may be in any of these realms; and movement among the echelons is always possible. For various complicated reasons that may include personal frustration or even innate inability, the lives of some people seem to get stuck in one state. Torquemada, Hitler and Stalin may have identified their own megalomania with an inner 'god'. But nothing we know suggests that the lives of these men ever rose above the Four Evil Paths. Perhaps from the very outset, they lacked the reflective powers to undertake the inward journey of self-improvement.

As is clear in works like *The Kreutzer Sonata*, Tolstoy's thoroughgoing idealism held that human beings improve themselves through the search for the holy and the sacred. What he had in mind is precisely the inward journey that leads to the Buddhist worlds of Bodhisattva and Buddhahood.

AITMATOV: The way to God begins with the self. But, as long as God remains solely in and for the self, the way to Him is on private property. In such a case, it can lead to abuse of God for mercenary aims and to the justification of all kinds of private and social injustice and violence. God cannot object, except in the first person singular; that is, as I. My opinion will evoke categorical disagreement on the part of many who believe that God exists independent of us and that we are entirely dependent on Him from birth to death. Nonetheless, for each of us, God exists only so long as we are alive. Alas, such is the dialectic of our mutual relations with Him.

Actually, it would be more fruitful to discuss the transformation, through the individual, of the divine idea into an all-embracing understanding of a divinity that is one for all of us and in whom we are all united.

The road inward into the self is as endless as the universe. Following it is to approach God by way of endlessly perfecting the soul. There is no limit to this process. Ideally, though none of us can see it through to the end, we should at all times follow that way.

Restoring Religion to its Rightful Place

IKEDA: All over the world, especially in the industrialised nations, society is dominated by carpe-diem hedonism, materialism and worship of money. It is therefore plagued with a variety of social ills including narcotics abuse and sexual violence. These phenomena represent the spiritual struggle to satisfy the desiccated spirit by means of external stimuli and desire-satisfaction. They reveal the spiritual hollowing-out of our era caused by the slow-but-sure advance of fundamental nihilism.

In the past, people found it impossible to restrain their unruly thoughts and actions without the aid of transcendent codes derived from sacred and awesome phenomena variously designated as God, the Law, the Way, Heaven and so on. Finding them futile, modern mankind has tossed these codes out as mere superstition. Liberated from restraints, our contemporaries have launched on what seems to them a brilliant, hopeful voyage, but without God to provide a compass. We are adrift on a tumultuous ocean where the wake of our ship creates new waves in the forms of scientific technology and governmental interference.

Metaphorically, the waters of the ocean stand for material goods, money and the pursuit of pleasure. When, driven to despair by longing, the passengers of the lost ship partake of them, these waters only aggravate their suffering, as seawater does physical thirst.

In *Crime and Punishment*, Porfiry Petrovitch, the inspector investigating Raskolnikov's crime, says,

> This is an obscure and fantastic case, a contemporary case, something that could only happen in our day, when the heart of man has grown troubled, when people quote sayings about blood 'refreshing', when the whole of life is dedicated to comfort.[3]

When Porfiry speaks of a contemporary case that could have happened only 'in our day', he is referring to something like the state of affairs that persists today, in your and my day, a century after the time in which Dostoyevsky set his novel.

To abandon standards of self control, no matter what designation they go by, is to lose ties with the invisible, spiritual world. Mesmerised by material phenomena, modern humanity has cut itself off from pre-birth and post-mortem possibilities and judges all things solely on the basis of the tangible world. The eye that sees only the mundane cannot penetrate to truth. Since life and death are essentially two aspects of the same thing, to question reasons for living has the same significance as questioning reasons for dying.

The world of concrete phenomena is a relative world where everything is ephemeral. Concentrating on it alone eliminates the possibility of discovering anything eternal or anything of absolute value and leads ultimately to futility. The social ills of our day arise from the futility haunting the modern human spirit.

A tree must have deep roots to be healthy. Similarly, for modern humanity to discover the meaning of life and the way to live better, we must delve to the eternal aspects of universal life deep within the phenomena of individual existence. This requires a revival of the religious spirit.

AITMATOV: Humanity does indeed find itself without rudder or sails on a raging ocean of ideological and political struggle – and, as you correctly point out, without a compass; that is, we find ourselves without God.

But are people aware of their desperation, of the horror of their position? Do they understand what kind of catastrophe awaits them? After all, to entertain apocalyptic apprehensions, human understanding must take into consideration comparative conceptions of good and evil handed down from generation to generation. Are we not deceiving ourselves? Are we not hiding the answer from ourselves? The following warning in the Apocalypse might serve as the apogee of blindness and delusion:

> And in those days shall men seek death, and shall not find it; and shall desire to die, and death shall flee from them. (Revelations IX: 6)

But are we to be blamed for euphorically ignoring philosophical issues and the well-being of future generations? Wherein lies the guilt of the hedonist who gives no thought for the consequences of his fecklessness? Is he guilty of anything at all? Must each individual bear the burden of responsibility for the fate of all humanity? Must we not admit that by no means everyone is capable of sensing the tragedy of existence? Suppose you and I feel it. Are we justified in demanding that everyone else feel it, too?

IKEDA: When you question the need for hedonists to awaken to a sense of the insecurity of life and to their responsibility for the welfare of the unfortunate, you sound a little like Dostoyevsky's Grand Inquisitor, who claims that most people need only bread, not liberty. I cannot believe you agree with him.

Like all the rest of us, hedonists cannot escape what Buddhism calls the four sufferings of life: Birth, Ageing, Illness and Death. The ancient Chinese emperors who searched for magical elixirs capable of making them immortal and eternally youthful and healthy searched in vain.

I have talked with individuals in all kinds of official positions and from all kinds of social and educational backgrounds. But, no matter who they are, I always address myself, not to their position or background, but to their fundamental humanity, as partakers of the common fate of Birth, Ageing, Illness and Death. I base all dialogues, including this one with you, on our common destiny, which makes possible exchanges transcending all other differences.

AITMATOV: We do share a common destiny in the shape of 'the end of the world', which philosophers of all schools find alarming. I sometimes think it would be easier to deal with the idea of ultimate cataclysm if we had jollier gods than those of modern theologians, gods like those of ancient Greece, for example.

IKEDA: Philosophers certainly find the idea of the end of the world alarming. Before the atomic age, however, in spite of some nagging fears about inescapable destiny, ordinary people worried little about the extinction of the whole human race. As a general rule, humanity has tended to consider itself immortal. Christians believe managing human fate to be God's purview and have preferred to resign their individual powers of judgement in this connection.

AITMATOV: I see what you mean. But nihilism, at any rate, religious nihilism, seems to be a natural reaction against religion's attempts to hobble and strictly control perfectly natural human physiological life-supporting, therefore essential, inclinations. In other words, it is a reaction against religion's attempts to substitute one gloomy god for what to the ordinary people appear human and cheerful gods. Fundamentally, the history of new religions is a history of a struggle in search of a true god, or a struggle between stagnant, conservative theology and the concept of the people's own divinity.

IKEDA: Yes. Rigidified theologies, what Emerson called dead formalities, try to impose a belief in the superior value of the hereafter. The people themselves, however, are in search of a religious emotion vibrantly vital within life itself. The struggle between the two can be called a religious revolution. It has occurred in the past, is occurring now, and will continue to occur throughout all time. As you say, people today seek their own divinity and no longer feel attracted to lofty supernatural beings unilaterally imposing controls on them. Indeed, the greatest religious issue facing contemporary humanity is discovering within itself that thing that can be called sacred – God in Christianity, wisdom or enlightenment in Buddhism. As Tolstoy said, the kingdom of God is within us. Dealing with this issue inevitably entails finding out how to deal with fundamental human instincts.

Physical desires, like those for food and sex, and psychological desires – like that for fame and glory – often have tragic consequences for individual and social life. Some people attempt to bind them in, repress them, or do away with them entirely. In Buddhist history, the Hinayana tradition has followed this course. But, as is already well known, such attempts have the paradoxical effect of denying human existence itself.

In contrast, Mahayana Buddhism teaches the oneness of earthly desires and wisdom. Earthly desires, in this case, equate with natural human desires and emotions. The task is, not to eradicate them, which is impossible anyway, but to control and purify them. In metaphoric terms, earthly desires – actually desires and emotions – can be compared to firewood, and wisdom and enlightenment to fire. Just as you cannot start a fire without firewood, so there can be no enlightenment if earthly desires are abhorred and renounced.

The purely analytical approach is incapable of solving all human problems. In this case, choosing between wisdom and earthly desires – the sacred and the secular – solely on a dualistic basis leads only to a dead-end where actual human existence drops from view. I feel certain that Avdyi in your *Executioner's Block* would understand what I mean.

AITMATOV: My Avdyi is different from the ordinary Christian: he is a born religious innovator, striving hard to relate religion to the vital needs of contemporary life, thus enabling human beings to turn to religion for answers to questions that it alone can answer.

Today, however, the situation is quite different. We are faced with new generations that believe in neither God nor the Devil and are indifferent to solutions to so-called eternal questions like the meaning of existence. They seem to need no compass and are willing to sail anywhere on any kind of ship, as long as it is comfortable.

Are they happy? I imagine they do not trouble their heads over that question either. And, if contrary to my expectations, they think about it at all, they give an affirmative answer. They have their own understanding of happiness. I see no need to pity them because they are not happy in our way. We can keep our pity to ourselves. But if we approach them with sermons on Christian morality, they are likely to wish we were somewhere else.

IKEDA: But can we stand silently by while such people perish before they have a chance to become real human beings?

AITMATOV: Judging others is difficult, but at least we can appeal to the human disposition within them.

IKEDA: Like Avdyi. But, unfortunately, Avdyi dies a violent death.

AITMATOV: Is there another way, as you say with my complete agreement, to restore religion to its rightful place? Contemporary society, in which the word has been drastically devalued, was born of a lie – either a willing lie or an unwilling lie arising from the so-called best intentions. But the lie no longer awakens a response in the souls of the people to whom it is addressed. Long suspicious of preachers of any kind, they now need a clear example of a truly just and worthy way of life.

Illness of the soul is one of the major causes of the pathological condition of contemporary society. There is no serious disagreement on its diagnosis: it is born of disparity between word and deed. We say one thing and do another. This condition has prevailed too long to persist much longer. Some people, naïve teenagers and odd-ball individualists, consider a life of lies an insult to themselves personally and to the highest humanistic ideals. For Avdyi, who is an Orthodox believer, the incarnation of these lofty ideals is the image of Christ.

In my opinion, restoring religion to its rightful place is not all that simple. Abrogating governmental orders assigning the Church a low social position and turning believers into second-class citizens or outcasts is one thing. And that must be done. But, as we have said, the Church and true belief are entirely different things. Old believers put it precisely when they say, 'God lives in hearts, not in buildings.'

Religion will not obtain its rights until the people and society experience an unquenchable thirst for God, or higher spirituality, realising that without this spirituality, the so-called good life is not all that good. This requires us to see ourselves as in a mirror and be terrified by the anti-human temptations of which we have become the victims. If we experience this horror, if shame burns our souls, then we can hope to begin living in a different way. I cannot say when this will happen. I know only that it will come to pass and that it is already taking place with certain people. That, of course, is reassuring.

IKEDA: We must be certain that the religious restoration will occur and must be determined to take an active part in bringing it about. In this, as in all important undertakings, we cannot afford to be passive bystanders. *War and Peace* teaches that defeat awaits the person who has not set a definite course, and that victory lies in store for the one who has made up his mind where he is going.

Gandhi said that, whereas violence leads ultimately to defeat, there is no defeating non-violence. Even cast into prison, the man who lives according to truth is always victorious. This, indeed, is the true meaning of victory. He went on to say,

> I remain an optimist, not that there is any evidence that I can give that right is going to prosper, but because of my unflinching faith that right must prosper in the end. Our inspiration can come only from our faith that right must ultimately prevail.[4]

A man of strong convictions is a mighty optimist with inherent ideas and powers to shake the world. Revolutionising the times demands, not changes in hard systems and structures, but the soft, internal revolution of the individual human being. We are witnessing a decided shift in emphasis from the hard to the soft; that is, from establishments to human beings. Oriented in the same direction, Soka Gakkai International is engaged in a widening struggle to create solid convictions in each human being.

Alienation and its Causes

IKEDA: Even now that He has been declared dead, people seek a replacement for God. Evgeni Pasternak, son of the Nobel laureate Boris Pasternak, once told a Japanese writer visiting Moscow, 'I have never known a true atheist.

Everybody believes in something. Even professed Soviet atheists idolise Lenin.'[5]

By relying blindly on reason, godless people stimulate the rapid development of scientific technology, while giving unbridled rein to their own greed. Faith in unaided reason has made life more convenient but has not liberated us. Paradoxically, the accelerated scientific–technological progress we ourselves have created now controls us and alienates us from one another.

Human beings have become parts of a social mechanism. Within standardised lifestyles and constructs, they have lost sight of their real selves. According to Carl Gustav Jung (1875–1961), the self rises from the subjective, which, located in the deep layers of the consciousness, supplies creative energy to the ego at the surface level. Take as an illustration a tree growing in a river. Roots sunk deep in the riverbed correspond to the true self. The waters of the river rushing by represent modern scientific civilisation. If the tree cannot withstand the force of the river, it snaps at the base. Then the trunk, now no more than driftwood, is lost on the current. The trunk stands for the ego alienated from the true self. Alienation of the ego from the true self illustrates the impasse into which modern Western civilisation has been driven by exclusive reliance on reason. Jung hoped that the great powers of what he called Oriental Wisdom could help the West find a way out of this dead-end.

Western philosophy, which can be said to have started with Descartes' *Cogito ergo sum*, posits a dualism between the subjective and the objective. While tremendously important to all intellectual operations, reliance on a dualist approach has reduced the self to the ego, or surface-level reason and intellect.

Like the modern civilisational impasse, the subject–object dualism is a closed system. People who have sensed this and who realise that knowledge in such a world is only partial knowledge are now trying to find an open system leading to a world of total knowledge.

In Eastern thought, thinking entails more than intellectual operations. It is excavation into the deep levels of life-force involving three categories of action (mental, verbal and physical) and a subjective search for the self. Consequently, in Eastern philosophical experience, the separation of ego from self is impossible. Jung was captivated by the oriental notion of the self engaged in an endless cycle of questioning and re-questioning.

AITMATOV: If I am not mistaken, the Danish philosopher Søren Kierkegaard (1813–55) advanced the idea that the human being is not what he thinks about himself but what he actually is. No doubt, considering civilisational progress as natural and inevitable, he foresaw the danger inherent in overconfidence in pure reason. His suspicions were right. After overturning and unmasking God, people were able to peer into secrets once concealed behind a veil of religious dogmas and statutes. Ostensibly having achieved absolute freedom in this way, humanity failed to see that it had stopped merely admiring reason and had come to worship it. Reason became a new power, enslaving humankind to it and to itself. The situation reminds me of an engineer trying to brake a train tearing along at top speed until it crashes, piling coaches on each other, then derails. Western civilisation is that train.

It is probably senseless to grumble about humanity's obsession with the tempting possibilities of technology and its ignorance of the consequences of dashing wildly into the future before ascertaining the obstacles on the path to the unknown. If splendour and radiant happiness await each and every one of us, why waste time? Let's get started. And then?

IKEDA: Unfortunately, radiant universal happiness has not arrived. How can we know that now, as we have already begun travelling in the vastnesses of the universe, we are not actually less happy than our forefathers, who thought the sun revolved around the Earth? The answer depends in part on interpretation of terms. But I dare say our ancestors did not worry prematurely about the issue but lived out their lives, accepting things as they thought they found them.

AITMATOV: You are right in saying prematurely. But when did they begin to worry? When did they begin to experience what the French philosopher and archaeologist Pierre Teilhard de Chardin (1881–1955) called the ailment of the *cul de sac*?

IKEDA: Anxiety, or a vague sense of insecurity, generally comes as a harbinger of the birth of a new era. At such times, people usually feel uncomfortable. They experience spiritual disharmony. They grow incapable of finding satisfaction in their unfamiliar, chaotic circumstances.

AITMATOV: And where does this feeling of chaos come from? What essentially is it? Here I think we encounter a tragic contradiction: ordinary, everyday consciousness is impotent to comprehend and therefore to explain our affiliations with the truly fantastic reality we live in and the technical blessings we employ. Unbeknownst to most of us, we live in a daydream, in a miracle apparently dropped from the sky. Why has this happened? Are we worthy of our condition? Deep in our subconscious, but none the less real for all that, lurks the fear of what would happen if our technological wonders should suddenly turn disobedient and, unresponsive to all urging, no longer serve us as they formerly did.

Suppose the television breaks down. Most of us would-be masters can do little more than bang on the set with our fists. We cannot repair it. We can turn the television on and off to see the amusing talking pictures; but when this particular technological miracle goes on the blink, the master becomes the slave. He is doomed. Unable to live without entertainment, he experiences an inexpressible, unexplainable fear of being alone with himself. Does *himself* exist? Did he ever? If he did, where has he gone? This condition, alienation from the self, is the apotheosis of the human estrangement you discussed.

IKEDA: This key issue for natural human existence in a science-fiction era relates to memory or, perhaps more accurately, to forgetfulness. Our age is a classical example of what Hamlet meant when he said, 'The time is out of joint.' For contemporary humanity, indispensable ties to the past and to other people have been weakened by a process that the French philosopher Simone Weil (1909–43) described as uprooting. We have fallen into a bottomless, black hole of loneliness. We have severed our roots. And, tragically, too many people fail so much as to discern the nature of their predicament.

AITMATOV: I have an image of man running forward as bridge after bridge collapses behind him. The familiar metaphor now has a new twist: humanity fails to notice what is going on in the rear. We seem to be in the grips of some kind of rabid euphoria. We are breaking our necks to get somewhere. But where? Reason flies ahead of the soul.

Instinctively we are afraid to look around. Perhaps a backward glance will reveal the dumbfounding spectacle of emptiness, or of scorched earth or desert, or perhaps of another Chernobyl. The mountains of trash and the lunar landscapes we see on all sides are just as incomprehensible as the technological wonders that spawn them. They are the price of progress and the culmination of a comfort that, instead of appeasing our spirit as it is supposed to do, only reinforces our vague anxiety.

To get out of this predicament, we must try to understand the cause of the anxiety gripping us. For one thing, we are bogged down in pride and satisfaction with our own achievements. In failing to go farther, we have allowed material things to assume existences of their own. They are alien to us, and we are foreign to them.

IKEDA: Though he would not relate in the same way to the technological miracle called an automobile, the hero of your story *The Piebald Dog Running along the Seashore* calls his kayak brother. His affection for his kayak arises from two causes. First, he made it with his own hands. Second, it embodies his spirit and the spirits of his forebears. When he speaks to it, he addresses history and memory. His universe is the sea, indestructible nature, a place uncongenial to humanity, a fierce chaos opposed to the hustle and bustle of civilisation.

AITMATOV: But the old man in the story comprehends the ocean, not with his reason, but with his entire being. Instead of thinking in everyday terms, he contemplates. Consequently, he comes to understand his own personal life and life in general. He finds out what he has lived for and perceives the essence of the law that formally he obeyed only instinctively. With this development, he has reached the stage where he must present a reckoning to his fate, the future and his own conscience.

Is the truly contemporary human being the kind of person who vainly expatiates on the so-called complexities of life and seems to believe that society is obliged to meet all his demands? Or is he grateful for the pristine wonder, beauty and wisdom of being and thankful to fate for the immense happiness of having been born? Poets belong in the second category. One of them, Boris Pasternak, said that the creator of all things gives more than is asked of him.

Pasternak was speaking as a single individual. But does one person have the right to possess what was given to all, or many? Egoism, that is, self-seclusion, is harmful. In the first place, it dooms the individual to lonely isolation from his fellows. Second, inevitably, the egoist shuts himself away in a kind of black box constituted of dubious pleasures which, alas, are fated to act ultimately as abrasives. The egoist's time passes fast. But he has nothing to remember because he was never blissful. His collocutor never invited him to the feast of the supremely blessed.

Aldous Leonard Huxley (1894–1963) calls man an evolution that perceives its own existence in time, with which it is equal. The realisation that this is so, produces a sense of immortality. As Huxley says, 'We are immortal, for a time.' And inclusion of the 'I' in history permits us to act, listen, speak, think and strive. How to attain such a state of 'Oriental Wisdom', on what such attainment depends, is another matter.

IKEDA: The interesting expression 'immortal for a time' relates both to my own idea of the 'eternity of the moment' and to Buddhist philosophy. The Buddhist idea of eternity is not a linear procession from past to present and from present to future. Instead, it postulates a living instant that is present yet subsumes past and future. Without the present instant, both past and future are delusions. This is why, in Oriental thought, the self not only is the subject of intellectual operations, but also is intimately connected with the nature of life. Presupposing this kind of self, let us change our viewpoint and think inductively.

A deductive interpretation of alienation in modern society inevitably breeds grave pessimism or, at worst, despair. Take, once again, television sets as an example. As you point out, generally turning them on or off exhausts the layman's powers to act on them. We are alienated from the technological devices we rely on. On a larger scale, political structures have become too hypertrophic for the limited powers of the individual to influence them. The consequent political anomie is the Achilles heel of modern democracy and parliamentary government. As estranged as we are from all these things, however, we cannot reject them. We have nothing to take their places.

We must, therefore, abandon deductive thinking and examine our circumstances inductively by expanding the self to embrace the invisible world subsuming the visible one and all the products of modern civilisation. Faust has something instructive to say on this point:

> Whatever to all mankind is assured,
> I, in my inmost being, will enjoy and know,
> Seize with my soul the highest and most deep;
> Men's weal and woe upon my bosom heap;
> And thus this self of mine to all their selves expanded,
> Like them I too at last be stranded.[6]

It is true that Faust's dauntless ambition to expand his self to include everything smacks of the arrogance of what Dostoyevsky called the man-god. Nonetheless, if rightly guided, it can integrate the microcosm (self) and the macrocosm (universe), as taught in Buddhist philosophy. Jung was probably thinking inductively when he spoke of 'Oriental Wisdom'. Indeed,

Jungian depth psychology tends to endorse the Buddhist concept of the self expanded in both space and time.

Verbally Explicit and Implicit

IKEDA: Cratylas, who appears in the eponymous Platonic dialogue, is an odd man. A follower of Heracleitus, he believes that all things are in a state of flux. Because he distrusts words as reliable conveyors of cognition, he points at things instead of talking about them. This would certainly be the logical outcome of thoroughgoing scepticism about verbal communication. Interestingly, one school of Buddhist philosophy contains a similar element of such distrust, an element that runs counter to Western logo-centrism as famously expressed in the passage from the Fourth Gospel: 'In the beginning was the Word, and the Word was with God, and the Word was God.' (John I: 1)

In his *Madhyamaka-kārikā* (*Verses on the Middle Way*), the great Indian scholar and philosopher Nāgārjuna, thought to have been active in the second and third centuries of the Common Era, criticises verbal communications as delusions in a strain similar to Cratylas' approach. The work opens with eight negations in which Nāgārjuna says:

> I pay homage to the Fully Awakened One,
> the supreme teacher who has taught
> the doctrine of relational origination,
> the blissful cessation of all phenomenal thought
>   constructions.
> [Therein, every event is 'marked' by]:
> non-origination, non-extinction,
> non-destruction, non-permanence,
> non-identity, non-differentiation,
> non-coming [into being], non-going [out of being].[7]

The eight negations symbolise the impossibility of grasping reality verbally. Nāgārjuna points out the fallacy and danger of trying to pin down Buddhist non-permanence. His thought, while not exactly the same, is something like Heracleitus' state of flux in words.

Articulate language distinguishes us from non-human animals. Ironically, even to point out the unreliability of verbal communications we are compelled to rely on words. Without them, we are reduced to Cratylas' clumsy pointing.

Still, precisely because of words' immense importance, we must always be on the lookout for falsehood in their use.

Words express meanings explicitly or implicitly. Failure to take into consideration the vast, fertile world of implication behind even explicit verbal expressions causes most of the friction in human relations. In the hope of finding a solution to this problem and of alleviating contemporary cultural impoverishment, philosophers like the French deconstructionist Jacques Derrida (1930–2004) strive to delve deeply into the world of implicit expression.

AITMATOV: We must assume that verbal expression, which the Kirghiz people call the bird of the soul, is a patriarchal property entrusted to us as a personal heritage for life. But, like any other heritage, the richness of its capital value is variable. Whether we increase and enrich it depends on personal socio-historical and cultural circumstances, but also to a great extent on individual and group effort.

I doubt that the majority of people regularly concern themselves about relations between explicit and implicit meanings or their transformations and metamorphoses. Still, to borrow a metaphor from nomadic life, words may be saddled with true content or unsaddled; that is, empty of internal content, or even reverse in significance. Be this as it may, it is absurd to expect to acquire knowledge of the world without words; gestures like those on which the Greek Cratylas relied are less than useful. We live with the aid of words. We live in words. But, from another viewpoint, 'the word uttered is a lie.'

Is this a contradiction? As long as it remains unexpressed within us, the word is primordial and true. What happens once it is spoken? The moment we have mouthed it, suddenly, willingly or unwillingly, it ceases to say what we want it to say. It fails to transmit even a small part of the truth that, a moment before, seemed so clear, so absolute. Whence and why does this lie emerge, contrary to our own good intentions? Does the falsehood of words make honest, true, cherished relations between people impossible? Are we doomed to eternal misunderstanding?

We require a code of relations. For good reason, scientists start their discussions by clearly defining the terms they intend to use. People with shared interests, no matter what — love for Dostoyevsky, Ryūnosuke Akutagawa, and Shakespeare — easily discover a common language.

You and I are engaged in a dialogue taking place in the face of eternity and against the background of a magical universe, whose image we are beginning to see and are keenly sensing because verbal expression makes it accessible and clear to us. The reality that opens itself to the genius lives, breathes, flows and changes. But, when I reflect on this phenomenon, I find myself trying to identify the nature of the magic that enables us to depict the labyrinthine world and the ceaseless flux of existence.

Because I wanted to draw the reader into the essence of the world I experienced while creating it, in writing the story *The Day Lasts More Than a Hundred Years*, I strove hard to find words that mean precisely what I intended. In this effort, I found an ally in the great Armenian poet St. Gregory Narekatzi (tenth-century) who said, 'And this book, in place of my body. And this word, in place of my soul.'

Who today has the moral right to join Narekatzi in saying this? It would reflect most balefully on us if I were to answer, 'no one'. But what moral justification does the poet or philosopher have to claim his words to be matter of the highest kind? He is justified if his spiritual life is pure. Only a spiritually pure person can decide, as Narekatzi did, to address 'To God, a word from the depths of the heart.' The very idea of standing face to face with God, of the possibility of His overhearing, is fearsome. Nonetheless, Narekatzi chose God to be the confessor of his, as he thought, weightiest sins. The responsibility of absolving them would be beyond all human agency.

IKEDA: Since Buddhism postulates no creator divinity, the Buddhist is compelled to confront and judge himself, without outside aid.

AITMATOV: For Narekatzi, the word *God* signified, not outside help, but his own conscience. Nonetheless, outside aid is comforting. Indeed to be able to trust another person without fear of being misunderstood or of having one's sincere, unguarded outbursts interpreted as signs of pathetic, unforgivable weakness, or worse, used inimically, is a source of supreme happiness.

IKEDA: Total mutual understanding of that kind seems to be what Ernest Hemingway longed for. His deep need for it depended, not on words, but on the will to comprehend the person behind the words.

You have said that, because you and I have been engaged in a discussion since long before our first encounter, our 'fireside dialogue' can be more accurately described as continuing rather than as having started at a specific moment. This idea fascinates me because of its apparent connection with the Buddhist doctrine of life extending from the past and continuing into the future. Though from a slightly different angle, Socrates subtly expresses the same thing in the Platonic dialogue *Meno*. Furthermore, Buddhism teaches that, far from mere coincidence, meetings in this life emerge from profound causes in past worlds.

For instance, in the twenty-seventh chapter of the Lotus Sutra, Shakyamuni introduces the story of King Wonderful Adornment, his wife Pure Virtue and his two sons Pure Storehouse and Pure Eye. The queen and the two princes, who are devout Buddhists, lead the king to become a believer, too. In his *Words and Phrases of the Lotus Sutra*, the founder of Tiantai Buddhism, Zhiyi (538–597; known as Great Master Tiantai) explains the story in the following way. In past existences, all four of these people were engaged in Buddhist discipline. But, to enable his companions to devote themselves fully to their study, one of them cooked and performed all other essential, menial tasks. With his support, the other three completed their training. The merit the fourth acquired by helping his companions enabled him to be reborn as King Wonderful Adornment. The other three were reborn as his wife and sons, who recompensed his former services by doing all they could to lead the king to belief in Buddhism.

I find it pleasant to think of our first meeting in conjunction with this Buddhist approach toward life and human relations. At the time of our first encounter, you were still living under the, at least ostensibly, atheistic Soviet system. Nonetheless, you demonstrated maximum understanding of Soka Gakkai ideals and activities. Our coming together and engaging in dialogue was too fateful an occurrence to be dismissed as mere coincidence. When we met in Luxembourg, you described our relation as true friendship. As someone has aptly remarked, true friendship means never being misunderstood no matter what one says. This definition hits the mark. True friendship is based on mutual trust and perfect congruence of opinions that eliminate the possibility of misunderstanding and antagonism and are the basic condition for error-free dialogue. Behind the marvellous feeling of true friendship that struck a chord in my soul at our first encounter I sense a karmic cause-effect relation.

AITMATOV: Mutual understanding supplies the meaning of any dialogue. It is sad to have to attend, even worse to take part in, conversations between people who are deaf to each other. Such deafness arises when one partner fails to consider what the other's words really mean. Understanding requires knowledge of the other's historical background.

The great classical Indian poet Ghalib (1797–1869) seems to have expressed profound knowledge of the meanings behind the words when he said: 'If they look at the lining, people will see the braided golden threads on the underside of my words' tattered garb.'

It is highly instructive that the Indian philosopher Abul Kalam Azad (1888–1958) quotes these verses in a letter to a worthy friend, a letter written from prison. Azad's commentary on the letter is as interesting as the letter itself.

> When I am free, my prison habits – constant self-control and
> self-analysis – will not change. My mind has no desire to be
> liberated from captivity to thought; my heart has no wish
> to abandon an abode graced with the ornaments of
> recollection. I was not made to be the soul of society, but
> I am proud that I have never abandoned my friends: part of
> my heart belongs to them.[8]

A person cherishes the hope of being accurately understood when he has grounds for thinking that he himself will not be abandoned by his friends, that a part of their hearts belongs to him. Truly heart-to-heart relations make words unnecessary.

IKEDA: Certainly this is the case among trusting and trusted friends. But on the political level, unfortunately, at least in current conditions, bargaining tactics assume primary importance, for, as Goethe wisely pointed out, political power lies in action, not in speech-making. Such Machiavellian conditions leave no room for implication or the emergence of merits like those of friendship.

AITMATOV: In general, that may be so. But today the interests of various nations are too mutually interconnected and depend too much on the same conditions to permit cunning. We need each other. We are indispensable to each other.

New thinking, which I hope is slowly but surely making a place for itself in our complicated world, requires sincere, honest language because, today as never before, humanity is more keenly aware of universal liberty as a gift of nature and the highest, general human value. Just as we in the former Soviet Union must now restore to its full rights a natural environment subjected to the malicious will of our social system, so, step by step, we must conform our language with our thoughts and with the interests of lucidity and justice.

For thousands of years, nature has been the hostage of human power-lust, oppression of one human by another domination of one nation by another and the division of people into slaves and masters. Human history has been justly called the history of the struggle for liberty. If this is true, the way out of the impasse in which contemporary civilisation finds itself is to learn to think in a new way and to express ourselves in the language of freedom and truth, a language understood by everyone. Such a language is a pledge of the solidarity of people of good will, a unity necessary at all times and especially today.

However, this does not mean, that truth in art or life can be attained easily. According to Dostoyevsky, one spoken word inspired by a passion for veracity can indeed express truth. When we say something in ordinary intercourse, we can modify or even disclaim it later. In literature, the hero cannot revoke a word once it has been uttered. Alexandre Dumas *père* said, 'God dictates, and I write.' All literary artists want this to be true. But God does not dictate to just everybody. Perhaps this is why we write so obscurely and vaguely today. We write that way because we live that way. Our words do not radiate the light of God.

IKEDA: As might be expected from a supporter of President Gorbachev's diplomatic philosophy, your words reverberate with a new idealism. Different from the pronouncements of what might be called the veteran diplomats – less flatteringly, the wily old foxes of the Metternich school – what you say inspires a feeling of warm humanism. The fresh approaches of John F. Kennedy in his day and later of Mikhail S. Gorbachev brought politics into agreeable prominence for the peoples of their two nations. The idealism of neither man went unopposed. As you know from having been at the very heart of events, Gorbachev encountered difficulties and frustrations. Kennedy did, too.

Scheming is often the order of the day in the world of politics. In spite of the smears and stains inherent in the field, I hope you will continue trying to bring political reality closer to the ideal state in which it is possible to express ourselves 'in the language of freedom and truth, a language understood by everyone'.

I am afraid that the frantic activity of the past few years may have tired you. In a society where, as you say, the value of the word had dropped drastically, it is only a few steps from weariness to despair and distrust of verbal communication. As my cherished friend, I hope you will continue fighting tirelessly for the sake of humanity. Without the 'one word' that

Dostoyevsky said can express truth, your sensitive soul may be easily wounded by the very emptiness of the plethora of words carelessly tossed around in society today. With that 'one word', however, you will be able to continue the struggle courageously.

Tiantai said the ultimate principle at first had no name. But the Sage (the Buddha) saw this principle and, when giving names to all things, finding the law of the simultaneity of cause and effect, named that principle the Lotus of the Mystic Law (*Myōhō Renge* in Japanese). The state in which the ultimate principle had no name indicates the chaotic, fertile state before things were verbalised. As I have said, Oriental philosophy, especially Mahayana Buddhism, is extremely cautious of fixing things by means of words.

This is not to say, however, that there is no single word that controls, or penetrates, the world of chaos and fertility. In this instance, the word takes the form of a verbal expression, the Lotus of the Mystic Law, that vitalises the infinitely diverse world of implicit meanings. To use an old Eastern illustration, this verbal statement adds the final touch, the enlivening eye, to the painted dragon, thus establishing exquisite harmony and balance. At one moment of incandescent tension, the verbal statement, the one word, suddenly concentrates all actions and thoughts in a single point. The spinning top suddenly stands still. For Descartes, *Cogito ergo sum* was just such a concentrating, illuminating verbal statement.

Humanity and Non-human Nature

IKEDA: In a speech at the United Nations, then President Gorbachev stressed the importance of environmental conservation measures. Your own writings, too, emphasise the importance of ecological balance. I vividly remember your plaintive yet impassioned indictment of blatant human arrogance in *Executioner's Block*, in which certain provincial officials organised technically sophisticated hunts of the Eurasian antelope called *saiga* in order to compensate for shortfalls in their meat-packing enterprise.

Tsunesaburo Makiguchi, first president of Soka Gakkai, was a great educational philosopher and a famous geographer. His book *A Geography of Human Life* is highly regarded as an outstanding and original treatment of the unity of man and nature and the influence the world of nature exerts on the human spirit and lifestyle. In his discussion of nature and human psychological development, he says that contact with plants cultivates a sense of beauty, suppresses violence and encourages generous sentiments.

Similarly, relations with animals and with such natural features as rivers and streams help manifest affection, courage and sensitivity to beauty. According to Makiguchi, experiencing the mystical activities of the natural world develops artistic sensitivity, ignites passion for truth, opens the eye of the mind and cultivates faith.

Throughout the whole ecological system, the magnificent force of life maintains a delicate balance within immense complexity. Although no more than a single factor in the system, human beings have deluded themselves into believing they are the lords of it all. Using the powers of science, man is now destroying the system of which he is a part, thus simultaneously spitting in the face of heaven and imperiling his own continued existence.

Not limited to the industrialised nations, environmental pollution is global. Once destroyed, the natural environment will take a long time to restore itself, if, indeed, full restoration is possible. For the sake of all-important environmental conservation measures, we must pool the wisdom of peoples everywhere to study the issue and propose concrete solutions. As the best place for such debate, I propose the creation of the Environmental United Nations. In order to prevent its recurrence, we must impartially and thoroughly examine the attitudes that have led to the current predicament.

Two anthropocentric attitudes constitute the background against which developing modern science has polluted the environment. First is the optimistic belief that nature exists for human beings to conquer and that, no matter how seriously it is damaged, the environment can always restore itself. Second is the conviction that man is lord of creation and monarch of the universe. In contrast to these fundamentally Christian approaches, Oriental philosophy is based on discovering ways to promote harmonious coexistence between humanity and nature.

The Buddhist doctrine of ecological harmony, known in Japanese as *eshō-funi*, teaches that the environment (*ehō*) and the entity living and acting in it (*shōhō*) are inseparably one (*funi*). Today, much of humanity ignores the principle of *eshō-funi*. The time has come to revolutionise the awareness of each individual to its truth and to the inexorableness of its operations.

Boundless human greed is at the heart of the anthropocentrism that has encouraged environmental pollution. In spite of the wealth modern Western civilisation has generated, the greed behind it has erupted like magma, destroying inner human life and polluting the external environment. Nuclear weapons are the extreme manifestation of this condition.

The human mind is the key to resolving the environmental issue. To solve the problem, we must think less in terms of environmental conservation and more in terms of revolutionising our attitudes and bridling rampant greed. Goethe told us that, if we seek our inner selves, we will find everything.

Revolutionising humanity itself on the basis of these Buddhist ideas can effect a shift from the domination–submission mode that has prevailed in man–nature relations in favour of harmonious coexistence. This, in turn, will both prevent environmental pollution and enrich our inner lives.

AITMATOV: Beyond this complex formulation of the theme, we encounter once again the global question of continued existence. Is the body, to put it crudely, of the planet big enough to satisfy the demands of human beings, the most voracious and pernicious of creatures? Or is human life threatened by complete bankruptcy and destruction in the madness of a universal catastrophe?

The Aral Sea, in Turkistan, was the sea of my childhood. I witnessed its conversion into a salt, grey desert. I first saw the Aral in April 1935, as a seven-year-old boy. Our family was travelling to Moscow, where Father was studying, and our train passed the sea. My first sight of it was unforgettable. Its waters splashed against the very railroad bed. Endless as the steppe, it was enlivened by sailboats and small steamships plying their ways here and there far from the shore. At a station near the water's edge, people sold bundles of golden smoked fish. Thereafter, for years, each passing of the Aral Sea was an exciting occasion. Such a great body of water in the midst of a limitless arid steppe is surely a natural wonder. Not long ago, I used these impressions in a story called *The White Cloud of Genghis-Khan*, from which I quote:

> Evening was approaching. The course of the Syr Darya gleamed a couple of times among the forest trees, as it snaked its way through the snowy lowlands. Soon, in the setting sun, the Aral Sea appeared in the middle of the steppe – first reedy bends, then a distant stretch of open water, then a small island. Before long, Abutalin saw waves crashing on the wet sand practically next to the train tracks. It was surprising to see in a single instance, snow, sand, seaside stones, blue windswept water and a herd of brown camels on a stony peninsula, all under a high heaven across which white clouds scudded.

I have heard that a Soviet space program once envisioned emergency catapulting of cosmonauts, in capsules, with the Aral Sea as the landing place. Given the condition of what was once a great body of water, you can imagine how horrified a cosmonaut today would be at the very notion. The water in the sea is nowhere deep enough to cushion his fall. He might as well be tossed out in the naked steppe.

What happened to the Aral Sea? Where did it go? Why are once seagoing ships beached high and dry on the former seabed as if trapped by encroaching dunes? What does all this mean, and what are the future consequences of the Aral catastrophe?

The trouble started long ago when dams and reservoirs were created along the Syr Darya and Amu Darya, the two largest rivers in Middle Asia. Their waters were diverted before they reached the Aral Sea to irrigate the world's most extensive cotton plantations, a monoculture of millions of hectares. By mercilessly exploiting nature and human labour, inordinate greed for profit sterilised a whole region and desiccated an entire sea, which, until then, fed by the combined Syr Darya and Amu Darya, had existed for millennia.

In spite of professed Utopian aims, human rapacity produced summer skies darkened by sandstorms whipped up by salt-laden winds blowing from the dry seabed. Along with this have come illness, epidemics, destruction of culture and traditions, hunger, poverty and persistent high infant mortality among the Asiatic populations.

The lamentable fate of the Aral Sea is only one episode in the history of the planet. How much similar evil have human hands wrought on Earth?

IKEDA: The loss of the Aral Sea, the fourth largest saltwater lake in the world, is an environmental disaster comparable in scale to Chernobyl. As a consequence of violence perpetrated by human instinct, a great body of water has all but disappeared. More disastrous still is the way in which deliberate, planned processes created an ethical environment where such things are possible. The intentions of the responsible Soviet planners may have been good, but their actions represent human egoism, which, as the crisis of the Aral Sea demonstrates, can have catastrophic effects.

Obviously the plan to divert the waters of the Syr Darya and Amu Darya rivers to irrigate an immense cotton-plantation was based on the Marxist doctrine that the value of a product is determined by the amount of labour that goes into its production. This idea deals not with the immensely diverse human labour of actuality, however, but with abstract, quantified labour. Sanctifying this concept into an absolute has caused great grief.

As Russian intellectuals S. Braginsky and Vitaly Shvidko wryly point out that, in the case of the Aral Sea, all other economic considerations, including land and natural resources, were relegated to second rank, behind the sacrosanct value of labour. Given such an approach to the issue, it is scarcely surprising that, after the collapse of the socialist system, environmental pollution in the states of the former Soviet Union turned out to exceed the gloomiest prognostications. Arrogant, ignorant authorities operated under the delusion that, since labour value can be objectively measured in terms of work hours, their economic plans had to determine the amount of labour value to be invested in each field. This was a fatal mistake. Nonetheless, the authorities not only entertained, but actually implemented these erroneous notions. In zealously and obdurately pursuing the Aral cotton-fields project, they completely ignored local environmental pollution. Neither they nor Soviet society in general considered the environment worth worrying about.

The idea of the absolute value of labour arises from mistaken anthropocentrism assuming the non-human natural world to be no more than an exploitable object on which human beings are entitled to operate unilaterally and at will. In such a philosophical climate, the idea of symbiosis is beside the point. Today, mistaken anthropocentrism is less all-pervading than it was when the Aral project was going ahead full steam. As you ask, 'Is the body of the planet big enough to satisfy the demands of human beings, the most voracious and pernicious of creatures?'

Rectifying mistaken anthropocentrism demands a revolution in our way of thinking and a proper ordering of our inner worlds because, sometimes, theoretically justified egoism can operate more savagely than the egoism of naked instinct. As Gandhi said, 'Rationalists are admirable beings, rationalism is a hideous monster when it claims for itself omnipotence.'[9]

AITMATOV: People began thinking about this problem long ago. A remarkable story, preserved today in Kirghiz epic culture, might serve to edify posterity in this connection. The tale, which relates the experiences of a young hunter named Kozhotash, is an ancient one intended to be recited before an audience. Its contents may be summarised as follows. The bold young hunter Kozhotash always returns from the mountains with rich catches of both grazing and fur-bearing animals, which he shares with his whole tribe. Generous to his fellow humans, he is a merciless hunter. But fate stalks him.

Once, he crosses a mountain pass to compete for the hand of a maiden. Some of his fellow tribesmen go along, bearing rich gifts of pelts – fox, marten, sable and snow leopard. The furs are spread out before the matchmakers, while the local bard sings the praises of the prospective groom – his strength, his keen eye, his speed in running. He can chase down a mountain goat and is strong enough to wrestle a snow leopard. He was born under a star of success. He defeats all competitors in free-for-all matches. The delighted matchmakers select him to marry the maiden and set the wedding date for the following autumn, after harvest. Kozhotash returns home triumphant.

But on his way, a magpie, starting from some bushes, flies overhead, chattering irritatingly and warning Kozhotash of coming trouble. It tells him of the danger of being intoxicated with his own glory and foresees that no wedding will take place. The hunter will take no bride. Kozhotash scoffs at the warning, which he finds ridiculous. How could a chatterbox of a magpie know anything? No doubt, the bird was put up to all this gossip by whispering, jealous people.

Back in his mountains, Kozhotash enjoys his old power and success. All winter, he hunts mountain goats, feeds his tribe and collects furs as new gifts for the impending wedding. Spring comes, then autumn. And one evening, Kozhotash accidentally witnesses a marten wedding.

In the quiet, moonlit night, the creatures emerge on a riverbank, forming a procession to accompany the bride-marten. According to some hunters, martens when in heat, conduct themselves almost like human beings, arranging weddings and processions to accompany them. This, it seems, is the best time to hunt them, because, engaged in these activities, they drop their customary guard. The martens dance around the supremely beautiful, sparkling-eyed bride. From the opposite direction appears another procession accompanying the groom-marten. After the two groups meld, the animals whirl about, singing.

Kozhotash admires the beauty of the bride-marten and is amazed by the animals' incautiousness. But, suddenly remembering that he needs still more costly presents for his own forthcoming wedding, he precipitately throws his fur coat over the engrossed martens, crushing and smothering them all.

The climax of the tale occurs somewhat later. During the following winter, Kozhotash decimates an entire local flock of goats, head by head, until only the great mother grey goat Sur Echki and her consort Sur Teke remain. The hunter pursues them, too. Having driven the animals up a mountain, Kozhotash draws his bow. Sur Echki implores him to spare Sur Teke so that their line may not be extinguished. Unheeding, Kozhotash lets fly. His keen shot hits its mark. The grey ram falls dead at the feet of Sur Echki, who curses the hunter for having destroyed their line. From the mountainside, she cries, 'You have slain our father and have put an end to our line. From this moment, a curse will light on your head. From this instant, you will never bag another animal. Shoot at me, a single, lonely, grey goat. I won't budge. But you'll miss.'

Kozhotash's contemptuous laugh shakes stones from the mountain. He takes aim. The arrow flies from his bow. It misses. He aims a second time and misses again. And yet a third time. Then, shouting out 'Now try to catch me!' the grey goat starts off, limping on one leg in pretended lameness. The hunter dashes after her, confident of catching up with this audacious goat in two leaps. But every time he draws near, the apparently lame Sur Echki manages to bound away and put distance between them. The chase lasts until evening. In the heat of pursuit, Kozhotash fails to notice that the goat is luring him deeper and deeper into mountains. Finally, he finds himself on a narrow ledge overlooking a chasm with unscalable sheer cliffs around him.

In a human voice reverberating like thunder throughout the mountains, Sur Echki, cries, 'This is the punishment for your cruelty to wild animals. You are cursed to bewail your fate until the last moment of your life, just as I bewail my dead children.'

Fellow tribesmen gather at the base of the cliff, and, to them, Kozhotash addresses a lament, famous in Kirghiz literature. He grieves for the animals he has treated cruelly, over his own fate, and over the fiancé with whom he will never be united.

Prepared to fall at her feet in entreaty for her prospective husband, the maiden herself travels into the mountains in pursuit of Sur Echki. She searches for centuries without finding the grey goat. But once, wandering through the mountains she, too, encounters a marriage of martens. By moonlight, the animals form a procession to accompany a bride-marten with eyes glittering like diamonds. Dropping to her knees, the human maiden bewails the impossibility of her ever knowing the happiness the bride-marten is experiencing.

IKEDA: I remember being deeply moved by that story when you first told it to me on a refreshing spring evening in May 1991, in the Soviet embassy in Luxembourg. Folklore teaches many valuable lessons. The numerous instances in which you make use of folkloric themes in your own writing signify your unjaded youthfulness and vigour. In return for your story of the hunter, I should like to share with you the story of the Crane Bride, a favourite example of Japanese folklore.

Karoku and his aged mother live together in a mountain village. He chars charcoal for a living. One winter, on his way to town to buy bedding, he comes across a crane caught in a trap. After releasing it, he seeks out the trapper and, with the bedding money, buys the bird and frees it. Back in their cold house that evening, he relates his action to his mother, who merely replies, 'Well, you've done it now. And I'm sure it was the right thing to do.'

The very next evening, a beautiful woman appears at Karoku's house, asking for a night's shelter. Though he tries to excuse himself on the grounds that his home is far too humble, the woman insists. Karoku gives in. Next the woman asks him to marry her. He says that he and his mother live from hand to mouth, and that he is unworthy to marry such a splendid person. Once again, the woman insists, this time with support from the mother. Karoku does as requested.

One day, the woman asks Karoku to shut her up in a closet for three days and under no circumstances to open the door. On the fourth day, she emerges. The other two express their sympathy for the hardships they imagine she has suffered and urge her to eat. But presenting them with a bolt of cloth, she says, 'Karoku, Karoku, I wove this while I was in the closet. Take it to town and sell it for two thousand *ryo*.'

Karoku takes the fabric to the mansion of the local lord, who is so delighted by its superior quality that he says he will pay two or even three thousand *ryo* provided he can have another bolt. Karoku says he must ask his wife, but the lord dismisses this as unnecessary and offers to pay at once.

At home, Karoku's wife says she will weave another length if given enough time to do it in. She must remain in the closet a week; and, as before, no one must spy on her.

By the end of the week, Karoku is so worried and so consumed with curiosity that he cracks the closet door to find inside a plumeless crane weaving cloth from her own down. The work is just about finished, and the bird says, 'Here is the cloth. But, now that you've seen me in this condition, you can't love me any more. I must go away. Before I go, though, I must tell you that I am the crane you set free that day. Now, take this cloth to the lord, as you promised.' Saying nothing else, the crane turns westward to be greeted by a thousand others, who fly away with her.

Both of our stories reveal the consequences of unbridled greed and the retaliation nature takes for it. In your stronger story, it leads to the young hunter's downfall. In the Japanese tale, greed makes Karoku rich but at the cost of losing a beautiful wife. Several Japanese writers have been inspired by this story, and a fine modern play has been written on the theme. Unfortunately, people today lack the sensitivity to detect the reality in folklore or to allow it to stimulate their imaginative powers.

AITMATOV: This immediately brings to mind one of Gauguin's striking Tahitian paintings of lovely, graceful, ochre-coloured women. Each line expresses self-contemplation, thought and silent questioning as to who we are, where we come from and where we are going. Patently, the only answers the pictures provide are the rustling of the palms and the soft murmur of sea expanses. The painting seems to be saying, 'Listen, guess and understand.' This implied message illuminates it with a bright sadness that leads to no despondency.

Who among our contemporary city-dwellers, our asphalt children, could fail to envy the peace and harmony of Gauguin's unending, immortal Paradise, where apparently primordial people sense their own happiness without artificial effort of any kind?

Of course, in this case the word *happiness* has a distinctive ring. It is neither as mono-semantic nor as flat as it sounds to us. We can scarcely know the blessed self-absorption of these people, absorption in the eternal, at the heart of which, in the words of the religious philosopher Vasily Rozanov (1856–1919), there is no evil. We all sometimes dream of life on such a paradisic island. I am afraid, however, that today the paradise survives only in Gauguin's wonderful paintings. Even in his own day, as he wrote bitterly, Tahiti was being favoured with the generosities of merciless, so-called civilisation.

Alas, we live in a world entirely different from the one known in the times of the Latin poet Lucretius (*c.* 99–55 BC). In his preface to *De rerum natura*, Einstein says that Lucretius' book is enchanting to a person not totally absorbed in the spirit of our own times, a person who can observe his contemporaries from the sidelines and evaluate their spiritual perceptions. It teaches us how the world looked to a vigorous, thinking man, interested in natural science but without knowledge of the achievements of modern science imparted to us in childhood, when we are incapable of opposing them. In another preface, this time to Newton's *Opticks*, Einstein said that the great English scientist combined in himself the theorist, the mechanic and the artist in exposition. In these two prefaces, Einstein sets forth what he considers essential conditions for the ability to derive happiness from the perception of primordial nature: childlike spontaneity, plenty of time and peace. For many of us today, these conditions represent unattainable luxury.

IKEDA: Used exclusively as the slave and means of satisfying human greed, modern science dissects the world of nature. In this process, some scientists have merely followed in the wake; others have been believers in the logical innocence of science. Einstein was most unusual in consistently placing science within a total human *Weltanschauung*. The following quotation gives an excellent idea of his religious views of the world and the universe:

> But whoever has undergone the intense experience of successful advances made in this domain, is moved by the profound reverence for the rationality made manifest in existence. By way of the understanding he achieves a far reaching emancipation from the shackles of personal hopes and desires, and thereby attains that humble attitude of mind toward the grandeur of reason, incarnate in existence, and which, in its profoundest depths, is inaccessible to man. This attitude, however, appears to me to be religious in the highest sense of the word.[10]

As you imply, this view of the world and the universe is intimate and closer to childlike spontaneity than to worldly-wise adult attitudes. The adults in Steven Spielberg's motion picture *E.T.* found their extra-terrestrial visitor weird and frightening. The children welcomed him as a charming friend. This seems to me in keeping with Einstein's words, 'Happy childhood of science!'

Although Isaac Newton never doubted for a moment that his own scientific discoveries demonstrated the providence of God, today modern science has departed far enough from its happy childhood to have spawned the evil of nuclear weapons. Perhaps this is why, in his late years, Einstein said, 'If I were a young man again and had to decide how to make a living, I would not try to become a scientist or scholar or teacher. I would rather choose to be a plumber or a peddler.'[11] Although pessimism never got the better of his gentle humour, Einstein did come to sense the ageing and decline of the age of science. But whatever pessimism this awareness inspired only stimulated his already intense pacifism and cosmopolitanism.

AITMATOV: How much longer will, or can, nature tolerate human imperialism? This question haunts me. Are we children of nature, as we like to call ourselves? Or are we creatures of uncertain descent, cast on Earth to perform diabolical experiments with our own hands? How do we explain the degree of the mindless cruelty within us? Is there a limit to it? And how will it end? In self-destruction?

What words can be used to express the nightmares of Hiroshima or of Chernobyl and the mutations, two-headed calves and so on, generated by nuclear pollution? Perhaps, in centuries to come, if we do not destroy the human race before then, our descendants will use a language of myth in speaking of this horror that has descended on humanity, a disaster analogous with the Flood, which, according to the Bible, covered the Earth as God's punishment for human sins.

IKEDA: Buddhists presuppose no external force or action, like the love or wrath of God. Buddhist philosophy is based on the idea that all things in the human and non-human natural worlds occur because of causal origination. A and B come into being in mutual dependence: neither can exist without the other. A occurs because of B, and B because of A. The outcome is a symbiosis in which relationship takes precedence over individuality.

In human affairs, too, unilateral action, wrathful or affectionate, on the part of a Creator God is unthinkable. Buddhism rejects the very idea of a single, once-for-all Creation, like the one related in the Book of Genesis. Whatever happens to us is caused by our thoughts and deeds. We have no one to blame but ourselves.

AITMATOV: As I understand it, then, attempted justifications like 'Science demands sacrifices' are unacceptable to a Buddhist.

IKEDA: Totally. They are unthinkable because they put the blame on God, in the form of science. Since its foundation is symbiosis, Buddhism cannot accept the idea of sacrifices. The fundamental injunction against taking life, setting aside the vexed issue of the extent to which it must be strictly honoured, is literally the life-line of Buddhism. In contrast with Christian history, marked as it is by bloody wars of religion and the horrors of the Inquisition, Buddhist history is permeated with the spirit of taking no life.

Why should it be permissible to take someone's life for any reason at all? No acceptable reason exists. Even the unintentional taker of life is doomed to indelible shame and unforgivable, eternal suffering – death itself. This is why Buddhist teachings require utmost caution in dealings with nature and fundamentally forbid destruction, even fortuitous destruction, of the orderly harmony of the world. Even on a minor scale, such destruction can have limitless ramifications.

AITMATOV: A certain story by the American science-fiction writer Ray Bradbury (1920–) illustrates your meaning. It tells of irreversible changes that occur in all creation because one man accidentally treads on some small creature. Understandably, the idea hit me very hard. For centuries we have had inculcated into our heads our right to take, without requesting, whatever we want from the world of nature. But, in Bradbury's story, the whole universe changes because of one small creature's death. After reading the story, I could no longer regard life as I once had. I felt as if some new man were being born within me. But, in those days, who could have explained what was happening to me? Bradbury taught me a great deal, even if it was only to plant doubt in my heart. In this different frame of mind, I took a new view of a poem by the Russian poet Tyutchev:

> Nature is not what you think it is:
> it's not a mould, not a soulless face.
> It has a soul. It has freedom.
> It has love. It has tongue.[12]

I seemed to have been brought to life. Shame woke me, as if it pulled me out of a prejudiced existence indifferent to other forms of life and ignorant of the pain even inanimate things, like stones, may feel.

IKEDA: Sooner or later, this was bound to happen to you.

AITMATOV: Why?

IKEDA: For a number of reasons. First, it is in your blood. Essentially and because of your background, you are a child of the mountains and plains. As is strongly reflected in your literary style, you always think of nature and non-human animals as friends. The death of an animal kills something in your soul. Second, as must be true of an artist who, even unawares, seeks spiritual support, you realise the bond, the common enigma, binding you to your environment. This is the logic of art, supreme humanity.

AITMATOV: Perhaps our inability to seek a common language with nature causes our sense of unhappiness. Again, as Tyutchev says,

> They don't see and they are deaf,
> living in this world as if they were blind.
> Suns don't breathe for them.
> The ocean's waves possess no life.

Rays have never come down into their soul.
Spring has never blossomed in their breast.
Forests don't talk in their presence
And starry nights are dumb for them.[13]

Why do people in whom the gene for understanding beauty survives fail
to seek spiritual union with the world? Probably because it is easier not to.
When the day of trial comes, they will plead for leniency on the basis of
having been 'voluntarily deluded'. It is one thing to do evil without realising
it. Doing wrong and knowing it are another thing altogether. Unfortunately,
not rare in our world, behaviour of this kind is sometimes elevated to the
level of internal or external state politics. It occurs in relations with non-
human nature, created, according to one view, solely to satisfy our needs:
as long as it fulfills our requirements, we have no further interest in nature.
If this is true, seeking communality with it is folly. As soon as we try,
however, we discover that nature is fully capable of talking to us. And we
may also discover that reluctance to enter into a dialogue with it is suicidal.

Willful perpetrators of evil are terrified that the 'benighted' majority will
find them out. Deliberate evil-doers, be they originators of so-called 'Projects
of the Century' or simple chemical plant managers who dump poisonous
wastes into rivers, are fully aware of the criminal nature of their actions.
But their secret operational principle is, 'There's enough for our century;
après nous le déluge.' Such people are murdering the future. Perhaps they do
not care because they have no children of their own. Are we encountering
some kind of tragic, or I might say pathological, phenomenon today?

Perhaps, without our being aware of it, the euphoria of gradual triumph
over nature has made us so cruel that we take criminal misbehaviour of this
kind for granted. Maybe our interest in preserving the human race has
atrophied. Perhaps exhaustion and satiety with victories have sapped our
taste for life to the extent that we are ready to give up on the whole thing
as a bad job.

But who is *we?* Who can assume the right to make decisions for all
humanity? Who is qualified to drag mankind into the grave, whither, in
'their' opinion, humanity is willing to go? *We* are all those people who,
until recently, ignored the price we must pay for technological progress and
its concomitant conveniences and services. Did we renege on responsibility
for the future by closing our eyes to the costs of the fruits of contemporary
civilisation? I have in mind barbarous destruction of nature, theft of natural
resources and, worse still, the sacrificing and abandonment to misfortune

of all those people who, at the risk of their own lives, warned us about the inevitable end of our bacchanalian intoxication with our power over nature.

How do we extricate ourselves? The Buddha's injunction 'Do not take what does not belong to you, for it will perish' is likely to meet with angrily sarcastic demands for a definition of 'belonging'. I have no answer. And no one else will have one until each person and all humanity experience a need to understand the language of living nature. Once we experience this need, we will know what is required of us; that is, to moderate our demands.

We are gluttons. Nothing satisfies us. Everything is insufficient. But we must not devour everything; we must leave something for others. That is the way of the natural world, even among predators. The wolf does not pick the carcass to the bone. And we are, after all, human beings, not wolves. If we live according to human laws in effect for millennia, we will see how splendid the world around us is and will be solicitous of each other.

To achieve this end, must Christians and Muslims convert to Buddhism? No! Such conversion is not absolutely necessary. Understood correctly, all the religions of the world are founded on love, beauty and humane-ness. All can come together in the Environmental United Nations, the creation of which I wholeheartedly support.

IKEDA: As I have noticed before, you dwell on the idea of religious conversion. This is understandable. Religions all have their own teachings, but strictly monotheistic religions like Christianity and Islam often compel people to choose between conversion or death.

In *Time of Parting*, the Bulgarian writer Anton Donchev, whom I have already mentioned, depicts one instance in which, during the seventeenth century, the Ottoman Turks employed atrocious, crafty devices to force Bulgarian Christians to convert to Islam. Trampling human dignity underfoot in the name of religious dogmas in this way is impermissible.

Expressed simply, my own ideas on the subject are as follows. First, in connection with such global problems as nuclear arms and environmental pollution, religious conversion is a secondary matter. Of primary significance are a religion's views on humanity, nature and the universe. These are the things that determine attitudes and judgements on how to deal with the evils confronting our world. The Buddhist approach to such issues evolves from the doctrine of *eshō-funi*, which embodies concern for harmonious, symbiotic, mutually beneficial relations between humanity and non-human nature.

Whereas anthropocentric Christianity denies a spiritual existence to all non-human nature, Buddhism recognises the existence of life not only in animals and plants, but also in inanimate objects. The humanisms of the two religions cannot be discussed on the same level. The gap between them is illustrated by two famous, written passages. First, in the first chapter of the Book of Genesis, occurs the following:

> And God blessed them and God said unto them, Be fruitful, and multiply, and replenish the earth, and subdue it: and have dominion over the fish of the sea, and over the fowl of the air and over every living thing that moveth upon the earth.
>
> And God said Behold, I have given you every herb bearing seed, which [is] upon the face of all the earth, and every tree, in which [is] the fruit of tree yielding seed; to you it shall be for meat. (Genesis I:28–29)

Instead of affording humanity a unique position superior to non-human nature, the writings of the Chinese Buddhist priest Miaole (711–782) list many characteristics in which the former is said to correspond to the latter. Our nasal inhalation and exhalation are compared with winds blowing through valleys over mountain streams. Human oral inhalation and exhalation are likened to winds blowing through empty space. The eyes are compared with the sun and the moon, and their opening and closing to day and night. The hair of the head is said to correspond to the stars and planets; the eyebrows to the Big Dipper. The blood vessels are compared with rivers, the bones with jade or other stone, the skin and flesh with earth and body hair with thickets and groves. On the basis of these correspondences, Nichiren said, 'Hence it is perfectly clear that if heaven itself crumbles, then the body of the individual likewise will crumble; if the earth breaks asunder, the body of the individual too will break asunder; if the elements of earth, water, fire, wind, [and space] perish, the body of the individual too will perish.'[14]

The Christian view is that non-human nature is made up of subordinates intended to be dominated by human beings. According to Buddhist teachings, on the other hand, the non-human world of nature is a friend with whom we must live in harmony. This distinction must be kept in mind.

Buddhism has established itself widely in Japan. But the extent to which this has influenced Japanese environmental policies for the better is dubious. Of course, compound global pollution requires a multi-angle approach and cannot be dealt with on the basis of one nation's performance alone.

With all respect to your good intentions, I cannot agree with you when you say, 'Understood correctly, all the religions of the world evolved on a foundation of love, beauty and humane-ness.' I consider this viewpoint somewhat naïve. Developing the ability to discriminate among religions demands a Socratic examination of their good and bad aspects. Without this ability, one has difficulty dealing with extraordinary situations like the rise of Islamic fundamentalism.

The disaster of the Aral Sea occurred not because people misunderstood the theories of the value of labour set forth in the para-religious ideology of Communism but because they understood them correctly. The problem was in the theories themselves, not in the way they were interpreted. In such instances, there is small choice between religions and para-religions. Instead of thinking of conversion from one to another, in the case of a deliberative group like the Environmental United Nations, different religious groups must join other organisations in cooperative discussions representing diverse viewpoints.

The Nine Stages of Consciousness

IKEDA: In this last part of our inward journey, I should like to discuss briefly the Buddhist teaching of the Nine Consciousnesses, which deals with the various aspects by means of which human beings make discernments.

First come the five kinds of consciousness based on information provided by the sensory organs of sight, sound, smell, taste and touch. Lives confined to sensory information never rise above the level of plants and non-human animals. The sixth stage of consciousness involves the operations of the mind, reason and intellect, in comparing and making judgements on sensory information. Even though equipped with reason, we all experience powerful impulses rising from the depths of our being to distort rational judgements. We all feel uncontrollable emotions running counter to what our intellects know to be true. The energy for these desires, emotions and impulses exists in vortices in the realm of the seventh consciousness, known by the Sanskrit term *mano-vijñāna* and extending to the subconscious substratum of the reason and intellect. The depth-psychology identity substratum can be said to be located in the *mano-vijñāna*. Meshed with the substratum of the reason and the self, are obsessive subconscious power drives and egoistic emotions that, when given manifestation, upset the discernment operations of the other six consciousnesses.

In his search for the nucleus of self-awareness, Jung identified self-consciousness and, deeper still, the individual subconscious where all mental experiences, some remembered and some suppressed, are stored.

The *mano-vijñāna* corresponds closely to Jung's individual subconscious. Jumbled impulses sway a life lived under its domination, causing it to oscillate frantically between polarities like love and hate or creation and destruction.

Buddhism penetrates deeper than the *mano-vijñāna* to identify an eighth consciousness representing the eternal, ceaseless flow of the life entity and called the *ālaya-vijñāna*. The word *ālaya* means storehouse; that is, the place where the life-seeds from which all phenomena germinate are stored. Everything we have said, thought, or done and all human historical experiences, too, are stored in the *ālaya*, where they leave traces of themselves, just as a perfume lingers in garments. By germinating, the seeds stimulate succeeding life activities in an infinitely repetitive process. The harmonious entity of the individual self is latent in the fundamental life-current, where its characteristics are never lost and where it may be dyed either good or bad.

Still deeper than the personal unconscious, Jung located the collective unconscious, in the upper level of which are stored attitudes common to various ethnic groups. Below these, are things that gush forth from the core of the cosmos. And on the lowest level is a conglomerate of the experiences of all races. This idea is very close to the Buddhist stage of consciousness called the *ālaya-vijñāna*.

With its customary perspicacity, Buddhist philosophy discerns yet another stage of consciousness beyond the *ālaya-vijñāna*. This ninth, called the *amala-vijñāna*, sometimes referred to as the fundamental pure consciousness or the palace of the ninth consciousness, the unchanging reality that reigns over all of life's functions, is the source of everything in the universe and the ultimate entity of life itself. It transcends relative distinctions like good and bad and generates all other entities. It might be called 'universal consciousness' or 'universal life'. The person who perceives this fundamental entity experiences a limitless expansion of the self. He becomes capable of controlling his own desires and impulses and of using them creatively as springboards for the self-perfecting process that I call the human revolution.

Morality and ethics alone are impotent to solve the problem of war and conflict, which inevitably involve egoism. This is true because morality and ethics arise from the intellect and therefore advance no further than the sixth of the Buddhist stages of consciousness. The only way to overcome egoism is to go beyond impulses of desire and emotion and to establish one's self firmly in the realm of universal life.

AITMATOV: It is annoying that, in their daily lives, the majority of people never so much as glance in the mirror of their own essential natures. I find the ordered Buddhist system of the conscious and subconscious a convincing psychological analysis. For me, it is a splendid discovery, one that contemporary humanity must learn and assimilate. Civilisation today must embrace the most diverse teachings about humanity. Bringing East and West together geographically is impossible, but all regions can pool their wealth in one great, human personality. How are we to achieve this? Perhaps the time has come for the universities of the world to establish East-West faculties for the study of all available sciences and philosophies about humanity itself.

Against this background of the Buddhist teaching of nine kinds of consciousness and psychology, I am subconsciously moved to mention a particular theme related to mysticism, or more accurately put, to the poetry of the mystical world.

In old Russian villages, before they were ruined by the revolution, certain widows were referred to as star-women (*Svezdnista*). According to popular rumour, they could actually communicate with their dead husbands, who, it was said, visited them by night in the form of falling stars. Fellow villagers eagerly substantiated the story, claiming often to have seen flying stars drop into the chimney of widows' houses. The star-women themselves told of wonderful meetings with their deceased husbands, who came in the night as stars and departed at dawn. These women were unafraid of being ridiculed or, worse, being accused of having truck with unclean spirits through black magic. Enjoying general respect and far from reticent, they trustingly passed on greetings from the spirits and shared their impressions with people close to them. They described how peacefully and pleasantly their meetings went and what they thought and suffered. Their discussions with their dead husbands touched on domestic matters, the children, village troubles and so on. Often the talk imperceptibly changed into the singing together of favourite songs. To themselves and for themselves, they sang just as in waking – softly – so no one could hear.

In connections with phenomena of this kind, we must bear in mind the power of human longings, the pain separation causes and efforts to revive a formerly cherished way of life. Consciousness higher than the ordinary arises in the heart. It is neither traditional nor everyday and, in itself, testifies to limitless possibilities for the transformation of the soul.

It is extremely curious to notice that something very much like the Russian star-women is to be found in Kirghiz mythology; that is, in a completely different geographical zone and cultural environment. The narratives follow generally similar lines, with a few minor differences. In the Kirghiz version, the longed-for stars fall, not into a chimney, but into the open-domed top of the yurt, or tent. At evening, the widow opens the top and leaves it open in the hope of a visit from a spirit-star. When he arrives, the visiting Kirghiz husband tells his wife to fetch both their saddles. Then, in the light of the moon, they saddle up their horses, staked nearby, and, as in times past, ride around the neighbouring fields, first at a muffled walk, then at a trot and finally at full gallop. Without making a sound, they fly away, birdlike, skimming the surface of the Earth. When dawn approaches, they return, unsaddle their sweating horses and put the saddles away in the accustomed places. Then the spirit-star disappears. Later, the wife displays the sweaty saddle cloths as proof that she and her star-husband spent the night riding horseback.

All of this brings to mind the limitless possibilities for transforming human consciousness, including such new phenomena of the post-industrial epoch as artificial intelligence.

IKEDA: Contemporary commonsense dismisses romantic stories of this kind as superstition. However, as the French philosopher Henri Bergson emphatically pointed out, this attitude is narrow and mistaken. In 1913, he was invited to chair and address a meeting of the Society for Psychic Research in London. In his message, criticising some prejudiced scientists for despising psychic studies, he said that people who rejected the efforts of the society in 'the name of science' were actually only semi-scholars. Then, as an example of this, he related the criticism a famous medical doctor had heaped on a certain psychic phenomenon.

The critical doctor is reported to have said something like this:

I find everything you say extremely interesting. But you must reflect before drawing any conclusions. I know of an abnormal occurrence, the truth of which I am prepared to guarantee because it was related to me by a highly intelligent lady whose words I trust absolutely. Her husband was a military officer killed in a certain battle. Just at the moment when he fell, his wife saw the whole scene in a vision that corresponded to actuality in all points. You probably would draw the same conclusion that the wife herself reached; that is, that some kind of clairvoyance or telepathy was involved. But you would be forget-ting one thing. Many wives dream of the deaths of husbands who are actually perfectly well. Attention is paid to the visions only when they

are accurate; otherwise, they are disregarded. Put clearly, you can see
that the correspondence is pure coincidence.[15]

Thus the doctor dismissed the wife's vision as strange, but coincidental.
Bergson, on the other hand, pointed out that the wife had given concrete
details of place, time and companions, which the doctor ignored. He criticised
the doctor for giving precedence to abstractions and references to laws of
probability over the wife's exact description. No matter how improbable,
the irrefutable facts are that the wife described a scene like the one that
took place when her husband died in battle and, in the vision, saw it at the
time when it actually occurred. No artist can reproduce graphically and
exactly a battle scene he has not witnessed. Similarly, the wife should have
been unable to relate the scene of her husband's death with exactitude. To
do what she did, she must have perceived the scene or something must have
somehow connected her awareness with it.

Bergson was correct. Given the existence of the vast time–space world
of the subconscious, the wife's experience was in no way strange. Rejection
of experiences like hers as abnormal or superstitious only reveals the spiritual
poverty of the rejecters. Ingenuousness and a feel for the universal are
essential to an accurate evaluation of such perceptions as hers and to the
appreciation of folklore like the Russian and Kirghiz stories you mention.
Sadly, today these qualities are steadily being eroded. Of course, in saying
this, I do not imply approval of passing fads for the occult.

AITMATOV: The thing that inspires me most about Buddhism as a philosophy
of life, is the way its teachings emphasise the responsibility of the human
being as an individual with unique values. They seem to say, 'Don't rely
on, don't hide behind, the Creator. You are the master of your own fate.
The quality of the life around you and of the whole world depends on how
you manage your destiny. You are your own judge.' There is no passing of
the buck. The individual must shoulder the heavy responsibility himself. It
is a great thing for a person to know he depends on no external will, neither
of concrete government nor of abstract deity.

The nine stages of consciousness are landmarks on the road to eternity,
passing consciously from one age to another, demanding both all-out spiritual
exertion and, accordingly, special behaviour at the new stage of existence.

Chekhov said, 'The desire to serve the general good absolutely must be
a need of the soul, a condition of one's own happiness.' I do not know at
what stage of understanding this need arises in the thinking man. No doubt,

its advent necessitates reviewing the past and ruthlessly reappraising one's values. Too many people refuse to grow up and face this soul-shaking experience. Their lives seem to have stopped in their salad days. They live, or think they live, by fleeing from problems until, in old age, they suddenly see it has all been in vain. This is a dreadful experience.

IKEDA: You have made some profoundly interesting remarks on the culture of thought and emotion. What essentially is it?

AITMATOV: Professor Luigi Volpicelli said that, according to an old definition, culture is everything remaining when one has forgotten what one has learned. Our own culture is everything from the human heritage of ideas that has become our own, that has melded with our personalities in everyday life. Knowledge attained only by way of communication remains dead. Though we can repeat it on demand, it is only dictionary or textbook knowledge. The sole, truly living knowledge is what exists in our profoundest personal manifestations and reflects our own significance and value.

IKEDA: That is quite right. This conception of culture has much in common with the Buddhist teachings of the *mano* and *ālaya* consciousnesses. Of course, unless we have learned and accumulated a great deal, we have nothing to forget.

AITMATOV: At the risk of yet another quotation, I know no better thoughts on culture than those expressed by Albert Einstein:

> What, precisely, is 'thinking'? When, on the reception of sense impressions, memory pictures emerge, this is not yet 'thinking'. And, when such pictures form sequences, each member of which calls forth another, this, too, is not yet 'thinking'. When, however, a certain picture turns up in many such sequences, then, precisely by such return, it becomes an organising element for such sequences in themselves unrelated to each other. Such an element becomes a tool, a concept. I think that the transition from free association or 'dreaming' to thinking is characterised by the more or less pre-eminent role played by the concept.[16]

What conclusion did Einstein draw for himself from this? He said that, for him, the history of physics was a drama of ideas. He approached his own life with the same criterion: 'The important thing in the life of a person of my cast of mind is what and how he thinks, not what he does or experiences.' Obviously for Einstein the scientist, thinking was a profession.

IKEDA: His personal disposition meant that Einstein the scientist was a philosopher, too. But philosophy is not the monopoly of the especially talented; it belongs to everyone. It is, therefore, a bad idea to repudiate one's duty by leaving thinking up to specialists like Einstein. Performed consciously or not, such repudiation amounts to a rejection of one's own fate and of one's responsibility before all humanity. Such a thing is unacceptable to a Buddhist.

AITMATOV: Or to anyone whose self-respect survives.

I have mentioned infantilism as a means of survival in the Soviet Union, where one was allowed to think only what was permitted to one's position. An unwritten, though strict, subordination governed everything. Meddling in matters that did not concern you could get you hanged. It is not surprising that people used to remark bitterly, 'I think differently, but I agree with myself.' In order not to say too much accidentally, people muffled and drove from their conscious minds what were called 'seditious' thoughts. To avoid upsetting those people whose positions obliged them to be omniscient, everyone was low-key and eager to remain inconspicuous. In the field of science, the Procrustean bed was used with immensely greater ferocity and refinement than elsewhere. Some observers have supposed that Soviet citizens enjoyed freedoms that were kept secret. Even if this were true, concealed freedoms are a cruel nightmare, a curse.

For an artist, his art is the pathway to freedom, in spite of everything. For its sake, he is ready to plumb the nine stages of consciousness or penetrate the nine circles of hell.

IKEDA: An ideology that treated freedom as rubbish spawned the tragic situation you describe. Its adherents adopted as their golden rule the idea that existence determines consciousness, and not the other way around. As long as this thesis obtains, consciousness is confined to perceptual existence, which, in the Soviet Union, was equated with production power and method, the reformation of which was accorded supreme importance. Everything else was superstructure of secondary or even tertiary importance. In such a philosophical atmosphere, spiritual liberty cannot exist; even affording it consideration is forbidden. In this respect, Soviet ideology smacked strongly of medieval Christian theology. Your frequent references to it, and the curse it brought, indicate the extent to which it permeated all aspects of Soviet life.

Buddhism makes no discriminations among people on the basis of things like occupation. It affords the same consideration to the artist and the ordinary man on the street. Fundamentally, Buddhists believe that actions, not status, differentiate human beings. The characters in your stories and novels are ordinary people, yet you describe them and their experiences in refreshingly epic language. Actually, of course, epic poetry by nature should sing the deeds of the ordinary people, but contemporary humanity has lost the epic-poetical spirit. The loss is immense.

AITMATOV: In the words of the French aviator and writer Antoine de Saint-Exupéry (1900–44), the peasant thinks with the plough. Can we translate the thought of a peasant into our daily language? Without so much as suspecting it, the peasant's forebears have thought with the plough for millennia. In the words of the German statesman and philologist Karl Wilhelm Von Humboldt (1767–1835), a peasant thinks in the highest thought, assimilating his own thinking to that of humanity as a whole. History speaks in him because he has preserved the proto-language with which he unceremoniously communicates with nature. This proto-language is, in fact, part of nature. I dare say the peasant is a truly happy man. Like Isaac Newton (1642–1727), for whom nature was an open book to be read effortlessly.

But does the peasant know he is happy? That is a question our pragmatic age asks. Jealous, because doomed to an unhappy state, we can neither believe nor admit that a person can be happy ingenuously and disinterestedly. Encounters with such a phenomenon stimulate protest within us: that cannot be. What kind of happiness is that? But these queries reflect only our own egoism. And, what is worse, egoism becomes arrogance when we find merit only in our own sufferings and display our sores to the world as proof of our own virtue.

IKEDA: The fulfilled person gives no thought to being fulfilled. We concern ourselves with fulfillment only when we lack something. The same is true of happiness. A certain classical philosopher said that the frequency with which we use a word is in inverse proportion to the frequency with which the thing signified by that word actually occurs. Long ago, people could listen in rapture to the rhyming of troubadours. We are no longer capable of feeling the joy this experience brings. People have tried so hard to be different and individual that they have ended up lonely, isolated and unhappy. Contemporary humanity has dug its own trap or built its own gallows. True happiness has nothing to do with the satisfaction of the desire of the moment: it is always accompanied by a profound sense of fulfillment.

AITMATOV: Egoism is a great given factor in our self-awareness. It is impossible for a human being not to be egotistical; that is, for him to be outside himself. It all boils down to defining the parameters of egoism. A thinking being whose egoism embraces all humanity, with all its dark and light sides, and who embraces this burdensome world, is a god. A human being whose egoism fails to extend even to his own children is a nothing.

Struggling with egoism is senseless. The important thing is for each individual's egoism to embrace as many people as possible; then all of us will exist in each of us. In the coming centuries, human evolution must follow the path of expanding egoism to a cosmic scale. The infant provides a convenient model of this process. At first, its egoism embraces only the mother. Then, gradually, it comes to include the family, kin, the nation and then the whole world. People of the future must be allowed to enjoy conditions favourable to this evolution.

But I fear that national egoism will remain an insuperable barrier for many generations. Giving rise to fanaticism and aggressiveness, it could be the fundamental cause of a third world war, God forbid.

IKEDA: As you put it, in characteristically poetical form, the important thing is expansion of egoism to a cosmic scale. This is what I had in mind when I said, 'The person who perceives this fundamental entity experiences a limitless expansion of the self. He becomes capable of controlling his own desires and impulses and of using them creatively as springboards for the self-perfecting process that I call the human revolution.'

Jung identified the inner *self* as the entity that touches the deep layers of universal life and strives to expand and merge with it. He named the more superficial self – the self of daily affairs – the *ego*. Modern philosophy and modern culture are both to blame in creating circumstances that diminish the self and isolate it from and oppose it to the objective world. Cut off from the self, the estranged ego is tossed hither and thither on the waves of life.

The vast number of teachings attributed to Shakyamuni, traditionally eighty thousand, though the figure must not be taken literally, are, as

Nichiren said, a diary of a human life. In addition to religious views, they include Shakyamuni's philosophy on humanity, the world, and everything in the universe. They reveal how he accomplished limitless self-expansion ending in integration with and affirmation of the cosmos. Passing through self-reflection leading to the rejection of actuality and the ego, the truly self-reflective, distant, inward journey leads to this kind of great affirmation.

The true meaning of the Buddhist doctrine of the absence of permanent self is not self-negation, but self-expansion, from the lesser to the greater self, or in Jungian terms, from the ego to the self.

AITMATOV: In my story *Piebald Dog Running along the Seashore*, I tried to examine overcoming cellular egoism. If you remember, in the story, having lost their way in a fog, three adults and a boy in a boat gradually come to understand the hopelessness of their situation. I see the role of art as elevating the human ability to overcome internal egoism born of the instinct for survival. Of course, in real life, things rarely turn out as we want them to in our abstract thoughts, for, at all but the cellular level, egoism is irresistible. During catastrophes at sea, when the ship is sinking, everyone fights to get a place for himself on the lifeboat. There are many examples of this. In my story, I tried to pit the force of art, of awareness, against this instinct. Surely, overcoming the power of egoism is the way to humanise human beings. Surely, such a triumph embodies the meaning and aim of cognition. Cannot the blinding flash of this feeling of internal victory over self illuminate an entire human life? Can it not, even at the very last, expand life into the limitlessness of space and time, thus connecting the individual with all humanity? Happiness is exultant ecstasy at liberation from the trammels and snares of daily life. Thus set free, the human spirit, birdlike, loses all fear of death.

Some people may object that the feeling of liberation is ephemeral. It is; but there is eternity in the instant of its existence. He who has experienced a sense of eternity is a human being in the full sense of the word.

Art is a special form of consciousness capable of fixing the immortal instant. While uniting generations, it forbids what the writer Dmitrii Sergeyevich Likhachev calls 'the naïve arrogance' displayed by those of our contemporaries who claim to be wiser than what they regard as our ignorant, inexperienced forefathers. If the ancients were so inadequate, why does their art remain a model that we strive, in vain, to emulate?

IKEDA: Art is assurance of immortality. I understand and agree with what you say. Why do ancient art and religion continue to attract innumerable visitors to the world's great museums and monuments? It would seem that the older the art, the stronger its attraction.

All religions are complemented by art in styles compatible with their natures and needs. This is not surprising because, to soar in time and space to limitless expansion, the life entity must have a form that provides energy for self-magnification. Art in any guise, painting, sculpture, literature, is the purest and most classical form for the purpose. This is culture. All superior art strives to transcend historical period and national boundaries to become the entirety, actually inherent in it, that links souls with souls. I emphasised this point in an address entitled 'Creative Life', which I delivered to the Académie des Beaux-Arts (Academy of Fine Arts) of the Institut de France, in June 1989. In this context, the word *entirety* equates with *poetic spirit*.

AITMATOV: Of course, because it preserves in its depths the limitless possibilities of the divine secret of being. Though inexpressible, intimate and understandable without words, this secret can exist only in true poesy, the music of verbal incarnation. I believe this was what the Russian poet Konstantin N. Batyushkov (1787–1855) meant when he said, 'O, memory of the heart! Stronger than the sad memory of reason.'

Batyushkov, by the way, considered art and creative work in general 'memory of the future'.

IKEDA: Is the memory of the future the special prerogative of the poet?

AITMATOV: Not at all. I believe in the justice of Buddhist philosophy, according to which all are equal before the absolute, before poetry. True, the 'vanity of vanities' (Ecclesiastes 1:2) kills the poetic understanding of life, thus turning human beings into gloomy, soulless creatures. But that is another matter. Cognition, no matter how many forms it takes, leads the human being to himself. Our dignity compels us to awaken the fantastic energy of the soul, energy that is most probably located in the subconscious. The visions of the star-women bear witness to this. I like to think that, when this energy has been awakened, everything monstrous, everything that hinders us from being truly human, will disintegrate into dust.

The Lotus Sutra – Drama of Life

IKEDA: The Buddhism of Nichiren is founded on the teachings of the Lotus Sutra. Of basic importance to Buddhism as a whole, this sutra is characterised by the doctrine that all human beings can attain Buddhahood; that is, can assimilate the doctrines of Buddhism and in this way reach a state of true happiness. In this vital respect, all human beings are equal. Indeed the concept of universal equality permeates the sutra: all are endowed with the same supremely reverence-worthy life as a Buddha.

The message taught by the Lotus Sutra unfolds as a great drama of life, the nucleus of which is the 'Ceremony in the Air'. During a magnificent assembly convened on *Gridhrakūta*, or Eagle Peak, a Treasure Tower made of the Seven Precious Substances (variously given, but generally gold, silver, lapis-lazuli, seashell, carnelian, pearl and agate) appears hovering in the sky. Thereupon the entire assemblage rises into the air, where the proceedings continue.

These apparently unreal occurrences embody profound meaning. The splendid Treasure Tower, which represents the entity of life and the fundamental Mystic Law pervading the universe, indicates the magnificence and vast expanse inherent in a single, individual life. Further, the sutra shows the Buddha life to be eternal by making it clear that Shakyamuni actually attained Buddhahood in the infinitely distant past. In other words, in the Lotus Sutra, Shakyamuni is not the historical personage of that name but a symbol of truth. His teaching, not resting on Earth, but elevated in the air, separates him from the historical Shakyamuni, who was subject to the ordinary restrictions of time and space.

Many Buddhas aside from Shakyamuni attend the Ceremony in the Air. First is the Tathāgata Many Treasures, who arrives in the Treasure Tower. Joining the assembly later, Buddhas of the ten directions and three existences of past, present and future symbolise the spatially and temporally limitless expansiveness of Shakyamuni's teachings. Shakyamuni's assuming a seat within the Treasure Tower symbolically represents the Buddha nature as a truth shared by all sentient beings.

Throughout the sutra, measurements of space and time are given in gigantic numbers intended, not as accurate information, but as indications of infinity and eternity. For example, the Bodhisattvas from the Earth, whom Shakyamuni summons forth, are said to be equal in number to the grains of sand in sixty thousand Ganges rivers. Though really part of a cosmic drama taking place in Shakyamuni's mind, to modern commonsense, these immense number make the Ceremony in the Air seem a preposterous fairy tale. Unfortunately, however, the fog of common sense, sometimes masquerading behind the good name of science, has dulled our sensibilities, enfeebled our imagination and impoverished us spiritually.

Many aspects of reality defy scientific and mathematical determination. The Russian philosopher Nikolai Berdyaev spoke of three kinds of time: cosmic, historical and existential. His cosmic time is measurable according to revolutions of the planets in the solar system and accompanied by cycles, seasons and hours. Historical time transforms the present into the past and moves in the direction of the future. Existential time is the eternal present, unconformable to mathematical time. It is time that transcends time. An instant of existential time embodies extended spans as understood according to the other two systems. Berdyaev's existential time has much in common with time as unfolded in the Lotus Sutra and exists on a plane apart from historical fact.

When confined to Berdyaev's cosmic or historical time, history itself becomes insipid and manifests neither drama nor the working of the imaginative powers. In discussing the merits and demerits of history in relation to life, Nietzsche said,

> The unhistorical and the historical are equally necessary to the health of the individual, a whole people and a culture. The unhistorical is like an enveloping atmosphere in which life alone produces itself in order to disappear again with the destruction of that atmosphere.[17]

In a perspicacious enumeration of the faults of modern history, he showed how increasing scholarly precision can run the risk of desiccating human life force and imaginative power.

AITMATOV: The topics you raise demonstrate the breadth of your field of inquiry and knowledge. Some of them are unique. Among the unique ones is the Lotus Sutra. My having been brought up and educated in the totally different atmosphere of dialectical materialism makes it very difficult for me to be your dialogue partner in the sphere of Buddhist philosophy. But, since no contemporary human being can be left indifferent by what you say, with your permission, here are some distant-echo-like thoughts inspired by your conversation.

I consider the drama of life our primordial paradigm. For this reason, thinking of the eternal drama within the limits of individual cases and a particular reality conditioned by definite fates may seem to be trifling with the issue. In such a case, the whole thing might boil down to explanations or censures. Or, in another variant, it might turn into an apology for the completely arbitrary facts of a given biography. Having made such an apology, the subject of the biography becomes satisfied with his life and devoid of desire to relive it differently; that is to say, more correctly and more righteously.

I think we reflect the spirit of the Lotus Sutra in the daily, inner awareness of our own shortcomings, our fates and the amounts of time we waste. Potentially, we could be much more significant, even in our own eyes. But as the Russian proverb goes, 'In age we know what we should have known when we were young; in age we long to do what we could do when we were young.' What is ironic, is that we try to understand and answer the eternal questions — and the drama of life is certainly related to them — directly on the everyday level within the confines of mathematically perceptible time and space. In this, as the Russian poet Prince Pyotr Vyazemsky said, we 'hurry to live and hasten to feel'. If it was possible to write about such haste in the nineteenth century, when Vyazemsky lived, what is to be said about the present day with its formerly unthinkable, mindless speeds? We live in a time when the world seems to change literally before our very eyes, like fashions. People knock themselves out to keep up with others, at all costs. Naturally, pragmatism is preferred to so-called higher matter, anything abstract.

IKEDA: You remind me of the stories told of lemmings and the way, during periodic population explosions, they dash headlong cross country, ultimately hurling themselves off cliffs to perish in the sea. The way greed-driven modern humanity dashes heedlessly on a headlong carpe-diem course cannot fail to awaken gloomy associations with these rodents. As a Buddhist, I do not despair. Still, is it not humiliating for the self-proclaimed Lord of Creation to find himself on a par with the lowly lemming? The association leads me to still another, more important one.

Dostoyevsky opens his novel *The Possessed* with a quotation from the New Testament concerning the Gadarene swine. Jesus has just cast out devils from a certain man in Gadara:

> Now there was there nigh unto the mountains a great herd of swine feeding.
> And all the devils besought him, saying, Send us into the swine, that we may enter into them.
> And forthwith Jesus gave them leave. And the unclean spirits went out, and entered into the swine: and the herd ran violently down a steep place into the sea, (they were about two thousand;) and were choked in the sea. (Mark V: 11–13)

Here communists are compared to the swine. The theme of *The Possessed* is the tragedy of atheism, used as a kind of reverse proof of the essential importance of religion. The spirit of religion can help people break free from obsession with pragmatism – I do not mean the pragmatism of William James – and subjection to materialism, which oppress and demean them, driving them recklessly on, like swine hurling themselves into the sea.

AITMATOV: In this connection, it is appropriate to call to mind Albert Einstein's sad comment to the effect that, in the epoch of scientific–technological progress, the essence of human existence is flight from wonder. At first, I considered this remark paradoxical. I now see that Einstein was talking about the speed with which we accustom ourselves to the startling achievements of human genius and come to accept them as if they had always existed. If they had not, we convince ourselves, how unfortunate our forefathers must have been! How did they get along without electricity, automobiles or aircraft? We find it very difficult to imagine that people in the past found their lives interesting, even fascinating. But, when we have finished congratulating ourselves on our good fortune in this, some of us may recall how, in youth, we wished we had been born in the age of chivalry, or the age of the samurai, with its noble code of honour. The thirst with which our imagination longs for heroic personal exploits in the name of high ideals, such as the good and the true, bears witness to this childhood wish. Are not these ideals the moral source of legends and tales? And, if they are, it is only because, once, they constituted the essence of real life, controlling real people whom memory now dubs heroes. They earned the title by having the power to perform immortal wonders, most of all wonders of the spirit.

Surely all of this is rooted in the sermon of the Lotus Sutra. Sermons are born and occur in the spirit. Everything truly great takes place in our spirits, which are, in contemporary language, models of the cosmos. We feast our eyes on the play of nature, its alterations of colouration and mood, the transition of young trees into maturity and wisdom. What if we could experience similar wonderful metamorphoses within our own essence! The careful, attentive gaze directed to the world around us is capable of making great observations leading to many conclusions. Once we have correlated these conclusions, we will understand that, since all things are born into this world in suffering, pain and suffering in general are not punishments but presages of a new life.

IKEDA: Why do human beings fear suffering?

AITMATOV: What is at the heart of Pushkin's now underestimated words 'I want to live to think and suffer?' As a human being and a poet, he understood and accepted the cosmic drama of life as a struggle with chaos and entropy. Thought overcomes both. But the victory must be achieved, not at a trifling cost, but in the sufferings of the entire being as an expression of innermost, primordial human nature. Herein lies the essence and purpose of the human vocation.

Many of us drive ourselves into a dead-end by refusing to experience life as a great drama. This is to renounce life and, finally, to become capable of cursing it.

But there is another approach: the affirmation of our right to life, to suffering and joy, and to appropriate recompense. This is what drives the very circulation of life, in the circuit of which we inevitably encounter the 'eternal question': in the name of what must we live? How can we become more human? Attaining greater humanity, again as Dostoyevsky knew, means developing greater imagination, expanding the understanding of life, and being, more accurately, striving to become, 'a witness of the invisible'. Through efforts of this kind, the human being becomes capable of awakening and drawing nearer to his own sense of experiencing the eternal, universal life. Not everyone, however, is endowed with this capability.

IKEDA: Goethe called faith, love of the invisible, trust in what one knows to be invisible and what one thinks cannot be. Since time immemorial, our imagination's ability to range far and wide through the realm of the invisible and the impossible, and to sense reality there, has been considered the greatest prerequisite of our humanity. This capacity is alien to the debilitated psychological climate of our time. Unfortunately, many people today are too engrossed in the struggle for material gain and the satisfaction of illusive, vain desires to savour the happiness inherent in the life of the imagination or, worse, even to be aware of its existence. Incapable of calling on their own imaginative powers, such people cannot see the tragedy of their lives. As D. H. Lawrence said, 'Ours is essentially a tragic age, so we refuse to take it tragically.'[18] If they could see their virtually pathological situation for what it is, there would be hope of alleviating it.

As you say, not everyone is capable of experiencing the eternal and the universal. Nonetheless, practical difficulties aside, in principle, the possibility of such experience is open to all. In this connection, the pre-eminent spirit of equality found in the Lotus Sutra shines bright.

Parallel with our underestimation of our own imaginative powers is our disregard for the powers of nature. Edigei, the hero of your story *The Day Lasts More Than a Hundred Years*, understands how puny we human beings are in the face of the ferocity of the natural world but, in spite of the unequal odds, accepts the trials imposed by nature as inevitable. Indeed, these very trials enable him to start a new life brimming with love for humanity and life. Merging with nature in an extraordinary fashion, he triumphs over fear of the incomprehensible and boldly faces past and future. Nichiren said that, in doing good, even a person who knows nothing of the Buddha is putting the Buddha's spirit into practice. Edigei instinctively puts the spirit of the Lotus Sutra into practice. He finds plenty of material ready to hand on all sides, in the eternally beautiful, natural world. However, being able to accept nature as he does, is not easy.

AITMATOV: I must admit that I find your viewpoint both unexpected and very interesting. You speak of the simple person Edigei as if he were a poet.

IKEDA: We all unconsciously create images of our worlds. You have given Edigei some of the poetry of your own world images.

AITMATOV: Perhaps. The pursuit of the fashionable good things of the world seems to shorten our earthly lives. Perhaps obsession with mere playthings that we think satisfy dubious desires deprives us of the ability to create real happiness. This, the source of the crisis of the imagination, is intractable. Not many are prepared to give up the conveniences of modern life. Few people would be willing to travel by car when they can take an aeroplane. Most are left indifferent by the argument that the pedestrian enjoys infinitely more wonderful sights than the passenger of a super-fast automobile. How many realise that the passenger is, in fact, a sacrifice, a mere adjunct, to scientific–technological progress? What is to be done? Does contemporary man want to live, not forever, but a long time? Many agree in wanting to live not so long, but better. Few would agree with Einstein that life is the most absorbing of all shows.

IKEDA: As you suggest, too many people today undervalue life and measure it solely in terms of material goods, to which they have become enslaved.

Still, I believe we all long for integration in the equality embodied in the Lotus Sutra. Sincere heart-to-heart exchanges on the truly important aspects of life can help us unite. Transcending boundaries of time and space, the teachings of the Lotus Sutra embody the capability of making the best of all other ideas and philosophies. Some day, the whole world will come to see and appreciate the integrating force of this capability. When that happens, the Lotus Sutra will inspire a spiritual revival for all humankind.

AITMATOV: Let us pray that such will be the case.

A Second Axial Period

IKEDA: The period between the eighth and second centuries BC witnessed the creative work of a whole array of brilliant, original thinkers, including Shakyamuni, Confucius, Laozi, Isaiah, Heracleitus, Plato and Archimedes. For this reason, the German philosopher Karl Jaspers (1883–1969) called it an axial period in the history of humanity. He characterises this period as follows:

> The new aspect of this epoch was that, in all three worlds, humanity became aware of its existence in its entirety, of its self and of its limitations.[19]

Our own age, too, is axial in the sense that it represents a great turning point. Possessed of nuclear arms, we can of course bring human history to a cataclysmic halt. To prevent this, and to create a cultural heritage that will determine the future flow of the eternal current, we must abandon the worn-out, nation–state frame of reference and think globally. To do so, we require a religion or philosophy capable of meeting the needs of all peoples for all times.

The requisite philosophy must have an inner universal element, what the Germans call a *Merkmal*. According to Jaspers, awareness of the dignity of the individual was the supreme value resulting from the original axial period. To attain this awareness, the individual had to transcend tribe and nation and realise connections with something universal. Only with this awareness is it possible to understand that all beings are equal and possessed of equal dignity before the eternal.

As subsequent history shows, the universal element assumed increasingly intense transcendental colouration. This is especially true in the case of

Christianity with its one transcendent God. But, to various extents, a similar tendency to transcendentalise can be seen in the Confucian idea of Heaven (*Tian*) and the Buddhist concept of Law (*Dharma*). Essentially, *Dharma* is an inner and immanent universal. But, in its diverse philosophical manifestations, it has not always functioned as it should.

Be that as it may, taking a cue from Jaspers, I think we are now experiencing a second axial period, which must evolve under the banner of an immanent universal element. Divorced from all discriminations on the basis of ideology, race, wealth, standing, sex or age, this universal element must help us uncover the power of human nature, the treasure deep within life itself. And, using this power, it must promote recognition of the equality of all peoples. Providing a shining example of how equality for all can arise from the individual life, Nichiren said that taking one person as a model, we see that all sentient beings are equal. The social role of Soka Gakkai is to manifest this equality by struggling against restricting forces like those of violence, oppression and cupidity.

The significance of the indispensable new religion lies in its initiating a transition from nationalism to humanism; that is, from emphasis on state interests to emphasis on the welfare of human beings.

AITMATOV: Synthesis of the philosophical thought of all epochs and teachings has exerted an important influence on the intellectual evolution of humanity. As a creator of literary subjects, I am afraid this topic falls outside my bailiwick. And perhaps, as the saying goes, the cobbler should stick to his last. Nonetheless, with no pretensions to learning, I shall make a few subjective comments.

In the synthesis under discussion, you discover a continuity of epochs. You prognosticate a new revival, or more accurately, a continuation of the second axial period in the future insights of the human spirit. Although a single lifespan is too short to carry the task out, you directly sense this synthesis. Doing so is a great intellectual attainment. Of course, the inner world of the human individual is the biggest of all banks for ideas and discoveries. Deposits in that bank invariably pay yearly increasing interest in the form of progress. Our supreme goal is to create ourselves as individuals. Ideals give meaning to both individual lives and whole civilisations.

In practice, however, things do not always work out the way we want. The path of the individual through the labyrinth of history is too long, excruciating, complicated and contradictory. Partly, this is because constantly emerging institutionalised forces enslave the individual to their own interests.

But the individual, too, contributes to the difficulty by failing to recognise its own great, decisive authority. Once again, the vanity of vanities spoils us and obstructs our perfection. This has been true in all epochs.

It took more than two millennia for us finally to see the truth in what some of the ancients had to say – for instance Heracleitus, who said that, though the majority of human beings are ignorant of it, agreement to the oneness of all things is a sign of wisdom, or Laozi's words: 'The knowledgeable person would follow the broad road. But I am afraid of the narrow pathways. The broad road is completely level, but the people love the pathways.' It took more than two thousand years for science to ascertain the oneness of the whole universe, to understand that stimuli in one part cause reactions in other parts and to realise the impossibility of arbitrary treatment of the environment, which, in spite of human meddling, will follow its own laws of self-organisation. Ultimately, science became convinced of the inflexibility of the laws of existence, which reject the alien. Independent of our wishes, some of those laws are propitious to us. The ancients were right to consider good, world reason and moral law primordial. These things preordain the course of evolution. Not everything depends on humanity, but humanity can give meaning to everything. Human beings appeared in this world in order to bring about self-knowledge of the spirit and general salvation: 'By means of igniting the human heart about all creation, about humanity, birds, animals, demons and all creatures.' In *Umozrenii o kraskakh* (Thoughts about colours), E. N. Trubetskoy recalls these words of Isaac Sirin and relates as follows:

> The question of the meaning of life, perhaps, has never been keener than now, when world evil and folly are exposed to view. Never since the beginning of the world has the spirit been as enslaved as it is today, this amounts to brutalisation elevated to a principle and a system; it is rejection of everything human that in the past has been, and remains, part of human culture.

And this managed to convince us to drain our cup to the bottom. Trubetskoy draws the following conclusion: 'The human being cannot remain just a human being. He must either rise above himself or fall into an abyss; he must evolve into either God or beast.'

Our only alternative is to choose between light and dark, before humanity is swallowed up in night. The choice must be made, not any old place, but within ourselves; not sometime, but now.

IKEDA: True. But humanity has generally left solutions of world problems in God's hands. Not everything, however, has gone well, since God and man are not always on good terms. Human beings want to be godlike, but cannot. Frustration at this inability gives rise to dissatisfaction and atheism. Whether to give greater weight to God or to oneself is a delicate question that has regularly been afforded serious consideration by all religions, especially the higher religions. As is revealed in condensed form in the Grand Inquisitor segment of *The Brothers Karamazov*, it was a cause of ultimate suffering for Dostoyevsky.

Buddhism confronts the issue by comparing one's inner power with external power. Some Buddhists call on outside aid; the classical example is evoking the name of the Buddha Amitābha (*Amida* in Japanese), for salvation.

Buddhist sects differ among themselves as to which is more important. I consider it erroneous to lay too much stress on either. As a certain poet has put it, the two are like inhalation (reliance on outside aid) and exhalation (self-reliance). Both are vital, just as our respiratory system operates correctly only when a delicate balance obtains between the two.

Buddhist texts sometimes illustrate this balance by reference to monkeys and cats. When danger approaches, the baby monkey clings to the mother and the two embrace as they flee to safety. A female cat, however, lifts her kittens in her mouth to carry them out of harm's way. Whereas the baby monkey does its part by holding on tight, the kitten merely dangles. In short, the kitten depends on outside help; but the baby monkey exerts effort on its own behalf.

Because they tend to emphasise outside help, religions have served as a cloak to conceal weakness and sloth. In this sense, and in this sense only, Marx was justified in branding them opiates of the people. As history shows, the opiate aspect grows stronger whenever ecclesiastical organisations institutionalise personal faith.

Perhaps as a reaction against such institutionalisation, too much stress on one's own power can lead to self-righteous, arrogant atheism. The question of balance between internal and external power, which is a perennial *aporia* for human kind, demands frank and open confrontation, because overlooking it threatens us with the fate of the lemmings of popular story or the Biblical Gadarene swine.

AITMATOV: Human beings were still firmly attached to God when the struggle against Him, theomachism, began gradually growing in intensity. In *On the Trinity*, Saint Augustine says that, in its sins and its proud, perverse, that is to say slavish, freedom, the soul strives to become like God. Thus merely exhorting them to be like God could incline our forefathers to sin. The subsequent course of events was thus determined because, when God is absent from the soul, anything is permitted and nothing is sacred. With Russia in mind, Dostoyevsky prophetically declared,

> For socialism is not merely the labour question, it is before all things the atheistic question, the question of the form taken by atheism to-day, the question of the tower of Babel built without God, not to mount to heaven from earth but to set up heaven on earth.[20]

Things have turned out just as he foresaw. What is the point of exhausting one's spirit in efforts at self-improvement, when one can simply sweep all obstacles out of the way, destroy all temples, internal and external, and demand subjection from the whole world.

By nature, when instructed to emulate God in thought and to assume his responsibilities and moral character, some people eagerly usurp the highest levels of the hierarchy. Bringing Heaven down to the level of Earth equates the high with the low. Ironically, however, this only results in unprecedented inequalities because it violates life's law of diversity within unity and the possibility of unimpeded circulation. It mistakes the potential equality of possibilities inherent in the nature of things for real equality. Confuscious said, 'In nature close to one another, in practice far apart.'[21] In order to be like everyone else, we abolish the spiritual, the heavenly, world. But, like the isolated halves of all dichotomies, Earth dies without Heaven. In the name of ostensible equality, we destroy everything outside that equality, everything individual and creative. Only the individual can establish connections with being. When we destroy individuality – personal or national – in the name of unity, we sever all such connections. Individuality comes to life in a cultural sphere.

IKEDA: The anti-religious propaganda of which the Soviet Union was abundantly productive often quoted Lenin's phrase 'priests without vestments'. To the socialist revolution and the building of socialism, pure priests were more harmful than depraved ones. The latter could easily be exiled or obliterated. The former, however, presented a more difficult problem. Similarly, a superior laity, priests without vestments, was a greater threat to the social extirpation of religion than the official clergy. This fits in well with the dictum that whatever advances the dictatorship of the proletariat is good and whatever hinders it is bad.

Surprisingly, Albert Einstein was censured as a priest without vestments. This peerless humanist once visited Japan, where, possibly because of the influence of the theory of relativity, he caused something of a cultural shock. The breadth of his personality, his warmth, his free-and-easy humour; and his unostentatious demeanour made an indelible impression. My own mentor, Josei Toda, who was young at the time, counted hearing Einstein lecture among the happiest experiences of his entire life. Incidentally, though extremely fond of Japanese traditional culture, as a great humanist, Einstein sharply criticised the *jinrikisha* as inhuman.

Einstein possessed a universal religious sense unshackled by sect or dogma. What you refer to as the individual cannot be cultivated when the possession of a universal religious sense brands such a person as a priest without vestments and therefore an enemy of the people and the revolution.

Nikolai Berdyaev said:

> Communism claims to have created not only a new society, but also a new humanity. There is much talk in Soviet Russia of a new humanity and a new mental structure. Foreigners who have visited Soviet Russia, too, like to talk about it. But a new humanity will emerge only with the dawning of the recognition of human beings as the supreme value in life. Considering human beings no more than individual bricks in the social structure or tools in the economic process indicates, not the emergence of a new humanity, but the extinction of humanity; in other words, a deepening of the process of human alienation.[22]

We now see clearly that Berdyaev hit the nail on the head. The humanism that I advocate accords with Berdyaev's assertion that a new humanity can emerge only when human beings are afforded supreme value. Positing a value higher than humanity, the God of the past, the proletariat of this century, or whatever else it may be, represents the transcendent universal or external universal that, in dominating, oppresses and alienates humanity. Such external values are fated to disappear sooner or later in the current of time.

AITMATOV: You speak of the necessity of a new religion or philosophy. Is it feasible? The Hindu religious philosopher Swami Vivekananda (1863–1902) believed such a religion would incorporate all spiritual elements that humanity has acquired and suffered for. Each person must cultivate his own individuality and approach full unity through self-revelation. Vivekananda revealed this thought in the following way:

> In the life of each nation and of each separate human being, a separate idea serves as the centre of existence. It is the basic note around which all the other notes in the harmony group themselves. The nation that discards this idea, the principle of its own vitality, the prescribed course handed down to it by the ages, perishes.

Believing in the divinity of each individual, Vivekananda urged all peoples to join in brotherhood. He prophesied that religious banners would soon bear not the word *struggle*, but the words *mutual aid*; not *destruction*, but *mutual understanding*; not *fruitless discussions*, but *harmony* and *peace*. His belief in humanity strengthened his convictions. His own teacher, the Hindu mystic Ramakrishna (1836–86), said, 'Are you seeking God? Then look for Him in Man. The Divine occurs in Man more than in anything else.'

Much is given to man! His personal capacities are enormous. Yet how few of his great possibilities are realised in him! In striving for peace, he stumbles over his own internal limitations, which, mirrorlike, reflect the perversions of the external world. External freedom is possible only when accompanied by internal freedom. Internal freedom presupposes a developed awareness and a moral sense. Upon attaining fullness, something, for instance, a person or a language, reveals its possibilities as unexpectedly as a flower gathers strength to burst into bloom. Individuality and openness are conditions for intercourse, ecumenicalism and unity of the highest order.

The principle of individuality normalises all relations, the whole man becomes the measure of all things. Individuality, the organ of the conscience, is not a part of a nation. It is said that nationality is a part of, and is located in, the individual, like natural content. Nationality is the environment that nourishes the individuality. This idea is a form of idolatry and slavery. Though they would seem close, in one sense, individualism and nationalism are opposite. One leads to freedom and salvation; the other, to servitude and slavery.

This is why the facelessness and featurelessness of party bureaucracy are frightening. All *apparatchiks* behave the same. They all obey a single, official logic built into the program from the start. If the individual is considered divine, then this lack of differentiation, this monotonous oneness, must be described as global diabolism. In the Soviet Union, it nearly proved fatal.

Failure to make the human being the subject of all; that is, interpreting human beings as objects and mere fragments of the mass, resulted in the victimisation of millions. Ours was a world of darkness, where everything was topsy-turvy: falsehood was called truth, monotonous undifferentiation was called unity. But why should unity deprive the human being, and entire peoples, of the very possibility of freedom?

The topicality of this issue scarcely requires comment. No matter what viewpoint one adopts, the new eon will be marked by the birth of a free humanity and the search for the individual way to perfection through knowledge of the age-old cultures of East and West and through self-knowledge and self-realisation.

IKEDA: The French philosopher Gabriel Marcel (1889–1973), who located the universal on a level where quantitative measurements are invalid, accurately criticised the Soviet misplacement of values. A certain famous French paleontologist, who professed himself a sincere Christian, repeatedly and militantly asserted his belief in socialist global progress. When Gabriel Marcel called his attention to the millions of people then dying in Soviet labour camps, the paleontologist disparaged the importance of a few millions in comparison with the limitless expanse of human history. An enraged Marcel replied:

> A really sacrilegious remark! Thinking in millions and billions, he can conceive only abstractions. For him, a numerical delusion conceals the unutterable, intolerable reality of the individual's suffering.[23]

This delusion of numbers corresponds to what you censure as lack of differentiation, monotonous oneness and global diabolism and to what I call the transcendental or external universal in opposition to the internal universal. Superficially similar to but essentially different from universality, this deluded approach leads, as you say, to slavery and servitude and is calamitous for both humanity and the Earth.

We must seek the universal within ourselves. It should be impossible even to discuss progress with an outlook so devastated that it ignores the suffering of a single human being. Though it may seem roundabout, in the long run, the only way to approach the universal is to, as Nichiren says, regard all individuals as equal and to empathise with their sufferings. Marcel said that the spirit, *l'esprit*, is the universal and that *l'esprit* equates to love. But he points out the danger of misunderstanding the meaning of the word *universal*:

We are led almost invincibly to understand by this (the universal) that which manifests a maximum of generality. But one can never react too strongly against that interpretation. The best thing is for the spirit to find its foundation in the highest expressions of the human genius; that is, in works of art of supreme character.[24]

The internal universal corresponds in many respects to the ideas you introduce from Vivekananda and is embodied in Ramakrishna's injunction, 'Are you seeking God? Then look for Him in Man. The Divine occurs in Man more than in anything else.' In a similar vein, Mahatma Gandhi once said:

To seek God, one need not go on a pilgrimage, light lamps or burn incense before or anoint the image of the deity or paint it with red vermilion. For He resides in our hearts.[25]

My many Indian friends and I share as a joint heritage the sentiments inherent in Gandhi's assertion that:

Only when it pervades all our actions does religion cease to be sectarian and assume the significance of faith in an ordered moral control of the universe.[26]

To allow sectarianism to harm friendship is to put the cart before the horse and is completely alien to the way the world religion of the future must be.

Our long inward journey, during which we have discussed your literary work, as well as the work of such writers as Dostoyevsky, Tolstoy and Pushkin, can be called an extended search for the universal. As of yet, no one can say how far humanity has proceeded or what future direction we will follow. Nonetheless, I am convinced that, unless we all pursue the path together, we will never attain the liberty and salvation you speak of.

A Parable for Mikhail Gorbachev

by Chingiz Aitmatov

Rumours about Mikhail S. Gorbachev are rife today (1991, as I write this). The twilight of his bright, contradictory epoch, occurring in view of everyone, leaves none of his contemporaries indifferent. Some sympathise with the former president, worry about him, and firmly shake hands at parting with him. From their viewpoint, a unique figure of the twentieth century is leaving the political arena after having suffered a crushing defeat. Others whoop as he goes, laugh, stamp their feet and hurl stones; in general, they publicly demonstrate the cynicism that has become the normal behavioural leitmotiv of the ranks that, like mushrooms, have recently parasitised the democracy of *perestroika*. But then, this is they way things had to be.

Another group of sincerely indignant people curse Gorbachev as they stand in lines at stores. And, beholding the ruins of the former superpower whose universal scale and formidability gave supreme meaning to their lives on Earth, a considerable number heap threats on the head of the hated radical-reformer. But, as God knows, the man they blame never wanted the collapse of the Soviet Union and now stands shattered and amazed by it. Perhaps this, too, is the way things had to be.

One day several years ago [in 1989], Mr. Gorbachev invited me to have a talk. He must have had something definite in mind, probably the situation in the Middle East, a national crisis at the time. But nothing very significant was said in that connection. Indeed, our meeting took an entirely different turn. Perhaps, I was innocently at fault.

In order to understand the essence of the situation, the reader must remember that *perestroika* as a process of unprecedented democratic reforms was in full swing at the time, not to everyone's satisfaction. The national economy was steadily declining. From right and left, from the democrats and the party bureaucrats, a rumble of latent dissatisfaction and ever-increasing criticism was growing distinctly louder. Everyone had his own ideas and arguments.

Undoubtedly, Gorbachev was uneasy in his mind the day I am talking about. He was his usual contained self. He smiled cordially and from time to time displayed the characteristic Gorbachev gleam, flashing animatedly in his eyes. Still, inner anxiety showed in his face. We sat opposite each other at a desk in one of his Kremlin offices.

In a perfectly natural way, before getting down to serious talk, Gorbachev asked about my literary affairs. What was I working on, a novel or a short story? Would it be out soon? Without realising it, he was introducing a very touchy theme because in those days I had practically no time for my own work. I decided to put my feelings on the table.

'Well, how can I tell you, Mikhail Sergeyevich?' I answered. 'It's getting harder and harder to do any writing. We've won total freedom, but I seem to be producing less. I don't have any time left over at all. We're all caught up in *perestroika*. The same wind's driving us all on.'

'It's more like the same seven winds,' smiled my companion, shaking his head in consternation.

'That's exactly it,' I agreed. '*Perestroika*'s bowled us over, swept us off our feet. I didn't expect this. Democracy has turned out to be a real time-devourer.'

'I understand. I know just what you mean,' said a thoughtful, sympathetically-smiling Gorbachev. 'Of course, we don't have enough time. But we have something else spiritually very important. All of a sudden, we have more to think about than we have time to think it in. Everybody – artists, philosophers, politicians – has something to say.'

As we talked on, I brought up a subject that had been on my mind a great deal: the fatal nature of power for the power holder. This fatality arises from the eternal contradictions, inevitably catastrophic, inherent in power itself. For a long time, the ideological pall of socialism had concealed it; but I suspected this question would influence the fate of Gorbachev, who was treading the still-unfinished path of a reformer-martyr in totalitarian conditions. In brief, we talked about the phenomenon of power and the methods and costs of dominion over many persons by one person.

Since I considered it not entirely tactful to broach this issue openly, I chose the roundabout way of relating an Eastern parable while talking about my own plans for creative work. Actually, the parable was a key factor in a literary subject I was contemplating. I related it to him as if thinking aloud.

'Look,' I said, 'A certain old fable has been on my mind. I think of it while travelling and during meetings, whether I'm alone or with other people. This is how it goes.

'Once a certain prophet, a soothsayer, came to a great ruler. The two of them shared a confidential and extremely frank conversation. The guest told the great ruler, "Your glory is known far and wide. Your throne is secure. But I've heard a rumour, strange at first encounter, that you dream of being a benefactor to your people for all times. You want to show them the way to complete happiness. In fact, you dream of giving them liberty, their full will, and total equality of rights." "Yes," replied the ruler. "I have been mulling over thoughts like those for a long time and actually intend to do what you say. That is my conviction and my decision."

'After a moment's silence, the wise guest said, "My lord, this great, praiseworthy undertaking for the good of many does you undying honour. It raises your image to the level of the gods. I sympathise with it, with all my soul. But it is my duty to tell you the whole truth. After I do, you must reach your own conclusions. You, my lord, face two ways, two fates, two possibilities. And you must do what you think necessary. One way is for you to strengthen your throne through strict government, continuing the traditions of your forebears. You are now at the pinnacle of solid power attained by heritage and right. You are now in the glory of your might. Fate decrees that, if you keep to the same path, you will remain in power to the end of your days, and when you die, your life will be honoured as a blessing to yourself and your people. Posterity will follow in your footsteps."'

All this while, Gorbachev remained silent, listening attentively to my parable, which, though transparent enough, was not too importunate, since, strictly speaking, it belonged to the never-never land of long ago. Next I related the old man's second prophesy.

'"Your second fate," said the soothsayer to the man on the peak of power, "is the hard way of the martyr. For know, sire, the people you enfranchise will repay you with black ingratitude. Such is the way of the world. But why? Why should such absurdity prevail? Should it not be the other way around? Where is justice? Where is reason? No one can answer. This is the inscrutable secret of heaven and the nether world. It has been thus in all ages, and always will be thus. Your lot will be the same. Once free, the people will become disobedient and will avenge their past on you. They will revile you in the crowds, ridicule you in the bazaars, scoff at and mock both you and your close associates. Formerly faithful comrades-in-arms will grow openly impudent and disobedient. And you, O Great One, will know sorrow and humiliation and will never be free of people, even people dear to you, who long to be rid of you and are eager to trample on your name. Sire, you are free to chose one fate or the other." And the sovereign said to the pilgrim: "Wait seven days in my court. I will think the matter over carefully. If I do not call for you in seven days, leave. Go your own way."'

Throughout this archaic tale, Gorbachev sat in silence but with a changed look on his face. Already regretting what I had done, I was about to say goodbye and go, when he commented with a bitter smile, 'I know what you're talking about. It's not just a new book. But there's no need to wait seven days for me. Seven minutes is more than enough. I've already made my choice. No matter what it costs me and no matter how my fate comes out, I'll stick to my course. Democracy, freedom, deliverance from the fearsome past, and no dictatorship over anybody. That's all! The people can judge me as they like. I'm going to stay on course, even if they don't understand.'

And with that we parted.

Chingiz Aitmatov
December 31, 1991

Epilogue

by Daisaku Ikeda

The End of One Age, the Beginning of Another

At the end of his book *The Grand Failure, The Birth and Death of Communism in the Twentieth Century*, the American political-scientist Zbigniew Brzezinski (1928–) gives a black-humourous forecast of the near future of the rapidly changing Soviet Union. According to him, in the year 2017, a century after the Bolshevik Revolution, Red Square will be renamed Liberty Square. Hidden by scaffolding, the Lenin Mausoleum will be undergoing reconstruction as the entrance to an underground parking lot for the growing number of tourists visiting a Kremlin exhibition entitled 'The Wasted Century, Fifty Million Human Lives Lost'.

Brzezinski claims a certain amount of accuracy for his prophecy. And, indeed, a few months after the collapse of the Soviet Union, it proved to be very much on course. As a matter of fact, it could come true long before 2017. The Russian tricolour replaced the red banner at the Kremlin. Statues of Lenin were toppled all over the Commonwealth of Independent States (CIS); and Anatoly Sobchak, former mayor of Saint Petersburg, now that Leningrad has its old imperial name again, spoke openly of demolishing the Lenin Mausoleum. The name Red Square (*Krasnaya Ploshchad*) predates the communists, *krasnaya* meaning splendid or beautiful as well as red. This one name, therefore, requires no alteration. But the pace of change in the country is so rapid that many other mementos of the Soviet past, including the mausoleum, may not last out the century. At the time of the publication of the first volume of the Japanese-language edition of this dialogue, memories of the shock of the burlesque, attempted coup d'état and the dissolution of the Communist Party were still fresh in our minds. By the time we published the second volume, the Soviet Union itself had collapsed, and the continued existence of the Commonwealth of Independent States (CIS) was in doubt. As the Roman poet Virgil says, truly time takes away all things.

Even if the name of Red Square persists, what fate awaits the place itself? In this vast space, Lenin, Trotsky and other revolutionary leaders once harangued the crowds. After the Second World War, trophies made of weaponry captured from the Nazi Germans were piled up there. On state occasions like May Day, tens of thousands of people waving flags or holding placards and balloons aloft used to throng the plaza while sabre-rattling parades were reviewed by supreme party leaders standing in ranks on top of Lenin's Tomb. Endless lines of tourists filed into the mausoleum, which was often visited by flower-bearing newlyweds fresh from their marriage ceremonies. On several occasions, I have trod the venerable cobblestones of Red Square. For me, it ranks with the majestic Gothic-looking tower of Moscow University rising high above the Lenin Hills – now once again known by their old name Sparrow Hills – as the two most memorable sites in the city.

The seventy-four years that transpired between the birth and the death of the Soviet Union signify the bankruptcy of a theory, the collapse of an idea and the frustration of an ideal. No one knows exactly how many human lives were sacrificed during that period, some people say thirty million, Chingiz Aitmatov says forty million and Zbigniew Brzezinski says fifty million. This very inability to state the cost accurately magnifies the tragedy. In this ideologically dominated twentieth century, the willful devastation caused by two monstrosities, Communism and Nazism, have left indelible scars.

Marxism-Leninism was an inclusive theory embracing a sweeping vision of a beautiful and, in a sense, complete human history. Its revolutionary application was to have abolished private property, collectivised agriculture and established a planned economy. In concord with ostensibly inevitable laws of history, the triumph of the proletariat was to have led humanity out of pre-history and into true history, ushering in a people's paradise, a golden age. Humanity itself, the driving force behind the process, was to be recreated in a form worthy of the theory. Furious learning projects were undertaken to this end. But an iron fist threatened anyone who either could not or would not be worthy of the ideal. As time went by, the entire Soviet Union was transformed into one 'gulag archipelago'. A fearsome abyss had opened between the vast, beautiful ideal and monstrous reality. The French sociologist and journalist Raymond Aron (1905–83) accurately said that Promethean ambition is an intellectual source of totalitarianism. In the Soviet Union, the very perfection of the ideal boosted the growth of limitlessly hypertrophic ambition, of which it actually became a means.

Human beings require dreams and hopes. The undeniably attractive aspects of Marxist-Leninist ideals appealed to many young people, especially during the so-called red thirties. Socialist ideology became their dreams and hopes. The sweet melody and inspiring lyrics of *L'internationale* promised justice and fairness to countless young souls: 'Arise, ye prisoners of starvation. Arise, ye wretched of the earth.'

The great tragedy is that, as Chingiz Aitmatov repeatedly laments, many of those socialist-inspired young souls were sacrificed to history.

Ultimately, a shallow, mistaken view of humanity brought about the bankruptcy of the theory, the collapse of the idea and the frustration of the ideal. Socialist ideology, which insisted that humanity is the sum total of all social relations, was global in scope but paid no attention to the life of the individual or the world of the mind. Indeed, it rejected the very idea of such concerns and was especially virulently antagonistic toward religion. Mr. Aitmatov's numerous comments throughout our book indicate how cruelly this ravaged the human heart. It was in recognition of this that we named the final chapter of our dialogue 'The Long Journey Inward'.

With his customary acumen, Mahatma Gandhi identified the cause of the catastrophic failure of the socialist experiment. Since, as Gandhi said,

> This socialism is as pure as crystal. It, therefore, requires crystal-like means to achieve it. Impure means result in an impure end . . . Therefore only truthful, non-violent and pure-hearted socialists will be able to establish a socialistic society in India and the world.[1]

Marxism-Leninism failed because it was defiled by its adoption of violence as the midwife of the revolution.

However, we must clearly realise that the so-called triumph of capitalism and liberty fails to illuminate the nature of the correct view to take of humanity. Socialist ideology strove for a world of equality and justice where people and nations neither dominate nor exploit each other. Socialism may have failed, but future prospects remain cold and desolate. The failure of the idea of a planned economy demonstrated conclusively that human beings are selfishly driven to work primarily in their own interests. Gone is the expansive, internationally-directed energy of early socialism, with its high hopes and bright dreams. The collapse of the international proletariat confronts us with the harsh spectacle of overt nationalist violence. We have no assurance that liberalism and democracy will be effective against a formidable array of pressing global problems like environmental pollution.

The dead of winter has not set in yet. But the autumn-scorched fields show no signs of fresh spring verdure. What new plants will emerge? We cannot afford to wait to see but must sow the hopeful seeds ourselves. Cultivation must begin with the individual inner life and its limitless possibilities.

I proposed the topic of a long inward journey, and my partner good-naturedly assented to it. As Mr. Aitmatov said, he and I seem to have been exchanging ideas since long before we actually met. Partly because our exchange has been largely epistolary, we have not reached the end of our way. We have much ground yet to cover. The journey goes on forever.

Daisaku Ikeda
March 1992

Notes

Chapter 1

1. Stefan Zweig, *Die Welt von Gestern* (The world of yesterday) (Frankfurt: Toscherbuch Verlag, Gmbh, 1944), pp.465–66.

Chapter 2

1. Victor Hugo, *Les Misérables*, trans. Charles E. Wilbour. Library of The Future, World Library, Inc., 1991–95. Screen 2429.
2. Anatoly Rybakov, *Deti Arbata* (Children of the Arbat) (Moscow: Knizhnaya Palata, 1988), p.344.
3. Jean-Paul Sartre, *Situations*, III – *Lendemains de Guerre* (Situations III, Morrows of war) (Paris: Éditions Gallimard, 1949, 1976), p.64.
4. William Shakespeare, *The Tragedy of Othello The Moor of Venice*; ed. Tucker Brook and Lawrence Mason. The Yale Shakespeare (New Haven: Yale University Press, 1918), p.98.
5. T. S. Eliot, *Notes towards the Definition of Culture* (New York: Harcourt, Brace and Company, 1949), p.27
6. Ōgai Mori, *Moso* (Delusion), trans. John W. Dower. *Monumenta Nipponica* (Tokyo: Sophia University, 1970), p.76.
7. Tōson Shimazaki, *Umi-e* (To the sea) (Tokyo: Chikuma Shobo, 1967), p.76.
8. Johann Peter Eckermann, *Gespräche mit Goethe in den letzten Jahren seines Lebens* (Conversations with Goethe in the last years of his life) (Wiesbaden: Insel Verlag, 1987), p.682.
9. John Steinbeck, *A Life in Letters*, ed. Elaine Steinbeck and Robert Wallsten (New York: Penguin Books, 1989), p.898.
10. Boris Pasternak, *Doktor Zhivago* (Moscow: Knizhnaya Palata, 1989), p.256.
11. Paul Valéry, *Variété IV* (Miscellany IV) (Paris: Éditions Gallimard, 1938), p.100.

12. Johann Wolfgang von Goethe, Johann Peter Eckermann, Frédéric Jacob Soret, *Conversations of Goethe with Eckermann and Soret*, trans. John Oxenford (London: Smith Elder, 1850), p.116.

Chapter 3

1. André Gide, *Retouches à mon Retour d l'U.R.S.S.* (Touching up my Return from the U.S.S.R.) (Paris: Éditions Gallimard, 1937), p.133.

2. Ryūnosuke Akutagawa, *Akutagawa Ryūnosuke Zenshu* (Complete works of Ryūnosuke Akutagawa) (Tokyo: Chikuma Shobo, 1965), p.277.

3. Alexis de Tocqueville, *De la Démocratie en Amérique* (Democracy in America) (Paris: Éditions M.-Th. Génin, Librairie de Médicis, 1951), p.252.

4. Sōseki Natsume, *Kusamakura*, trans. Meredith McKinney (New York: Penguin Books, 2008), p.3.

5. Albert Einstein, Cited from 'Principles of Research', a speech delivered on the occasion of Max Planck's sixtieth birthday in 1918. Published in *Mein Weltbild* (My world view); reprinted in *Ideas and Opinions*. p.225.

6. Aleksandr Blok, *Iskusstvo I Revolyutsiya* (Art and Revolution) (Moscow: Sovremennik, 1979) p.267.

7. Matthew Arnold, 'The Study of Poetry', *The Norton Anthology of English Literature*, Fifth Edition, Volume 2. (New York: W. W. Norton & Company, Inc., 1962), p.1441.

8. Plato. *Phaedo*, trans. Benjamin Jowett. Retrieved from <http://ebooks.adelaide.edu.au/p/plato/p71pho/phaedo.html>

9. John Reed, *Ten Days That Shook the World* (New York: Penguin Books USA, 1997), p.39.

10. Gabriel Marcel, *Les Hommes Contre L'Humain* (Men against mankind) (Paris: Éditions Universitaires, 1991), p.99.

11. Norman Cousins, *Human Options* (New York: Berkley Books, 1981), p.45.

12. Johann Wolfgang von Goethe, *Faust*, Part I, trans. George Madison Priest. Library of the Future, World Library, Inc., 1991-1995. Screen 69.

13. Nikolay A. Berdyaev, *The Russian Idea of Religion and the Russian State*, trans. R.M. French (London: Robert MacLehose and Company Ltd., 1948), p.146.

14. Werner Kaegi, Preface to the Japanese-language edition of *Historische Meditationen* (Tokyo: Chuokoron-sha, 1979)

15. Cousins, *Human Options*, p.27.

16. N.I. Boukharine, *Report of Court Proceedings in the Case of the Anti-Soviet Bloc*

of Rights and Trotskyites, March 2–13 (Moscow: People's Commisariat of Justice of the U.S.S.R., 1938), p.777.

17. Friedrich Wilhelm Nietzsche, *Human, All Too Human: A Book for Free Spirits*, trans. Marison Faber and Stephen Lehmann (Lincoln, NE: University of Nebraska Press, 1996), p.226

Chapter 4

1. Albert Einstein, This comment was made in a telegram sent to prominent Americans and published in the *New York Times* on May 25, 1946.
2. *The Writings of Nichiren Daishonin*, Volume II (Tokyo: Soka Gakkai, 2006), p.934
3. Paul Valéry, Extract from a lecture given at the University of Zurich in November, 1922. *Oeuvres I*, ed. and annot. Jean Hytier (Paris: Bibliothèque de la Pléiade, Gallimard, 1957), p.1014.
4. Joseph Needham, *Science in Traditional China – A Comparative Perspective* (Hong Kong: The Chinese University of Hong Kong, 1981), p.3.
5. Cousins, *Human Options*, p.84
6. Shin Hasegawa, *Nihon Horyo-shi* (Japanese Prisoner Records) Vol.1 (Tokyo: Chuokoron-sha, 1979), p.9.
7. *The Writings of Nichiren Daishonin*, Volume II, p.844
8. Confucius, *The Analects of Confucius*, trans. Burton Watson (New York: Columbia University Press, 2007), p.108

Chapter 5

1. Mohandas Karamchand Gandhi, *All Men Are Brothers – Life and Thoughts of Mahatma Gandhi as Told in His own Words*, ed. Krishna Kripalani (Paris: UNESCO, 1958), p.67.
2. Stefan Zweig, *Joseph Fouché, Bildnis eines politischen Menchen* (Joseph Fouché, Portrait of a politician), *Gesammelte Werke in Einzelbänden* (Collected works in separate volumes) (Frankfurt am Main: S. Fischer Verlag GmBH, 1950), p.106.
3. Simone Weil, *Écrits historiques et politique* (Writings on history and politics) (Paris: Éditions Gallimard, 1960), p.236.
4. Eckermann, *Gespräche mit Goethe in den letzten Jahren seines Lebens*, p.664.
5. Sōseki Natsume, *Kōjin*, (Tokyo: Iwanami Shoten, 1930), p.368.
6. Mohandas Karamchand Gandhi, *The Collected Works of Mahatma Gandhi*

(New Delhi: The Publication Division, Ministry of Information and Broadcasting, Government of India, 1969), p.292.

7. Ibid. p.294.

8. Hugo, *Les Misérables*, Screen 80.

9. Fyodor Mikhailovich Dostoyevsky, *The Brothers Karamazov*, trans. Constance Garnett. Library of the Future, World Library, Inc. 1991–95. Screen 494.

10. Ibid. Screen 519.

11. Jean-Jacques Rousseau, *The Social Contract*, trans. Maurice Cranston (London: Penguin Books, 1968), p.179.

12. Stefan Zweig, *Menschen und Shicksale* (Men and their fates) (Frankfurt am Main: Fischer Taschenbuch Verlag, 1990), p.167.

13. V.I. Lenin, *Sochineniya* (Works), Vol.15, March 1908-August 1909, 'Lev Tolstoy kak zerkalo Russkoi revolutsii' (Lev Tolstoy as a Mirror of the Russian revolution) (Leningrad: Gosudarstvennoe Izdatel'stvo Politichiskoi Literatury (State Publisher of Political Literature), 1952), p.180.

14. Chingiz Aitmatov, *I den' dlitsya dol'she veka* (The day lasts more than a hundred years), *Chingiz Aitmatov, Izbrannoe* (Selected works of Chingiz Aitmatov) (Frunze: Kyrgyzstan, 1983), pp.29-30.

15. Confucius, *The Analects of Confucius*, trans. Burton Watson (New York: Columbia University Press, 2007), p.73

16. Aitmatov, *I den' dlitsya dol'she veka*, p.117.

17. Plato, *The Republic*, trans. Desmond Lee (New York: Penguin Books USA, 1987), p.392.

18. Ibid. p.393.

19. Lev Nikolaevich Tolstoy, *Voina i Mir* (War and Peace), *Sobranie Sochinenii* (Collected works), Vol.7 (Moscow: Khudozhestvennaya Literatura, 1974), p.53.

20. Aitmatov, Selected works, p.265.

21. Daisaku Ikeda, *Songs From My Heart* (New York: Weatherhill, 1978), pp.75–76

22. Aitmatov, Selected works, p.260.

23. Dostoyevsky, *The Brothers Karamazov*, Screen 478.

24. Gide, *Retour de l'U.R.S.S.*, p.463.

Chapter 6

1. Anton Donchev, *Vreme Razdelno* (Time of Parting), 1964. Quoted passage translated for this book from the Japanese translation by Rokuya Matsunaga. 'Wakare no Toki' (Tokyo: Kobunsha, 1988), pp.312-13.

2. Hristo Botev, *My Prayer*, trans. Kevin Ireland, ed. Theodora Atanassova (Sofia: Sofia Press, 1982), p.83.

3. Fyodor Mikhailovich Dostoyevsky, *Crime and Punishment*, trans. Jessie Coulson (New York: Oxford University Press, 1981), p.437.

4. Gandhi, *All Men are Brothers*, p.177.

5. Tōru Kawasaki, *Fukugan no Moscow Nikki, Olympic Mura no Ichinen* (Ommateal Diary in Moscow, One year in Olympic village) (Tokyo: Chuokoron-sha, 1987), p.511.

6. Goethe, *Faust*, Screen 97.

7. Nāgārjuna, *Mūlamadhyamakakārikā,* trans. Kenneth K. Inada (Tokyo: The Hokuseido Press, 1970), p.39.

8. Azad, Abul Kalam.

9. Gandhi, *All Men are Brothers*, p.172.

10. Albert Einstein, *Out of My Later Years* (New Jersey: The Citadel Press, 1956), p.29.

11. Albert Einstein, Quoted in *The Reporter*, November 18, 1954.

12. Fyodor Tyutchev and Frank Jude, *Nature, Love and Politics: the Complete Poems of Tyutchev in an English Translation*, Retrieved from <http://www.cultinfo.ru/fulltext/1/001/001/241/1.htm>

13. Tyutchev, *Nature, Love and Politics*

14. *The Writings of Nichiren Daishonin*, Volume II, p.850

15. Henri Bergson, *L'Énergie Spirituelle* in *Œuvres* (Paris: Presses Universitaires de France, 1970), p.865

16. Albert Einstein, *Autobiographical Notes* (Chicago: Open Court Publishing Company, 1979), p.7.

17. Friedrich Wilhelm Nietzsche, *Unzeitgemässe Betrachten* (Old-fashioned considerations) (Frankfurt am Main: Insel Verlag, 1981), p.101.

18. D.H. Lawrence, *Lady Chatterley's Lover* (London: Penguin Books, 1993), p.5.

19. Karl Jaspers, *Vom Ursprung und Ziel der Geschichte* (On the origin and goal of history) (Frankfurt am Main and Hamburg: Fischer Bücherei, 1959), p.15.

20. Dostoyevsky, *The Brothers Karamazov*, Screen 41.

21. Confucius, *The Analects of Confucius*, trans. Burton Watson (New York: Columbia University Press, 2007), p.120

22. Nikolai Aleksandrovich Berdyaev, (The Origin of Russian Communism) Quoted passage translated for this book from the Japanese translation by Seijiro Tanaka and Keizaburo Araya. *Berdyaev Chosakushu* 7 (Tokyo: Hakusuisha, 1960), p.245.

23. Gabriel Marcel, *Les Hommes contre l'Humain* (Men against humanity) (Paris: Éditions Universitaires, 1991), p.161.
24. Ibid. p.162.
25. Gandhi, *All Men are Brothers*, p.65.
26. Ibid. p.59.

Epilogue

1. Gandhi, *All Men are Brothers*, p.83.

Index